DID I KISS

Marriage

GOODBYE?

TRUSTING GOD
WITH A HOPE DEFERRED

CAROLYN McCULLEY

CROSSWAY BOOKS

A DIVISION OF
GOOD NEWS PUBLISHERS
WHEATON, ILLINOIS

Cover design: Josh Dennis

Cover photo: Getty Images

First printing 2004

Printed in the United States of America

Unless otherwise noted, Scripture references are from *The Holy Bible, English Standard Version.* Copyright © 2001 by Crossway Bibles, a division of Good News Publishers. Used by permission. All rights reserved.

Scripture marked NIV is taken from the *Holy Bible: New International Version®.* Copyright © 1973, 1978, 1984 by International Bible Society. Used by permission of Zondervan Publishing House. All rights reserved.

The "NIV" and "New International Version" trademarks are registered in the United States Patent and Trademark Office by International Bible Society. Use of either trademark requires the permission of International Bible Society.

Library of Congress Cataloging-in-Publication Data
McCulley, Carolyn, 1963-
   Did I kiss marriage goodbye? : trusting God with a hope deferred / Carolyn McCulley.
     p. cm.
   Includes bibliographical references.
   ISBN 1-58134-579-8 (tpb : alk. paper)
   1. Single women—Religious life. I. Title.
BV639.S5M33   2004
248.8'432—dc22   2004007761

BP		14	13	12	11	10	09	08	07	06	05	04
15	14	13	12	11	10	9	8	7	6	5	4	3	2	1

Carolyn's transparent, insightful, and wonderfully hopeful testimony to God's tender and lavish love for her will be an encouragement to every woman who longs to find God's joy and blessing in her singleness.

> —Ken Sande, President,
> Peacemaker Ministries

When a man married for twenty years can enjoy a book written for single women, you know the author has done something special. That's the case with Carolyn McCulley's *Did I Kiss Marriage Goodbye?* Carolyn's sense of humor, biblical insight, and deft handling of Scripture, together with a refreshingly unsentimental view of sin and the human heart, has produced an inspiring and spiritually uplifting book. *Did I Kiss Marriage Goodbye?* is engaging, honest, real, insightful, fun to read, and spiritually inspiring—all this, plus it has a perfect ending. I highly recommend this fine book.

> —Gary Thomas, author of *Sacred Marriage*
> and *Sacred Pathways*

Did I Kiss Marriage Goodbye? is an insightful and cross-centered look at faithful obedience lived out in a life spent in singleness. Carolyn McCulley doesn't mince words about the real struggles singles face, but she won't leave you in despair, either. Instead, she consistently focuses on the gospel and the good news that soon there will be a wedding ceremony where the sorrows and disappointments of this life will be swallowed up in unbounded joy. In the meantime, though, happiness and delight can be yours as you learn how to pick up the basin and the towel and rejoice in the fellowship of believers.

> —Elyse Fitzpatrick, author, founder of
> *Women Helping Women Ministries.*

DEDICATED TO . . .

My nieces:
Natalie Oman, Claire Barber, Stephanie Barber, and Abigail Barber
May you find this book to be a trustworthy guide
in your single years,
and may you be fruitful and God-centered in them!

My nephews:
Patrick and Matthew Oman.
May the Lord faithfully guide you to your own
Proverbs 31 wives one day,
and may you follow Him all the days of your life.

CONTENTS

ACKNOWLEDGMENTS

Like all things in the kingdom, this book is definitely a collaborative effort, one for which many have earned my deep thankfulness. My gratitude goes to:

The team at Crossway Books for your vision for this book. It is a privilege and an honor to be among the authors you have developed and published throughout the years. *Soli Deo Gloria!*

Marvin Padgett for being willing to sign another author named Carolyn from Covenant Life Church and for patiently answering all my e-mails and questions.

Jill Carter for your cheerful administration of those e-mails and questions and your personal encouragement in response.

Lila Bishop for your fine editing skills and your conviction that single women would find Christ to be more than satisfying.

Joshua Harris, not only for the title but also for the personal writing tutorials. More importantly, please receive my deep appreciation for your life and example as one of my pastors. I've sought to emulate your model of personal humility, transparency, and Christ-centered writing. Thanks for setting the standard.

Gary Thomas for your enthusiasm and interest many years ago in a new member of the Northern Virginia Christian Writers Fellowship and for your ongoing friendship and mentoring.

Nancy Leigh DeMoss for your godly example of solo femininity, your friendship, and encouragement to a tired writer on deadline. I remain indebted to *Singled Out for Him.*

Mark Dever for all that you've invested in Covenant Life Church and Sovereign Grace Ministries over the years. More importantly, thank you for preaching that superb message on Ruth and allowing me to build chapter 3 on the foundation of your outstanding teaching.

Bo Lotinsky for more than five years as my boss, friend, and faithful brother in the Lord. No doubt you have a special reward in heaven for all those observations you've invested! So many illustrations wouldn't have been possible without your godly forbearance with me. Thanks for your generous support in this new venture.

My friends and colleagues at Sovereign Grace Ministries for patiently enduring the short-term memory loss of your sleep-deprived coworker. Special thanks to the Media Group—Kevin Meath, Martin Stanley, Matthew Wahl, Jessica Evers, Steve Cook, Dave MacKenzie, and, of course, Bo—for years of fun, friendship, sanctification, and overcoming deadlines together. ("Core value—deadlines!")

Doug and Sandy Wilda, John and September Robertson, Claude and Jann Allen, Karl and Jen Graustein, Doug Gerber, Pam Wilbur, Janeen Buck, Marzio DeSpirito, and Mindy Hooper for your friendship, prayers, care, good questions, and faithful service to me as my caregroup leaders over the years.

Gene and Liz Emerson (my ultra-patient first pastor and his wife), Rick and Christine Darby, and Bob and Marsha Dixon—and all the wonderful people of Kingsway Community Church—for everything you invested in me as a new believer and for your faithful care and discipleship while I lived in Richmond.

The First Draft Team—Maya Brewer, Vivian Saavedra, Larry Lie, Erin Sutherland, Jen Wahl, Carol Mills, Patti Brown, Mindy Hooper, Karin Moses—for the countless hours you spent reading, your gracious comments, and your insightful corrections. You made this process fun, and I'm deeply indebted to you.

Andy Farmer for your priceless mix of editorial and theological comments. Thanks for sharing your own writing gift with me.

Jeff Purswell for your theological instruction and biblical insight. Thanks for the covering and the counsel.

Janelle Bradshaw and all the ladies of the single women's "trial run" discipleship group at Covenant Life Church. I'm grateful for your candid feedback as well as your passion to grow in godliness.

The pastors of the singles ministry over the years at Covenant Life—Mark Mitchell, Eric Simmons, and Isaac Hydoski. Thanks for challenging us that "to live is Christ."

Susan DiDomenico (the new Mrs. Pat Moran) for your years of praying with me and for your good cheer and patience as your housemate disappeared for months behind a laptop and a huge pile of reference books.

C. J. and Carolyn Mahaney—none of this would have happened if I hadn't first heard C. J. preach the gospel in South Africa in 1993. Thank you for making that trip, C. J.! Carolyn, thanks for all the wise teaching I've received from you. The Lord used you to radically change my understanding of femininity. You've both been so generous to support, review, correct, and promote this project while under your own book deadlines. Thanks for being my champions and my covering.

The members of Covenant Life Church who not only supported this project in prayer, but whose godly lives and service made many of the illustrations possible in this book. May your high view of the local church only increase!

My family, who mean so much to me and who were my most faithful reviewers. My parents, James and Rosalind McCulley, for decades of love, guidance, and listening. My sisters, Alice Barber and Beth Oman, for being my best friends and always making me laugh long and loud. My brothers-in-law, Fred Barber and Andrew Oman, for the way you love my sisters and for your friendship and counsel to me. And last but not least, to my "munchkins," who have responded favorably to my big campaign to be their favorite aunt. Your hugs and your drawings are my treasures. I love you all!

Deut 6:67

FOREWORD

By Joshua Harris

Here's a book that I've always wished existed—one that I've wanted to hand to specific people I've met. But I've never found it. And it's a book that I could never be qualified to write myself.

On many occasions since I wrote *I Kissed Dating Goodbye*, single women have told me, "Josh, it's fine for you to hold these standards about relationships; you're a guy. You can initiate a relationship with a woman when you're ready. But I'm a woman, and I have to wait for a man to get his act together! And, Josh, you got married when you were twenty-two! You don't know the first thing about the challenges I face as an older single!"

Of course, they're absolutely right. That's why I'm so glad to say that Carolyn McCulley has written the book I've always wished existed. *Did I Kiss Marriage Goodbye?* speaks to single women of all ages, but particularly to women who are concerned that marriage may have passed them by. Carolyn writes with honesty, understanding, and a God-centeredness that keeps this book from being just about sympathy. She relates to your circumstances—she's right in the middle of the questions herself—but she constantly points your gaze upward toward the wonderful Savior.

I've known Carolyn for many years. We've worked together, and she's a member of my church. She's the real thing. She lives what she teaches on these pages. She's a feminine, godly woman. And I'm confident that the time you spend with her reading this book will leave you wiser and more confident in God's goodness.

PREFACE

No, I didn't come up with the title of this book. Joshua Harris actually did. As my pastor, colleague, and friend, I entreated him for help. A pithy wordsmith, I knew of few who could rival him for memorable titles. Halfway through this book, he sent me a short e-mail:

> How about . . . *Did I Kiss Marriage Goodbye? Trusting God with a Hope Deferred*
>   I'm actually being serious.

After laughing a long time, I sent it to Crossway, and within hours the title was approved.

Some might wonder at the close connection of the title to Josh's best-selling book, *I Kissed Dating Goodbye*, but to me, it's appropriate. I remember eagerly devouring his book when it first came out in 1997. At the time I was leading a small book study with girls ranging from thirteen to thirty-five. We had just finished another relationship book, one full of stories about missionaries in faraway places and romances from distant eras. I could tell the teens weren't quite connecting. So then here comes this book about relationships from a young, single man! The teens connected instantly, of course, and I read it with a sense of relief after years of confusion: *So this is what I'm supposed to be doing!*

That same year Josh moved from Oregon to Maryland to begin a pastoral internship at Covenant Life Church. A year later I moved from Richmond, Virginia, to Gaithersburg, Maryland, to join Covenant Life Church and work at Sovereign Grace Ministries. Josh later wrote *Boy Meets Girl*, which I appreciated even more—possibly because I knew many of the people he quoted and the relationships he profiled. I knew that the principles he outlined weren't impossible because I saw them embodied every day in the relationships around me.

But even so, I remained single. So did most of the women in that orig-inal book study. I began to wonder what Girl is supposed to be doing if Boy isn't meeting her. What good purpose could God have in keeping me sin-gle? Was there something wrong with me? Or with the men around me? Am I stunted in my femininity because I'm not a wife or mother? What about my friends—what should our lives look like? How are we to prioritize demanding careers, a home with a constant parade of roommates, shifting relationships as others marry, and so on? Should I continue to hold out hope, or did I kiss marriage goodbye without even realizing it? So many questions—and all those questions led directly to the most important one: *Am I trusting God with this hope deferred?*

It's my prayer that if you are asking the same questions, you will be refreshed and cheered through this book. More importantly, I hope you will close this book with an increased passion for our Lord and Savior, who is fully worthy of complete trust.

PART ONE

SURVEYING

SINGLENESS

1

"You're Still Single?"

*The LORD bestows favor and honor. No good thing does he
withhold from those who walk uprightly.*
PSALM 84:11

I stood outside in the crisp autumn night, rekindling twenty-year-old
memories. As I hesitated, numerous laughing couples passed through
the hotel doors. Would I be the only one attending my high school reunion
alone?

Taking a deep breath and exhaling a brief prayer, I opened the door and
strode purposefully to my target—a paper-skirted table with multiple rows
of plastic nametags. With a sigh I pinned on the evidence: Twenty years had
passed since high school, and my name was unchanged.

I was still single.

Back home various friends were praying for me—that I would be gracious, focused on others, and above all, that I would have evangelistic
opportunities. *My* goals were much smaller: Keep smiling, keep moving,
and keep the mascara in place. No tears, no quivering lower lip, no self-pity.

With a practiced smile, I entered the reunion, a collision of high school
trauma and middle-aged reality. The music was loud, the lighting dim.
Thankfully, the nametags were in large print, sporting our graduation pictures. I marveled at the number of people I never would have recognized
without the tag.

I was making my way toward some familiar faces when I heard my
name half-shouted, half-slurred on my right. Turning toward the sound, I
was greeted by an exhaled puff of beery breath from lips O-shaped in surprise and disbelief.

"Carolyn *McCULLEY*? Is that right? You're still single?!"

I looked at the unfamiliar bloodshot eyes and then stole a quick glance at his nametag. I barely recalled this man.

Dear God, please give me the grace I need to make it through tonight.

"Yes, I am." *Smile. Look him in the eyes. Be gracious.* "It's so kind of you to remember me. Where are you living now? Did you have to travel long to get here?"

After a few moments of small talk, I moved on to mingle elsewhere. The participants changed, but the questions didn't vary: *So what's a nice girl like you doing still single? Why aren't you married? Didn't you want to get married? How's the single life these days—do you still have to hang out in bars to meet men?*

It was a singularly long night.

UNHELPFUL QUESTIONS

Extended singleness ushers in a season of difficult questions—questions for which few gracious and informative answers exist. (My definition for extended singleness is one day past the marriage of a close high school friend, your younger sister, or even your own niece or nephew.) Being single also requires a healthy sense of humor. This Top Ten list is from my witty friend Vivian Saavedra:

Top ten things never to say to a single woman at a wedding . . .

1. You're next.
2. Why aren't you married?
3. Maybe you should lose some weight.
4. What about (insert name here)? He's a nice boy.
5. You're next.
6. Maybe you're called to singleness.
7. Can you baby-sit tonight?
8. Did you ever consider being a missionary?
9. Just don't think about marriage, and it will happen.
10. You're next.

"Why aren't you married?" Here's a common question, usually posed by a brand-new acquaintance. Believing the best, I must assume they ask because they are genuinely interested in my situation. But because I often lack a good, pithy answer to one of life's mysteries, it *feels* like a tabloid reporter's inquiry to uncover what's really wrong with me.

"Don't you want to get married?" Shortly after my fortieth birthday, a college friend wondered whether I was really serious about getting married. She wanted to know why I wasn't more proactive about achieving that goal. Had I considered Internet dating? I couldn't just sit around and expect it to happen. She was trying to be helpful, to express her care. But her words fueled a slow boil of despair in my soul.

"Don't the guys in your church want to get married?" The only way to answer this one is with another question: "Why don't you ask *them*?"

I'm sure the people who ask these questions don't mean to embarrass me. Still I find myself awkwardly fumbling for an appropriate answer.

The questions others ask, however, can't compare to the kinds of questions that bubble up from within me during a lonely moment at a wedding or late at night when the house is still but the emotions rage: "Does God really know what He's doing? Is He really in control? Can I trust Him with my desires? *Has He forgotten me?*"

GODWARD ANSWERS

If you've ever been asked those questions, you have my sympathy. And if you've responded graciously, you have my respect. Well done! But if you opened this book hoping to find a specific, concrete answer to your own situation, then let me first introduce you to a mystery.

> *There are three things that are too amazing for me,*
>   *four that I do not understand:*
> *the way of an eagle in the sky,*
>   *the way of a snake on a rock,*
> *the way of a ship on the high seas,*
>   *and the way of a man with a maiden.*
>   (Prov. 30:18-19 NIV)

This biblical passage shows us that there are things too amazing, too wonderful for even a wise man to understand. Now you may say to yourself that modern science can explain the first three items. What's the big deal? Number four still has us though. Wise men and women remain confounded by the mystery of attraction and romance. We really don't know why some relationships bud and bloom, and others do not. It takes humility—a sober recognition of our limitations—to be comfortable with that mystery.

I hope you're not tempted to close the book right now because I have some good news for you: There is One who *does* know.

We don't know the ways of the heart, but God does. He perfectly understands the things that are too amazing for us to understand. He created the eagle, the snake, the high seas, and men and women. He knows how everything operates, and nothing is a mystery to Him.

Even better, He is lovingly involved in His creation—with the eagles, the snakes, the ships, and also our wily hearts. He didn't just make us all and then stand back to have a good laugh. He is Lord over His creation, lovingly ruling over all things to accomplish His purposes—even (especially!) in the affairs of the heart: "The king's heart is a stream of water in the hand of the LORD; he turns it wherever he will" (Proverbs 21:1).

Are you tracking with me here? This means if the Lord can direct the heart of an absolute monarch, He can certainly turn the affections of our future husbands to us.

(Silence.)

(Crickets: *brrrpp, brrrppp.*)

"Uh . . . well, does that mean God is holding out on us?" you might ask.

It can feel that way, can't it? But only if you forget whose heart He has already changed—yours. If you are a believer in the Lord Jesus Christ, if your life has been radically changed by a personal relationship with Him, then you know this to be true. He softened your once hardened, rebellious heart and gave you affection for His Word and His people. You may remember what you were like before your Christian conversion. I certainly remember what I was like! I mocked Christians. They made no sense to me.

I didn't know I needed a Savior, but that wasn't a mystery to God. I didn't know then that my heart needed to be changed, but that wasn't a mystery to God—nor was it impossible for Him to do. What we can't control, what we don't even understand, is clear to Him. As hard as it can be at times to be single, doesn't that put it all in perspective?

Dear friends, the whole Bible testifies of God's faithfulness to us even in the face of our own faithlessness to Him. God has not forgotten anything at all. The gentle words of my pastor, C. J. Mahaney, are a good reminder: "Your greatest need is not a spouse. Your greatest need is to be delivered from the wrath of God—and that has already been accomplished for you through the death and resurrection of Christ. So why doubt that God will provide a much, much lesser need? Trust His sovereignty, trust His wisdom, trust His love."[1]

A BETTER QUESTION

So the infamous question about why we're not married is the wrong question to ask. It implies lack. But our heavenly Father has said He withholds no good thing from His children (Ps. 84:11; Matt. 7:11). The better question to ask ourselves is: *What is God doing with and through my singleness?*

Maybe this perspective is all new to you. If you're uncertain of the statement I just made, or if you're not entirely sure what the gospel really is (and I remember what that was like), then I encourage you to read the Afterword at the end of this book *before* you read further. That's the foundation for this book, and the rest of the chapters will make a *lot* more sense after you read the Afterword.

Maybe the gospel doesn't confuse you, but you're living as though it doesn't make much difference in your life. You don't see how God could possibly have any purpose for your being single, and you're wondering what you have to do to "earn" the privilege of marriage.

Maybe you don't trust God to bless you. You look at your life and wonder at what age you need to shut down hope and start making long-term goals for solitary confinement—*oops*, that's singleness, of course.

Maybe you *say* you're content now, but your actions and decisions reveal that you are *really* waiting for your life to begin when a man comes along.

Maybe you are still young, and you've only recently started to wonder if you are going to get married. But you see lots of older, discontented single women around you, and you're hoping this book will tell you how to make sure you don't end up like them.

Maybe you'd honestly say you fit that description—an older, discontented single woman—and you have no idea how to change.

Maybe you just want to know what God has planned for your future so you could prepare for either marriage or singleness (because you would not prepare the same way, right?).

Maybe none of the above applies to you. You love the Lord, and His gospel is precious to you, but you need to be encouraged in how to apply His Word to your daily life as a single woman.

For all of you, may you find in these pages some answers and a sympathetic friend. As we go along on this journey together, I'm not offering myself as a role model for "successful" singleness. But I have been the beneficiary of much rich, grace-filled teaching that has deeply affected my life, and I want to refract that through the prism of single adulthood. I hope if you ever receive a high school reunion invitation, and you are unmarried, that this book will help you respond with true joy—not ashamed of what God has done in your life throughout the intervening years.

So let's ask ourselves the better question: What is God doing with and through our singleness? If your answer begins with "Uhmm . . ." and then a long pause, I pray you'll continue to read. I believe there is much encouragement ahead!

• In the next chapter, we'll look at why God calls singleness a gift. We'll examine the definition, value, purpose, and context of this gift.

• In the third chapter, we'll explore why God is worthy of our trust as He sovereignly, wisely, and lovingly chooses which gifts to give and when.

• In the fourth chapter, we'll see that we don't need to know *now* whether we'll be ever be married in order to prepare for our futures. The Bible shows us, married or single, that the emphasis is on our *femininity*. Our preparation is the same in almost every respect.

• Chapters 5 and 6 will look at matters of the heart and our relationships with men.

• Then we'll spend the rest of this book exploring one worthy role model who shows us how to make the most of our femininity now.

My prayer as you read this book is the same one I prayed as I wrote it: *Lord, please give me Your comfort, encouragement, and wisdom as I examine Your Word as a single woman. Impress it upon my heart that You are worthy of my complete trust, and change me as I study and write these truths about You. Then please use these words to inspire and edify my sisters—Your daughters— as they read. All to the praise of Your glory and for the advance of Your kingdom. I pray this in the compassionate and mighty name of Jesus. Amen.*

2

ESTEEMING THE GIFT

But each has his own gift from God, one of one kind and one of another.

1 CORINTHIANS 7:7

M om blew out the lone birthday candle on her slightly lopsided, lumpy cake and then smiled at all of us. My sisters and I were just old enough to pitch in on family birthday celebrations, and as I recall, the cake was one of our first creations. I don't remember if it was any good, but I do remember how good it felt to do something for Mom for a change.

Although Mom had already opened all of her birthday gifts, my youngest sister suddenly announced there was one more. Darting upstairs, she scurried around in her room. Above our heads, we could hear the frantic movements of a four-year-old desperate to get a last-minute gift together. Moments later Beth came downstairs holding a heavily taped box with a hair ribbon wrapped around it.

Pleased with herself, she offered her gift to Mom, who opened it with surprise and delight, wondering aloud what it could be. Beth's smile broadened as Mom inspected the contents. It was a box of . . . tissue wads—not used tissues but thoughtfully pre-wadded, clean ones—ready for any action-packed day with the kids. I remember my mother receiving that gift as if it was the best present anyone had ever given her. I also remember snickering, as a know-it-all oldest child often does. *A box of tissue wads?! That's not a real present!* I was evaluating only the "worth" of the gift and not my sister's motivation in giving it.

A few months later, it was Christmas. I was eight, and I had scraped together enough money to actually buy my first "real" gifts for my parents.

I purchased them at our school holiday fair, an event created to help children buy inexpensive items for their families. Of all the items there, I selected an acrylic "thingy-do" to give my mother. I don't think there is any other name for it because there is no useful purpose for such an item. This particular thingy-do had a clear acrylic base with about ten black six-inch wires springing up from it. Each wire was topped by a colorful acrylic half-orb. That's it—a multicolored spray of acrylic blobs that swayed slightly in the breeze. No self-respecting household should be without one!

With my limited resources, this strange token of my affection was all I could afford. To her credit, Mom seemed just as delighted to receive the acrylic thingy-do as she was the box of tissue wads. At least my father, the pilot, got a model airplane made out of nuts and bolts. They received these gifts with sincere appreciation and effusive thanks, a sincerity that is evidenced by the fact that both of these items are still in my parents' family room.

In both cases, we gift-givers were limited by our resources, abilities, and even taste. We wanted to give something extravagant, but we presented token gifts instead.

GOD'S GIFT OF SINGLENESS

This is how I can think about gifts when I consider the biblical passage that calls singleness a gift (1 Cor. 7). Calling marriage a gift doesn't surprise me. I understand that. Over the years, I've tried to beg, bribe, borrow, and buy *that* gift. It simply can't be done! I am now convinced I must wait to receive it. But how and when did I get this gift of singleness? I don't recall putting it on my "wish list" or asking anyone to give it to me. I don't remember opening it up and saying, "Ooohh, thank you! Singleness! How did you know? It's *perfect!*" No, this is how I have viewed singleness: While others walk down the wedding aisle to receive the golden gift of marriage, I'm standing to the side, sullenly holding my useless thingy-do of singleness. (Unlike my mother, I'm not even grateful to get it.)

When we talk about gifts, it's easy to think about them in self-centered, human terms. We evaluate whether we like a particular gift and want to keep it or return it. We at times wonder if the giver spent much money or effort on the gift. We consider whether we would ever use it. To call singleness a gift certainly opens the door for more questions—legitimate questions. Why does the Bible call it a gift? Is it the gift I will always have? And for what good purpose could singleness be given anyway?

This is why we're going to start this book with a discussion of the gift of singleness, as controversial as that can be. I bet you are used to thinking of yourself as I do: "I'm a single woman." The first word that describes you is single. The second is woman. I believe the Bible would put it the other way around. But because culturally we've been camped out on singleness, let's start there.

This is a meaty chapter—I'll be honest. But whenever I've engaged women on this topic, I've encountered a great thoughtfulness and eager scrutiny of the Bible about this gift. I've seen a real hunger to understand what God's Word says about it. So, ladies, in this chapter, we'll look at five important aspects of singleness:

- The context of the gift
- The definition of a gift
- Who assigns the gift
- The purpose of a gift
- The timing of any gift

SINGLENESS IN CONTEXT

Did you ever notice that it was a single man who wrote the longest passage in Scripture about singleness? It's also the only place in the Bible where singleness is called a gift—and a *good* gift—which may be surprising to some.

Let's look at this excerpt, which is from chapter 7 of the apostle Paul's first letter to the Corinthian church. As you read, please keep in mind that Paul was addressing some specific questions or views that the Corinthian church had previously sent to him—questions that we don't have access to today. Paul begins in verses 1 to 5 by addressing married people. In fact, he quotes a statement from the Corinthians that he's going to correct ("it's good for a man not to have sexual relations with a woman"), and then he turns to singleness in verse 6:

Now as a concession, not a command, I say this. I wish that all were as I myself am. But each has his own gift from God, one of one kind and one of another.

To the unmarried and the widows I say that it is good for them to remain single as I am. But if they cannot exercise self-control, they should marry. For it is better to marry than to be aflame with passion. . . . (1 Cor. 7:6-9)

The next part of this letter addresses those who are married, and the commands that the Lord gave regarding marriage. Then he addresses those who are legally committed to marry but have not yet consummated the marriage, which is what betrothal was during those times. Now if you're like me, you might be tempted to skip over a long passage of Scripture, but I hope you won't—for God's words are the only ones with power.

> Now concerning the betrothed, I have no command from the Lord, but I give my judgment as one who by the Lord's mercy is trustworthy. I think that in view of the present distress it is good for a person to remain as he is. Are you bound to a wife? Do not seek to be free. Are you free from a wife? Do not seek a wife. But if you do marry, you have not sinned, and if a betrothed woman marries, she has not sinned. Yet those who marry will have worldly troubles, and I would spare you that. . . .
>
> I want you to be free from anxieties. The unmarried man is anxious about the things of the Lord, how to please the Lord. But the married man is anxious about worldly things, how to please his wife, and his interests are divided. And the unmarried or betrothed woman is anxious about the things of the Lord, how to be holy in body and spirit. But the married woman is anxious about worldly things, how to please her husband. I say this for your own benefit, not to lay any restraint upon you, but to promote good order and to secure your undivided devotion to the Lord.
>
> If anyone thinks that he is not behaving properly toward his betrothed, if his passions are strong, and it has to be, let him do as he wishes: let them marry—it is no sin. But whoever is firmly established in his heart, being under no necessity but having his desire under control, and has determined this in his heart, to keep her as his betrothed, he will do well. So then he who marries his betrothed does well, and he who refrains from marriage will do even better. (1 Cor. 7:25-28, 32-38)

Why would Paul say this? As we look at this passage, it's helpful to understand the cultural context of first-century Corinth and the church there. With its busy seaport, Corinth was a major city and one of the most culturally diverse cities in the Roman Empire. It was originally Greek, but had been a Roman colony for about a century before Paul's letter was written. It was once prosperous, but history shows there were food shortages in Corinth during this period. As one commentary notes:

> This is the longest discussion of sexuality and related matters in all of Paul's letters. It contains vital information on issues not touched upon elsewhere. Failure to understand the circumstances which gave rise to

the problems written about in 7:1 and 7:25 has meant that valuable teaching on singleness and marriage has been ignored.

Concerning the circumstances: one clue rests in the letter itself, for Paul refers to *the present crisis* in 7:26 which gave rise to Christians rethinking the appropriateness of engaged couples getting married (7:25). There is firm archaeological and literary evidence which indicates that there had been food shortages in Corinth during this period. . . . Tacitus also records earthquakes and famines. Many believed that these were divine portents. . . . Here Paul not only answers their immediate questions but also provides an important framework in which Christian marriage is to be seen.[1]

Thus Paul not only addressed their immediate concerns, but also the clashing cultural perspectives on sexuality and marriage that affected this young church. His answer would have challenged the current thinking of both his Jewish and his Greco-Roman readers. To the Jewish mind, marriage was the expectation and the norm. A spouse and children ensured that the family line would continue, and caregivers would be available in one's old age; barrenness was seen as a point of shame. But Greek culture was being increasingly shaped by the idea that marriage was a distraction and that sex without marriage was acceptable, as long as one's sexual appetites didn't control the emotions. Additionally, the Roman law of the time not only permitted prostitution, but only forbade pre- or extramarital sex if both parties were of aristocratic birth.[2]

No wonder the young Corinthian church needed guidance!

Paul's answer shows how well he knew his readers and how skilled he was in presenting biblical truth in a relevant manner. In this passage, he validates marriage, promotes the advantages of singleness, acknowledges that not everyone will be equipped for singleness, recognizes the reality of sexual tensions and human passions, and advocates just two alternatives: self-controlled singleness or monogamous marriage with only limited periods of mutually agreed-upon abstinence. His primary concern surrounding the issues of marriage and singleness is found in verse 35: "I say this for your own benefit, not to lay any restraint upon you, *but to promote good order and to secure your undivided devotion to the Lord*" (emphasis added).

THE POWER OF A GIFT

Against this cultural backdrop, we read that Paul calls both marriage and singleness a gift from God. He doesn't refer to either as a state of being or as a function, but as a gift. The Greek word Paul used here is *charisma*. There are several Greek words that could be translated as "gift" in English. One word denotes a gift presented as an expression of honor. A second euphemistically infers that a gift is more a matter of debt or obligation. A third denotes a free gift of grace, used in the New Testament to refer to a spiritual or supernatural gift.[3] This is the word Paul uses in this passage— *charisma*.

Despite all the modern connotations of the word *charisma*, it means much more than the nuances found in either the Pentecostal/charismatic theology of spiritual gifts or the functional "identifying your spiritual gifts" lists common in evangelical circles. As a gift of grace, it stresses the fact that it is a gift of God the Creator freely bestowed upon sinners—His endowment upon believers by the operation of the Holy Spirit in the churches.[4] Theologian Gordon Fee says that Paul's use of *charisma* throughout this letter to the Corinthians stresses the root word of "grace," not the gifting itself. Fee writes:

> Thus, even though Paul has concrete expressions of 'grace' in view . . . and even though in ch. 12 these concrete expressions are understood as the direct result of Spirit activity, there seems to be no real justification for the translation 'spiritual gift' for this word. Rather, they are 'gracious endowments' (where the emphasis lies on the grace involved in their being so gifted), which at times, as in this letter, is seen also as the gracious activity of the Spirit in their midst.[5]

Are you still with me here?

This grammar lesson is important because we need to understand what *kind* of gift we are talking about when we discuss "the gift of singleness." It's not a gift that we have to spend time trying to identify, that we should worry about having. If we're single, we have the gracious gift of singleness. How we may feel about it—"Do I like being single? Do I desire marriage?"—is not part of the equation. The emphasis here is on a gracious God who gives good gifts and ultimately on His purpose for giving them. It's also not a "spiritual gift" in the sense we've come to use that term in our churches today. It's not an activity or a role, but a blessing—like the free gift [*charisma*] of eternal life (Romans 5:15) that was given to us without any merit of our own.

What about the future? To paraphrase verse 17, "Only let each [woman] lead the life that the Lord has assigned to [her], and to which God has called [her]." God may change your assignment and calling. Or you may find that, as the years go by, you are increasingly contented with being single. *There's grace for being so gifted either way.*

GOD ASSIGNS THE GIFTS

That truth might help you rest in God's current assignment for your life, but you may be wondering what purpose God would have for anyone being single. Paul addresses this question a few chapters later in this same letter:

> *Now there are varieties of gifts, but the same Spirit; and there are varieties of service, but the same Lord; and there are varieties of activities, but it is the same God who empowers them all in everyone.* To each is given the manifestation of the Spirit for the common good. *To one is given through the Spirit the utterance of wisdom, and to another the utterance of knowledge according to the same Spirit, to another faith by the same Spirit, to another gifts of healing by the one Spirit, to another the working of miracles, to another prophecy, to another the ability to distinguish between spirits, to another various kinds of tongues, to another the interpretation of tongues.* All these are empowered by one and the same Spirit, who apportions to each one individually as he wills. (1 Cor. 12:4-11, emphasis added)

Paul uses the same word—*charisma*—here that he used in 1 Corinthians 7:7. As Gordon Fee notes, the emphasis here in Paul's writing is not on the list of gifts, but on the God who gives them:

> Diversity within the unity belongs to the character of God. Although there is but one Spirit, one Lord, and one God, a great variety of gifts and ministries characterizes each of the divine Persons (vv. 4-6). Such diversity in God manifests itself, Paul argues further, by God's distributing to the many of them different manifestations of the Spirit for the common good. Paul then offers several of these as illustrations (vv. 7-11).[6]

We have each received a *variety* of gifts. First Corinthians 7:7 says that as a single woman, I have received the *charisma* of singleness. First Corinthians 12:4-10 lists other gifts that I may also receive. I may yet one day receive the gift of marriage. However, two things are important to remember about any spiritual gift:

• "All these are empowered by one and the same Spirit, who apportions to each one individually as he wills" (1 Cor. 12:11);

• "To each is given the manifestation of the Spirit for the common good" (1 Cor. 12:7).

Let's look at the first point. God apportions gifts as He sees fit in His infinite and sovereign wisdom. Here Paul is returning again to the point he raised in chapter 7. God gives us our assignment, and He calls us to the task. Here now we see that He apportions gifts to each of us to accomplish these purposes.

Do you see God's will at work here? *Ultimately, we are single because that's God's will for us right now.* That's it. It's not because we are too old, too fat, too skinny, too tall, too short, too quiet, too loud, too smart, too simple, too demanding, or too anything else. It's not wholly because of past failures or sin tendencies. It's not because we're of one race when many of the men around us are of another. It's not because the men we know lean toward passive temperaments. It's not because there are more women than men in our singles group. It's not because our church doesn't even *have* a singles group. Though perhaps these things seem like valid reasons, they don't trump God's will. One look at the marriages we know or the ones announced in the newspaper will assure us that these factors are present in many people's lives, and they still got married. We are single *today* because God apportioned us this gift *today*.

One more thought: I've often heard married people say to singles that we won't get married until we're content in our singleness, but I humbly submit this is error. I'm sure that it is offered by well-meaning couples who want to see their single friends happy and content in God's provision, but it creates a works-based mentality to receiving gifts, which can lead to condemnation. The Lord doesn't require that we attain a particular state before He grants a gift. We can't earn any particular spiritual gift any more than we can earn our own salvation. It's all of grace. However, we *should* humbly listen to our friends and receive their input about cultivating contentment; we just shouldn't attach it to the expectation of a blessing.

(If you are single again due to divorce or death, I realize it can be challenging to reconcile your current experience with the concept of a gift that God has allowed or even willed, but this is the testimony of Scripture. I trust the expanded definition of "gift" has helped you to understand better your current situation. And I hope you'll stick with me as we explore this idea in the next chapter.)

GIFTED FOR THE COMMON GOOD

Now let's look at the second point: Spiritual gifts are given for the common good. The good news here is that the singleness is not about you—either your good qualities or your sinful tendencies. You have a "gracious endowment" that is for the good of those around you! (So the next time someone asks you why you're still single, you can reply with a straight face, "It's for your good!")

To amplify Paul's point, let's look at 1 Peter 4:10: "As each has received a gift [*charisma*], use it to serve one another, as good stewards of God's varied grace." The New International Version translates this passage as "faithfully administering God's grace in its various forms." A steward is a good administrator. She knows her purpose, employs her resources, and brings in a good return. Theologian Wayne Grudem notes that the word *varied* here is *poikilos*, which means "having many facets or aspects; having rich diversity."[7] Not everyone is going to receive the same gift, but the ones we do receive are to reflect the many facets of God's character. Even though this gift of singleness is not a *charisma* defined by an activity or an obvious role as other gifts are, it's still meant for the common good—the implication being the good of the local church.

Friends, we have to stop here and ask ourselves if being gifted for the benefit of the church is important to us. This passage from 1 Corinthians 12 shows us that singleness gives us a *context* for the other spiritual gifts we may have and is a *resource* to be faithfully administered. This is what we'll explore in chapters 4 through 13. But this biblical passage also goes on to give us a *place* to invest our gifts. Verses 14 through 26 present the analogy of the church as literal members of a body and emphasize the interdependency of the members. Verse 15 says, "If the foot should say, 'Because I am not a hand, I do not belong to the body,' that would not make it any less a part of the body." Do we ever act like that foot? Are we saying (in thoughts, words, or actions), "Because I am not part of a couple, I do not belong to the body"? We *are* part of the body, and we have a vital function within our churches. Those other members need us, and we need them.

As I've become older, I've grown in my gratitude for my church. Many times I've looked around the Sunday worship service or at my friends in a small-group meeting and silently thanked God for the fellowship I have there. Not only am I grateful for the wealth of relationships, but I am grateful for the grand vision before me. When I think of how much Christ loves His bride, the church, and how in His merciful kindness He has rescued me and made me a part of this body, I am even more grateful for the purpose I find in the church.

Without the context and eternal purpose of the church, singleness can seem like the waiting room of adulthood. *Within* the context and eternal purpose of the church, singleness truly is a gift for the common good of others. We can love the bride of Christ by joyfully investing the "firstfruits" of our resources, affections, and time in our churches. In the coming chapters, we'll look at specific examples of how we can invest this gift into the body of Christ.

BUT WHAT ABOUT MARRIAGE?

I hope you are encouraged as you read this chapter and see the loving purposes God has in the gifts He gives. But you may be wondering if it's okay to still want to get married and even have children. Yes! Those are also good gifts from God. It's not wrong to desire marriage or to ask God for it. The problem is when we do not humbly and peaceably accept God's will for our lives *right now*.

Paul started chapter 12 by writing: "Now concerning spiritual gifts, brothers, I do not want you to be uninformed. You know that when you were pagans you were led astray to mute idols, however you were led" (1 Cor. 12:1-2). Many of the singles I know were converted as adults, as I was. I have a very clear memory of being "led astray to mute idols." They may not have been little metal or wood figurines, but I still worshiped (exalted) them for the privileges I thought they could bestow. The most dominant was the idol of self: self-centeredness, self-fulfillment, selfish pleasure, selfish freedom. Though I had been raised attending church and participating in those rites, I hadn't yet repented of my sins and trusted Jesus as my personal Savior—so I really was an unbeliever. Throughout my twenties, I pursued various sins. I can remember laughing at the "old-fashioned ideas" of the few Christian women I knew who were willing to abstain from sex until marriage. I was blinded to the selfishness of the men I was involved with and completely deceived by my own desires. I thought I would get married at some point, but I didn't have any compelling vision for marriage.

That changed when I became an authentic, believing Christian at age thirty. My pastors taught their flock well about God's purpose for marriage and family. What had once been a washed-out, unfocused concept took on contours and hues that I had never considered. So I wanted it. *A lot.* Thus, a new idol was created: Husband of My Dreams, the reward for my new obedience in chastity. When this wonderful husband didn't immediately materialize, I sometimes found myself shaking my puny fist at the Lord of the universe, unhappy with His provision for my life.

You see, even as a believer indwelt with the Holy Spirit, my heart is a "factory of idols," as sixteenth-century theologian John Calvin noted. Because of this, good gifts are in danger of becoming idols, too. "The evil in our desire typically does not lie in what we want, but that we want it too much," Calvin wrote. Our desires so quickly turn into demands. When these demands are not met, it's tempting to create another set of "mute idols" that may bring about what we want. If I see younger, thinner, more reserved women being pursued and wed, then I think those must be the keys to marriage. If I see more engagements in one church or singles group, I can think the pastors there are better at encouraging the men to step out and pursue. If I perceive that one kind of man is more often getting married than another, I can be tempted to disrespect the men around me who are not like that. That pattern of thinking reveals where I'm wrongfully putting my trust. *When any of us is tempted to think that the power to bless and satisfy resides in something other than God, this is idolatry.*

Ten years after my conversion, I remain single. I find myself thinking that marriage and children, while still possible, are unlikely. (I like to joke with my friends, though, that now I'm in good company with Sarah, Rebekah, Hannah, Elizabeth, and other biblical heroines who had to rely solely on the God of the impossible.) If I peer into the future, all sorts of things seem uncertain and, well, lonely. Left to the clichèd outcome, my future looks suspiciously like a one-bedroom apartment with two cats named Bitter and Resentful. But then I remind myself that's a cultural view, not a biblical one.

FORECASTING THE FUTURE

Will I always be single? I don't know. But I do know that singleness is a gift that *everyone* has at one point. Marriage will be given to most, but it's only a gift for this world. Jesus made that clear when He said, "For in the resurrection they neither marry nor are given in marriage" (Matt. 22:30).

I also know that I can trust God with my desire to be married. The same grace extended to Paul, when the apostle petitioned God three times to remove the "thorn in his flesh," is available to me today. As Paul wrote, "Three times I pleaded with the Lord about this, that it should leave me.

But he said to me, 'My grace is sufficient for you, for my power is made perfect in weakness'" (2 Cor. 12:8-9). I have no proof, but I suspect these weren't three quick prayers in a row. I assume Paul learned the reality of God's sufficient grace over a period of time.

Am I "called" to singleness? I've been asked that question several times, although no one asked until I reached my late thirties. I still don't know how to answer. Honestly, I don't know if one can apply that phrase to singleness. We're all *born* single; so don't we have to be called to something different? In my opinion, the question is not whether we're called to singleness but whether we're called to marriage. The weight of evidence—both in the Bible and in what we can observe around us—is that most people *are* called to marriage. But that's only proven through the experience of receiving the gift of marriage. Everything else about it is unreliably subjective until that point. (My anecdotal evidence: The numerous testimonies I've heard from men now married who, upon conversion, were convinced they'd be "bachelors 'til the Rapture." They felt "called" to remain single, but God obviously had other plans.)

Sometimes I ponder the assumptions that appear to lie behind that question. I wonder if we can assume that being single requires us to live differently from other Christian women who are married. I've thought this, too, in the past—and even wondered when I might need to make some sort of shift to living permanently as a single woman. I suspect that this concept has worldly roots—roots planted during the late nineteenth century when many women were shaking off both the institution of marriage and the authority of God to carve out a lifestyle independent of men and religion. While I am grateful that these women demanded changes in the law that benefit me today—such as a woman's right to vote—I see where they also introduced the model of lifelong singleness that spurned any aspect of traditional femininity.

We want to emulate a biblical model. We need to think of ourselves not as single women, *but as women who are single*. The emphasis in Scripture is first on our femininity. The Bible gives us one seamless portrait of femininity. We don't see women in the Bible making a wrenching switch from singleness to marriage—as though these states are completely foreign to one another. Obviously, there are different roles in the various seasons of our lives, but roles are all built upon the same bedrock. (This is what we'll explore starting in chapter 4.)

I like Elisabeth Elliot's perspective:

If you are single today, the portion assigned to you for *today* is single-ness. It is God's gift. Singleness ought not to be viewed as a problem, nor marriage as a right. God in His wisdom and love grants either as a gift. An unmarried person has the gift of singleness, not to be confused with the gift of celibacy. When we speak of the "gift of celibacy," we usually refer to one who is bound by vows not to marry. If you are not so bound, what may be your portion tomorrow is not your business today. Today's business is trust in the living God who precisely measures out, day by day, each one's portion.[8]

My business today—what I know now—is that I'm single, and I'm called to do something with this *charisma* for the common good and the glory of God. If God has marriage for me, He will bring it about. In the meantime, I want to live to the fullest of this "gracious endowment," pour-ing His gift of singleness into the church—the place and people *He* loves.

FOR FURTHER STUDY

❖ If you are struggling with what other people think of you because you're single, you may want to read *When People Are Big and God Is Small: Overcoming Peer Pressure, Codependency, and the Fear of Man* by Edward T. Welch (P&R Publishing). I highly recommend it for everyone, but I would consider it a "must read" for single women.

❖ *Singled Out for Him* by Nancy Leigh DeMoss was one of the first encouraging resources for single women that I encountered. This com-bined audio message and booklet is based on some interviews she did with the FamilyLife Today radio show. You can order it from either FamilyLife Today (www.familylife.com) or Nancy's ministry, Revive Our Hearts (www.reviveourhearts.com).

❖ *The Rich Single Life* by Andrew Farmer (Sovereign Grace Ministries) is one of the most grace-filled books ever written for singles. It contains helpful advice for both men and women, written with Andy's wonderfully wise and humorous words.

3

GOD'S QUIET PROVIDENCE

I have spoken, and I will bring it to pass; I have purposed, and I will do it.

ISAIAH 46:11

Though summer was waning, my soul was already autumn-dry. I felt as brittle and fragile as a fallen leaf, its edges curled and ragged from lack of water. I knew it was time to schedule a personal retreat and seek refreshment alone with God.

I drove to the retreat center that late August afternoon with my windows down, enjoying the tantalizing hint of unseasonable evening coolness. Forsaking the highway, I chose a longer route across winding, two-lane rural roads. As I drove, the sun sank languidly to the horizon, tinting the sky with soft peach and baby pink hues that lingered long into the early evening. Interrupting the twilight serenade of crickets, I popped a sermon into my car stereo. The message was from pastor and author Mark Dever,[1] given at a conference just a month prior. He titled it "The Kindness of God in the Book of Ruth." I hadn't planned on studying Ruth on my retreat, but the title intrigued me.

Partway through his sermon, I was startled to hear a clear diagnosis of my spiritual state. I rewound the tape and listened again, stunned. Again I rewound, pondering his words. One more time—yes, it's true! Why hadn't I noticed this before? Though Dr. Dever uttered only a few sentences on this point and then continued with his sermon, I was transfixed. I stopped the tape and started meditating on the scene that had just unfolded for me . . .

Circumstances and Conclusions

Naomi knew the gnawing emptiness of hunger. Ten years earlier, driven away by withered crops and hard soil, her husband had decided to flee the Promised Land—the land of milk and honey—to seek refuge in the land of a longstanding enemy of Israel. From their hometown of Bethlehem (which meant, ironically, "house of bread"), it was possible to see the hills of Moab to the east across the Dead Sea. Elimelech calculated the risk, deciding it was better to take his wife and two sons on the nearly 100-mile trek to a hostile nation ruled by foreign gods than to starve in Bethlehem.

But now Elimelech was dead, and so were her two adult sons. Naomi was a childless widow—bereft of rights, income, or someone to care for her in old age. Worse, she had two dependents—her own widowed daughters-in-law. One day she overheard field workers say the famine was over in Israel. A flicker of hope rose in her soul. Perhaps she could return home and find someone who might extend care to her.

The trio of widows packed their meager possessions and left before dawn. But as Naomi walked, she began to reconsider the wisdom of taking Ruth and Orpah with her. In the golden glow of the late afternoon sun, Naomi studied the two young women before her. What kind of future could she offer them? Her life once held promise, but now she would have to rely on the uncertain charity of extended family. Would they also obligate themselves for these foreign women?

Suddenly she blurted out, "Go, return each of you to her mother's house. May the LORD deal kindly with you, as you have dealt with the dead and with me. The LORD grant that you may find rest, each of you in the house of her husband!" (Ruth 1:8-9).

Then she kissed them goodbye. But they wept aloud, refusing to leave her. Naomi would have to be blunt: "Turn back, my daughters; why will you go with me? Have I yet sons in my womb that they may become your husbands? Turn back, my daughters; go your way, for I am too old to have a husband. If I should say I have hope, even if I should have a husband this night and should bear sons, would you therefore wait till they were grown? Would you therefore refrain from marrying? No, my daughters, for it is exceedingly bitter to me for your sake that the hand of the LORD has gone out against me" (vv. 11-13).

Orpah understood and returned to her family in Moab. But Ruth could not be dissuaded. She clung to Naomi and vowed not to leave her. So the two women journeyed on.

When Naomi and Ruth arrived in Bethlehem, they were greeted by the women of that town, who marveled that Naomi had returned. But to Naomi, overcome with self-pity, their greetings were hollow. "Do not call me Naomi [*pleasant*]," she said. "Call me Mara [*bitter*], for the Almighty has dealt very bitterly with me. I went away full, and the LORD has brought me back empty. Why call me Naomi, when the LORD has testified against me and the Almighty has brought calamity upon me?" (Ruth 1:20-21).

Naomi had surveyed her circumstances and concluded that the Lord had no further blessings for her. But *God* was not finished. For standing next to Naomi was the Lord's provision for material and relational blessing— Ruth. And just beyond Ruth, the barley harvest was ripening in the fields of her kinsman-redeemer, Boaz. God's quiet providence was already at hand, but Naomi couldn't perceive it.

UNEXPECTANT APATHY

The German poet Goethe once called the book of Ruth "the loveliest complete work on a small scale."[2] While God is never mentioned in it, His kindness and provision are highlighted throughout. Because of its apparent matchmaking theme, the book of Ruth is usually well known to single women. But how many of us have stopped at this point in the story and considered how relevant Naomi's words are to our own lives? Here we have two single women, one of whom has evaluated her present unhappy condition and decided that God was always going to be dealing bitterly with her. Naomi assumed her future was as barren as she was, but that wasn't true. Even as she uttered her complaint, God was quietly orchestrating the circumstances that would lead not only to the redemption of Naomi's family line and property, but also to the ancestry of Jesus Christ.

This is the point that made me rewind that tape over and over again. I know I have been like Naomi. I've looked at my circumstances and concluded that God had "abandoned" me to unwanted singleness. I've actively complained about it. I've made snide remarks. I've been bitter when others have received the blessings I desire. I've even been outright angry with God for not answering my demands on my schedule.

But I thought I'd grown out of it.

Before that retreat, I honestly thought I was doing fairly well. What God showed me then was a more subtle form of unbelief: When our prayers seem to go unheeded, we can learn to live in unexpectant apathy. We go through the motions, but we're not convinced that God will bless us. Bottom line, ugly truth: We really don't trust God. This is no minor issue. As author and theologian Jerry Bridges wrote, "God views our distrust of Him as seriously as He views our disobedience."[3]

SAVORING SOVEREIGNTY

How do we change then? How can we grow in trusting God? I'll provide some simple suggestions here. One way we can change is to immerse ourselves in the Bible passages that highlight God's promises to fulfill all that *He* has planned. If we are to weather the ups and downs of our lives, we must meditate on these truths. (This practice isn't just for singles. I'm reminded by married women that they need this discipline more than ever when they are also trusting God for the safety, fruitfulness, and even salvation of a husband and children.) When waves of doubt and despair threaten to capsize our faith, we must look with eyes of faith at the specific revelations of God's loving and wise sovereignty in Scripture. We must, in effect, feed on it.

Some of the clearest declarations about the Lord's ability to bring about all He has planned can be found in the book of Isaiah. The prophet Isaiah lived in a bloody, tumultuous time when the Assyrian Empire brought about the fall of the northern kingdom of Israel and the siege of Jerusalem in the southern kingdom of Judah. It might have appeared to the Israelites that God was no longer in control. But that's not what God told Isaiah:

> *For I am God, and there is no other; I am God, and there is none like me, declaring the end from the beginning and from ancient times things not yet done, saying, "My counsel shall stand, and I will accomplish all my purpose." . . . I have spoken, and I will bring it to pass; I have purposed, and I will do it.* (Isa. 46:9-11)

"I will accomplish all my purpose." Over and over again in Isaiah we read the Lord's reassurance to His people that He is fully in control and has a plan for glorifying His name and blessing His people. In fact, these prophecies speak not only to current and future events for the nation of Israel, but they also point to the coming Messiah and even to the new creation when Christ will rule as King! Such assurance is sweet to savor.

A second way we can change is to emulate the model of trust found in Psalm 131. I've memorized this short psalm to help me put these truths into practice:

> O LORD, my heart is not lifted up;
> my eyes are not raised too high;
> I do not occupy myself with things
> too great and too marvelous for me.
> But I have calmed and quieted my soul,
> like a weaned child with its mother;
> like a weaned child is my soul within me.
> O Israel, hope in the LORD
> from this time forth and forevermore.

This is a picture of how we can savor the sovereignty of God. There are three principles in this psalm. First, we must humble ourselves and not think too highly of ourselves. We must keep our minds free from speculation and not be preoccupied with "things too great and too marvelous" for finite creatures to know. Second, we must calm and quiet our souls. A weaned child knows from experience that her mother is going to feed her. She doesn't need to cry with every hunger pang. She trusts her mother to provide for her. Third, if we know we have a limited view of our circumstances, and if experience has shown us in other ways that God will provide, then we can choose to put our hope (trust) in God in our seemingly bleak circumstances and wait quietly.

But here's one thing you might have missed. The psalmist addresses not an individual but the community—"O Israel, hope in the LORD." Why? Let's return to Ruth to see.

GOD'S BIGGER PICTURE

Naomi's experience reveals God's faithful provision for one individual. But this biblical account highlights another aspect of God's loving and wise sovereignty: He works on a scale much larger than our individual lives.

I've often daydreamed about the testimony I hope to have on my wedding day. I want to stand up and say that the long wait for my husband was worth it. I want to say that the Lord is fully trustworthy. I want to give Him all the glory should He give me the gift of marriage. It's as though I've been running a grueling race, and having flopped over the "finish line" of marriage, I can stand in the winner's circle with an inspiring story about the reasons for the delay.

Those aren't necessarily bad dreams. But they *are* puny. They start and stop with my individual blessing. I'm rarely daydreaming about how God may be using my life (single *or* married) to accomplish a grander purpose for numerous people. This finite creature has finite plans. But our infinite God has infinite plans to accomplish His purpose of redemption in our generation and beyond. The book of Ruth displays for us God's grander purpose.

In the opening narrative, we saw Ruth as she arrived in Bethlehem. Her prospects weren't rosy. Ruth was a Moabitess, from a group of people who historically had been enemies of Israel. She had to know enough about Israelite customs and history from Naomi to know that she might be snubbed for this. Certainly, her chances of remarriage would be dim among a people who historically had been warned against marrying foreign wives. She was also arriving in Bethlehem during the time of the judges—a time of disorder prior to the unifying rule of a king. The book of Judges concludes with this ominous line: "In those days there was no king in Israel. Everyone did what was right in his own eyes" (Judges 17:6). And let's not forget that Ruth was flat broke.

Ruth had been married to Naomi's firstborn son, Mahlon, which means "the sickly one" or "invalid."[4] Perhaps this marriage and her subsequent widowhood had refined Ruth's character. By the time we meet her in Scripture, she is obviously a submitted woman. She immediately goes to work to provide food for the both of them. Under Jewish law, she had the right to glean in any field, but in God's quiet providence she ends up in the field of a kinsman-redeemer, Boaz. The Bible says she "happened to come to the part of the field belonging to Boaz, who was of the clan of Elimelech" (Ruth 2:3). As Jerry Bridges writes, this was no mere coincidence:

> But still Ruth must gain Boaz's attention and favor. Undoubtedly many of the poor gathered from Boaz's field since leaving the leftover grain was part of the Mosaic law (Leviticus 19:9-10), and hence a common event in the life of Israel. We would suppose that a landowner such as Boaz would not normally notice one poor woman gathering up leftover grain. But Boaz notices Ruth, verse 5: "Boaz asked the foreman of his harvesters, 'Whose young woman is that?'" Finally we see Boaz responding favorably to Ruth, verses 8-10.
>
> The right location, the right timing, being noticed, and gaining Boaz's favor were all key links in the chain of events that eventually resulted in

Ruth's marriage to Boaz. None of the events were extraordinary and all give the appearance of "just happening," nothing more than a coincidence in a romantic story. But the reverent reader of Scripture cannot fail to see the sovereign hand of God arranging those ordinary circumstances to accomplish His purpose.[5]

Because gleaning is an antiquated practice, it may not seem very significant to us today that Ruth gleaned in a kinsman-redeemer's field. But as one commentary says:

> Strong family ties in Israel meant that the verb "redeem" was in common use; it belonged to the realm of family law. Each member of a family or clan had an obligation to defend and provide for any other who was destitute or a victim of injustice. . . . The book of Ruth extends his duties to providing an heir for a male relative who has died childless. Usually this duty fell to a brother (Dt. 25:5-10), but in the case of Ruth who had no brothers-in-law, a more distant relative was expected to marry her, as Naomi revealed (ch. 3).[6]

Because it was common then for parents to arrange the marriages of their children, perhaps Naomi felt obligated to do the same for Ruth. In sending Ruth to Boaz, Naomi was initiating what was her right to request as an Israelite widow (the protection of a kinsman-redeemer). We should also note that Naomi instructed Ruth on her next steps. Ruth was not acting on her own, despite our modern interpretation. By asking Boaz to spread the corner of his garment over her, Ruth was using, according to one commentary, a "vivid expression for providing protection, warmth and fellowship. The phrase spoke eloquently of marriage."[7] Because Ruth had sought a husband who could be a kinsman-redeemer and provide for Naomi—instead of holding out hope for a younger husband—she was being selfless. Boaz recognized that and blessed her for it. His generous nature was also revealed in his willingness to redeem Naomi's property and to marry Ruth:

> Elimelech had a right to an heir. Ruth the Moabitess, his daughter-in-law, was still living, and the man who bought the field had the duty of raising an heir for the dead man through her. If a son were born, the land would revert to him and Elimelech's property would remain in his family. The kinsman would then lose what he had bought and would have another family to keep. . . . The generosity of Boaz in accepting these financial losses becomes the more apparent.[8]

Indeed, this is what happens. Note how the women of Bethlehem direct their words to Naomi upon the birth of Ruth's son:

> *So Boaz took Ruth, and she became his wife. And he went in to her, and the LORD gave her conception, and she bore a son. Then the women said to Naomi, "Blessed be the LORD, who has not left you this day without a redeemer, and may his name be renowned in Israel! He shall be to you a restorer of life and a nourisher of your old age, for your daughter-in-law who loves you, who is more to you than seven sons, has given birth to him." Then Naomi took the child and laid him on her lap and became his nurse.* (Ruth 4:13-16)

I trust that Naomi joined the voices of these women when they praised the Lord for the reversal of her financial and relational losses. God had kindly provided for these two destitute widows against tremendous odds. That was noteworthy enough, but these women could not have known the bigger picture. This child was Obed, who became the grandfather of King David (the author of Psalm 131) and an ancestor of Jesus. Both Boaz and Ruth are listed in the opening genealogy of Jesus in the Gospel of Matthew—a fulfillment of their words about Boaz, "may his name be renowned in Israel!"

Naomi and Ruth undoubtedly were encouraged by what the Lord did for them in their lifetimes, but I suspect they would have been shocked to know how God worked through them to bring about His glorious plan of redemption and salvation.

GOD IS NOT THROUGH YET

I will always be grateful that I selected that message from Dr. Dever as I drove to my retreat. I left that weekend convicted that my unexpectant apathy was really sinful unbelief toward God. He refreshed my determination to remember that, of the two of us, *only* God is the omniscient being. I simply can't comprehend the big picture, even though my pride tempts me to think I can. Later, when I discussed this lesson from Ruth with a friend of mine, she observed a precious detail I had overlooked: The seeds for the barley harvest were planted while Naomi and Ruth were still in *Moab*! The harvest was ready in time for Naomi's arrival.

Since that retreat, I endeavor to look around whenever I find I am judging God. When I *look* for the barley harvests of my life, I see many things for which I can be grateful. I may desire the companionship of a husband, but standing with me now are loving family members, good friends, and the amazing fellowship of my church. I may desire the joy of being the object of masculine pursuit, but standing with me now are godly men who are faithful brothers and friends. There are even blessings in my life that I didn't ask God for and others that I take for granted.

God is still working—let's never forget that. *What we can see of our circumstances is not all that is there.* Whether we are single or married, God is working to glorify Himself through those circumstances, and only He knows the best way to accomplish His plans. At any given time, we can't see the grand panorama of His grace. But, secure in the reality of it, we can rest in the promise that still echoes across time: "'My counsel shall stand, and I will accomplish all my purpose.' . . . I have spoken, and I will bring it to pass; I have purposed, and I will do it" (Isa. 46:10-11).

FOR FURTHER STUDY

❖ *Trusting God* by Jerry Bridges (NavPress) is another "must read" book. Chapter 4, "God's Sovereignty Over People," chapter 11, "Trusting God for Who You Are," and chapter 13, "Choosing to Trust God," will make your highlighter run dry.

❖ Read Isaiah chapters 40 to 49, and highlight the passages where God speaks of His purpose and plan. Spend at least a week in your daily devotions meditating on each highlighted passage. Pray these Scriptures back to God, thanking Him for His sovereignty in your life as you make your requests of Him.

❖ Make a list commemorating as many evidences of God's faithfulness to you as you can recall, and remind yourself often of these events. "I will recount the steadfast love of the LORD, the praises of the LORD, according to all that the LORD has granted us . . ." (Isa. 63:7).

❖ After I wrote this chapter, Dr. Dever gave this message again at a conference for single adults and made what was already an outstanding message into a stellar one! Do yourself a favor and order your own copy. He spoke at Joshua Harris's New Attitude 2004 conference. The message was titled, "Ruth: God's Providence in a Single Woman's Life." You can order this from www.sovereigngraceministries.org.

PART TWO

FINDING A GUIDE FOR RELATIONSHIPS IN THE PROVERBS 31 WOMAN

4

A WOMAN OF
NOBLE CHARACTER

A wife of noble character who can find? She is worth far more than rubies.

PROVERBS 31:10 NIV

I thought I'd be married by now," she said, her eyes downcast as she absently twirled her coffee stirrer.

I nodded, waiting. This was a familiar conversation.

"I'm beginning to think that I might be single for the rest of my life."

Kristi spoke in a half-whisper, barely audible above the whistling hiss of the cappuccino machine. As she looked up, I could see the tears of disappointment brimming, threatening to paint her cheeks with black mascara.

"If God doesn't have marriage for me, then I have to rethink what to do with my future," she continued. "I feel like I'm on hold, just hanging around waiting to find out the plan."

"What would you do differently now if you had known?" I gently asked.

"Well, that's the thing—I don't really know," she said. "I guess I would take my career more seriously. Maybe take some classes so I could get a better job. Or maybe do something really radical, like move to Africa and serve in a church orphanage. I just didn't plan on being single for so long, and I feel like I need a roadmap for this detour."

Kristi's words stayed with me for a long time after our conversation. At twenty-nine, she was facing an internal deadline for marriage. Most of her childhood friends and all of her siblings were married. Yet she was a godly woman who actively served her church. She didn't lack theological instruction, and she wasn't bitter. She just didn't have a *plan* for flourishing in extended or even lifelong singleness.

I could empathize with her. I had often voiced similar questions myself, and heard them from many other women. Then God mercifully showed me a portrait of fruitful singleness in Scripture—a plan that I could follow. I did have a roadmap that, more importantly, does *not* point to a detour.

A Personal Guide

As we might expect from a God who once lived among us, the roadmap He has provided is actually a personal guide. We find her at the conclusion of Proverbs—the famous Proverbs 31 woman. This epilogue is a twenty-two-verse acrostic. Each line starts with a successive letter of the Hebrew alphabet. The chapter is attributed to the mother of King Lemuel, who instructed her young son through this memory game in both the alphabet and the qualities of a virtuous wife. In other words, she wanted this future ruler to know by heart what to look for in a *single* woman to ensure that he would find someone who would make an excellent wife.[1]

When I considered this for the first time, I laughed out loud. The very passage I often skipped because it was about an excellent wife was the key to understanding my singleness! Here was the guide I needed to show me how to invest my gift of singleness in the church. As I studied this woman, the priorities for my life came into focus. The *role* described in this passage is that of a wife, but her godly, noble character is what all women should desire. It will serve us in every season of our lives. As author Douglas Wilson says:

> [T]he time a person spends when he is single should be time spent in preparation for marriage. This is important even if he never gets married. This is because biblical preparation for marriage is nothing more than learning to follow Jesus Christ and to love one's neighbor. In other words, preparation for Christian marriage is basically the same as preparation for Christian living. Christians are to prepare for marriage by learning self-denial, subduing their pride, and putting their neighbor first.[2]

Isn't this great news? If we're floundering in our singleness, wondering what we're supposed to do, we find it all in this passage. We don't need to know what God has planned for our whole future. We just need to take the next step. It's all right here for us. The Proverbs 31 woman is a concrete example of this kind of others-focused spiritual maturity, a maturity required for every Christian woman. While many translations call her a wife, the original Hebrew word is *ishshah*, or woman.[3] The King James Version refers to her as "a virtuous woman." The New International Version calls her a "wife of noble character." The English Standard Version calls her "an excellent wife." No matter her role, this woman is virtuous, noble, and excellent. She is commended as "a woman [*ishshah*] who fears the Lord" in verse 30. These are virtues for all Christian women, whatever our marital status.

As we saw in chapter 3, God can be trusted to deliver a husband if that is His will. We don't have to snag one. Our job is to work on becoming women of noble character. We have much to learn from the example of the Proverbs 31 woman; so we will explore some of her stellar character qualities for the rest of this book.

Right now, let's dive into the first virtue of our wonderful role model.

BE THE RIGHT WOMAN

In this chapter, we will focus on verse 10: "A wife of noble character who can find? She is worth far more than rubies" (Prov. 31:10 NIV). There are three important ideas in this verse. The first is *ishshah*—she is a woman. The second is her noble character. The third is her worth.

Believe it or not, I've discovered that I must state the obvious: We are women. The Lord only made two types of creatures to bear His image: men and women. He didn't make third-wheel hybrids. I know that singleness can tempt some of us to think we've slid into a neutered gender somehow, but that's not the case. The Lord God made Eve as a woman *before* He brought her to Adam. It bears repeating: Eve was fully feminine *before* Adam laid claim to her as bone of his bone, flesh of his flesh.

It is immensely important that we single women acknowledge that our femininity is God's initiative and creation. We aren't more feminine because a man is pursuing us. We aren't less feminine because no man is pursuing us. Our femininity is not dependent on marriage or motherhood to be fully expressed. We are feminine from the moment we are conceived because that is God's design, and He has a purpose for our femininity throughout the various seasons of our lives. (The rest of this book is devoted to exploring what this looks like when we're single.)

The second idea in verse 10 is the importance or influence of character. You often hear it said today that "she's just a wife," or "I don't want to be just somebody's wife," as though there is no value or significance in that role.

The Bible is very clear about the influence a wife has—for better or for worse. One of the more chilling indictments of a woman is found in 2 Kings 8:18 in connection with Jehoram, king of Judah. Despite the influence of his father, Jehoshaphat, who did "what was right in the sight of the LORD" (1 Kings 22:43), the Bible says Jehoram "walked in the way of the kings of Israel, as the house of Ahab had done, for the daughter of Ahab was his wife." Why did Jehoram ditch his father's instruction and example? Because of his wife, the daughter of the notorious Israelite king Ahab, who tangled with the prophet Elijah at Mount Carmel and lost. Ahab worshiped false gods, and so did his daughter.

The Bible doesn't seem to be concerned with the difficulty of finding a wife. Rather, it is full of exhortations to find the *right woman* to be a wife (i.e., Prov. 12:4; 19:14; 31:10). We shouldn't want just to be someone's wife. We should want to be known as women of noble character who are a blessing and an influence for good in any relationship.

The third idea in verse 10 is the worth of a woman with a noble character. The Hebrew word used to describe her noble character was *chayil*. That word has the connotation of a wealth of resources, including valor, ability, strength, and riches. It implies a multitude, an army.[4] Her worth exceeds a valuable and rare jewel. The Hebrew word *paniyn* has been translated in many English Bibles as ruby, but its exact meaning is uncertain.[5] No matter the specific stone, the point is that such a woman is priceless.

BE UNCOMMON

History is littered with bloodthirsty kings, selfish queens, corrupt princes, and vengeful knights. It's unfortunate that noble birth with all its privileges rarely produces noble character. However, the concept still stands: A noble is a person of rank, someone who is not a commoner. A noble character, therefore, is one that is not common—one that possesses dignity and is above whatever is low, mean, degrading, or dishonorable. When a woman is demanding or high maintenance, we often joke that she is being a princess. But that is a distorted view of nobility. The best princesses are gracious and uplifting. Their brows are not furrowed with bitterness or discontent; they are not scowling; they are serene.

One of the first people I met in church as a new believer was a single woman pushing forty. She had a history of active fruitfulness in the church, but as she got older, she grew bitter about being single. She would decline invitations to baby and bridal showers and withdrew from small-group activities with married women. You had only to talk with her for a very few moments to hear how discontented she was with being single.

I vowed then that I did not want to emulate her example. I couldn't control whether or not I'd be single, but I could certainly control my attitude about it. But I also arrogantly judged her and kept my distance from her, not wanting to be associated with any "unhappy leftovers." Ten years later I better understand her temptations, and I regret my attitude. This woman left my church years ago, and I don't know where she is now, but I trust that God has helped her change, just as He has helped me to change. When I was younger, I sinfully judged single women who were the age I am now; time has humbled me. I still don't want to be an "unhappy leftover," but now I understand that there are no leftovers with a sovereign God who purposefully plans our futures and who graciously gives us good gifts (like singleness). Once I got that straight, it was easier to avoid being chronically unhappy.

As I've pondered the common temptations of singleness, I've noticed five character qualities that help exhibit noble character in this season:

- Trust in God when your hopes are deferred
- Contentment while you're waiting
- Faithfulness to sow to the future even when you're in tears
- Graciousness when others receive what you would like
- Humility to pray to *be* a blessing, rather than to receive a blessing

This isn't an exhaustive list, of course, but I think as we explore each quality, we will find in our singleness some practical ways to honor God before the watching world.

TRUSTING GOD WITH DEFERRED HOPES

I once read that the opposite of fear is not courage; it is love. When you love someone, you naturally look for his best qualities and give him the benefit of the doubt in situations you don't understand. When you fear someone, you distrust his motives, actions, and words. You certainly don't go the extra mile for him.

This is the situation Jesus addressed in the parable of the talents (Matt.

25:14-30). Three servants each received a vast amount of money. One received five talents, a second received two talents, a third received one talent. The Bible notes that the master gave "to each according to his ability." Now a talent was a monetary unit worth about twenty years' wages for a laborer;[6] so this master had been generous to all. But the third servant viewed this man as a harsh taskmaster. He hid his one talent in the ground. When his master returned, this servant expressed his great distrust: "Master, I knew you to be a hard man, reaping where you did not sow, and gathering where you scattered no seed, so I was afraid, and I went and hid your talent in the ground. Here you have what is yours."

The third servant had a low view of his master—and perhaps even of what he had received in comparison to the other servants. So he made no effort to multiply his talent. An extended season of singleness can present a similar temptation. We can think that God has given us very little. So we do nothing with it. Despising the "one talent" of singleness, we don't invest it to have something to show when He returns. We don't try to multiply what He's bestowed; we ungratefully just put it in a hole in the ground and sit down to have a pity party.

Our lack of trust is revealed in our lack of investment in the Lord's dearly beloved body—the church. When we view God as a generous master (for that is the truth), we will embrace what He's given us and look forward to giving Him an account of what we've done with His gift. We'll tell Him of the many ways we invested it in the church and got a return. We'll tell Him about the lessons we taught in children's ministry. We'll tell Him about the tithes and offerings we gave. We'll tell Him about our prayers for the sick. We'll tell Him about all the people in our small groups that we helped. We'll tell Him about the plans we administrated and the meetings we attended that were for outreaches that impacted our communities. None of this will be news to Him, of course, but what a joyous account that will be—*if we trust Him*.

The parable of the talents reveals to us the sad consequences of not trusting God when He's been generous to us. Precisely because the Lord is not a "harsh taskmaster," He fully understands that there is suffering in living with deferred hopes. We can read His compassion in Proverbs 13:12: "Hope deferred makes the heart sick, but a desire fulfilled is a tree of life." God's Word recognizes how difficult it is to live with unfulfilled expectations. But this proverb simply notes the obvious. We can find the remedy for our sick hearts in what I call the "chain of hope" in Romans 5:3-6: "[W]e rejoice in our sufferings, knowing that suffering produces endurance, and endurance produces character, and character produces hope, and *hope does not put us to shame*, because God's love has been poured into our hearts through the Holy Spirit who has been given to us. For while we were still weak, at the right time Christ died for the ungodly" (emphasis added).

As we persevere in doing good, we find the endurance to continue by the grace of God. This perseverance produces that noble character in us, and noble character produces hope. Hope doesn't put us to shame because we are hoping in a God who has shed His blood for us and poured His love into our hearts!

What we find here in Romans is that years of waiting on God should produce more hope, not less. Is that an upside down thought to you? It's certainly not the way we would rationally think about hope. Waiting on God often shifts the *content* of our hope. As we wait, we see the many ways He proves His faithfulness to us—starting with the cross and ending with the bright promise of heaven—and all the big and little mercies in between. That vista of grace can't help but dwarf the outstanding request we have before God!

Let me get personal here. Now that I'm forty and still single, I see that I haven't died of deferred hopes. Actually life is pretty good. I would still like to be married, but this hope doesn't consume me the way it used to. I am trusting that when I get to see the big picture from heaven's viewpoint, I will agree that God's plan for my life was the best, that the years I spent single were worth it for the ways God used me. If being single means that God is using me to reach many unbelievers, I know I'm not going to stand in heaven and resent His decision! There was a point in my early thirties, however, when you couldn't have convinced me this would be the way I would feel now. I remember talking then to a single woman in her forties who told me it really wasn't that bad to still be single. I just stared at her as she said those words. She might as well have been speaking a foreign language.

One thing I've learned to do is praise God in the middle of my dashed hopes. Years ago when a hoped-for relationship wouldn't happen or a friendship wouldn't kindle into a romance, I would crash and burn emotionally. Sometimes it would take weeks to recover. But now I've learned something from the prophet Habakkuk and his closing psalm. He acknowledged the reality of suffering, but still aimed his emotions and will toward the One who is his salvation and strength. In recent years, I've trained myself to respond similarly. When I receive the disappointing news, I will retreat with a worship CD and sing with tears coursing down my cheeks—willing myself to praise the Lord in the midst of crushed hopes. I've learned to paraphrase Habakkuk 3:17-18 this way:

> *Though this friendship does not blossom,*
> *nor love be in his heart,*
> *though he chooses to pursue someone else,*
> *and my prayers seem to go unanswered,*
> *though others walk down the wedding aisle,*
> *and I remain behind,*
> *yet I will rejoice in the LORD;*
> *I will take joy in the God of my salvation.*

CONTENTMENT IN THE WAIT

The apostle Paul wrote that he had "learned to be content whatever the circumstances" (Philip. 4:11 NIV). I am grateful for one word in that incredible phrase—*learned*—because I tend to focus first on the "whatever the circumstances" part. If the venerable apostle had to learn to be content, I can expect no less.

What does contentment in varied circumstances look like? It is a gracious spirit that is steady and constant. A woman who has learned to be content "takes a licking and keeps on ticking," to quote the old Timex ad. That slogan has its roots in nautical history. Prior to the development of a timepiece that could accurately keep time aboard a ship, sailors had no way to gauge longitude, and navigation remained hazardous. They needed a timepiece that could withstand the changes in barometric pressure, humidity, and temperature, as well as the pitch and roll of the ship. The scientific challenge was so daunting that in 1714 Queen Anne signed an act offering a vast sum of £20,000 to the one who could solve the problem of measuring longitude. One man, John Harrison, dedicated his life to the cause, and he was ultimately successful.

When we experience changes—the pressures of life, the heat of sin, the cold drafts of loneliness, the damp chill of disappointment, the pitch and roll of shifting circumstances—but we keep a steady pace, we are exhibiting contentment.[7]

One woman who knew what it was like to wait on God was Hannah. In 1 Samuel 1:7 we read that she endured both the shame of being childless and the provocation of her rival wife. "So it went on year by year," the Bible says matter-of-factly (v. 7). Even after she cried in prayer to the Lord and

Eli the priest blessed her petition, she still had to wait. In verse 20, it says "in due time" Hannah conceived and bore a son. We don't know exactly how long that was, but it still took some time.

In *The Art of Divine Contentment*, Puritan author Thomas Watson notes one very important aspect of how Hannah handled her emotions during the wait: "When any burden is upon the spirit, prayer gives vent, it easeth the heart. Hannah's spirit was burdened; 'I am' says she, 'a woman of a sorrowful spirit.' Now having prayed, and wept, she went away, and was no more sad; only here is the difference between a holy complaint and a discontented complaint; in the one we complain *to* God, in the other we complain *of* God."[8]

Are we not to have cares or concerns? Of course we still have them. But contentment comes from knowing *where* we can take our concerns and *who* cares for our concerns. As 1 Peter 5:6-7 (NIV) says: "Humble yourselves, therefore, under God's mighty hand, that he may lift you up *in due time*. Cast all your anxiety on him because he cares for you" (emphasis added). What are we to do in the "due time"? We are to give our anxieties to God and wait patiently because we know He cares for us.

A contented woman is not impatiently proud. Contentment calls for humility. We have to intentionally humble ourselves under God's mighty hand when our circumstances don't work out to our liking. Without a doubt, it *is* humbling to go year after year with a hope deferred! It's *very* humbling to keep showing up at family events as the only single sibling or to go to the wedding of a former boyfriend without a date. But we have to remember that, as Christian women, we're not here to promote our personal success stories anyway. We're here as trophies of grace—broken clay jars carrying around incredibly valuable treasure. Even if the Lord should grant our petition for marriage and a family, our witness and purpose do not change. Only our circumstances change.

Finally, as single women, I think we can take special comfort from Paul's words. He learned to be content in whatever the circumstances, and singleness was among them. When he wrote that he had learned contentment in all things, he was a single man, imprisoned in chains! I appreciate this description from an article about contentment in the *Journal of Biblical Counseling*:

> One hesitates to include singleness in a list of Paul's problems since he did not view it as a problem. Nevertheless, undesired or unexpected singleness surely provided temptations for discontentment in Paul, and it has been a problem for many people since him.

Paul lacked the support, comfort, and companionship of a wife and family. As a single man he had no spouse with whom he could share his life and find consolation. Yet Paul learned contentment in every circumstance, including his single status. In fact, he even found this state preferable (1 Cor. 7).

Again the message of the gospel is clear: Whatever the cause of your single status—never married, widowed, or divorced—you who believe in Christ are all sons and daughters of God and heirs of His promises (Gal. 3:26-29). You can know God's contentment. Even if your friends or church members don't fully know or understand you, Jesus does. He can provide inner satisfaction.[9]

FAITHFUL TO SOW, EVEN IN TEARS

All of my food comes in plastic wrap. The only seeds I ever see are the sesame seeds on my hamburger bun. I don't even plant seeds in a *garden*! If I bother to put out any plants, I buy them half-grown and stick them in containers.

But every day I am sowing.

The Bible says that I'm either scattering the right seed, or I'm scattering the wrong seed. "Do not be deceived: God is not mocked, for whatever one sows, that will he also reap. For the one who sows to his own flesh will from the flesh reap corruption, but the one who sows to the Spirit will from the Spirit reap eternal life" (Gal. 6:7-8). Every action and every thought is dipping into one bag of seed or another—all of which will one day produce an inevitable harvest.

The discipline we must have as single women is to avoid despair and persevere in sowing to a harvest of righteousness. I like the imagery of Psalm 126:4-6:

> *Restore our fortunes, O LORD,*
> *like streams in the Negeb!*
> *Those who sow in tears*
> *shall reap with shouts of joy!*
> *He who goes out weeping,*
> *bearing the seed for sowing,*
> *shall come home with shouts of joy,*
> *bringing his sheaves with him.*

For those who have experienced loss, this is an especially poignant psalm. One commentary calls this psalm "the tension of experience." I like that title very much. This commentary notes:

Joy seems to lie in the past, tears occupy the present. If only the Lord would act now as completely and dramatically as he did then! So we pray for streams in the Negev, a sudden flash flood, transforming dried-up watercourses, making the scorched land into a garden! But no, in God's providence, following on his mighty acts, the metaphor of the harvest takes over. There will be songs of joy but only when the toilsome task of sowing has been done and the crop has matured for harvest.[10]

When we're battling cynicism, wrestling with grief, or overcome with discouragement, it's hard to take a long-term view. But the Holy Spirit will help us to do so as we rely on Him for help. At times I've felt like I've trudged along with one handful of used tissues and the other limply trailing seed behind me. I've cried on the way to and from bridal and baby showers, but I've gone. I've cried as I've held my nieces or nephews in my arms (as much as I love them with all my heart) because I want my own children—but I've still cared for them. I've listened to countless hours of girly talk about the new boyfriend and saved the tears for later. I'm not boasting in myself here. I'm boasting in the grace of God. He *does* provide the strength to keep doing the right thing even when all we want to do is pull the covers over our heads and never leave our beds!

There is one memorable scene in the life of Jesus that I meditate upon often. In John 11:35, the Bible simply says, "Jesus wept." This short verse is found in the account of the death of Lazarus. What's stunning about the tears of Jesus is that He knew what was going to happen! Not only was He going to resurrect Lazarus in this age, but He was also going to the cross in order that Lazarus be resurrected at His second coming. All that was planned for Lazarus in the mind of God was glorious; yet Jesus still paused to grieve with His good friends, Mary and Martha. He recognized their present pain and didn't minimize it. What a sympathetic God we have!

There is legitimate grief in deferred hopes and an unfulfilled desire for marriage and children. But I wouldn't be honest if I didn't say that many of my hot tears have been motivated by self-pity more than anything else. I wish the plight of those who reject God would move me as much, but I must confess I've not cried as much for their souls as I have for my own desires. Author and pastor John Piper says, "Self-pity is the response of pride to suffering."[11] *Ouch!* But so true.

"Self-pity sounds self-sacrificing," Piper writes. "The reason self-pity does not look like pride is that it appears to be needy. But the need arises from a wounded ego, and the desire of the self-pitying is not really for others to see them as helpless, but as heroes. The need self-pity feels does not come from a sense of unworthiness, but from a sense of *unrecognized worthiness*. It is the response of unapplauded pride" (emphasis added).[12]

When I am weeping out of self-pity, I am indulging a sense of unrecognized worthiness—the unapplauded pride that I should not be passed over for marriage. I do have a compassionate Savior, but in those particular moments I suspect that if Jesus is weeping at all, He's weeping because I've grieved Him with my unbelief and distrust. At those moments, I think of a song lyric that rings so true—"bearing gifts as if they're burdens."[13] What's especially egregious is that I know what Mary and Martha *did not* on their day of mourning—the Father has accepted the sacrifice of my Savior on the cross, and my future is secure in Him! My fortunes have been more than restored; they exceed anything I could ask for or imagine.

When tempted by self-pity, I endeavor to recall all the ways that God has been faithful to me, starting with my regeneration and conversion, and ending with His promise of life everlasting. In between, I have a long list of other blessings that are merely a foreshadowing of all that is to come. I want to sow to right thinking as well. Psalm 104:34 says, "May my meditation be pleasing to him, for I rejoice in the LORD." If I'm meditating on all the ways I feel I've been wronged, cheated, or overlooked, it's impossible for my thoughts to be pleasing to God. Those thoughts are seeds that will produce a ruinous harvest.

We must evaluate our thoughts and actions with a long-term view. Most single women will one day get married; so what we're sowing to now will suddenly bloom in marriage. For those called to lifelong singleness, we can never forget that our lives are a mere mist, a vapor, a ray of sunshine on the grass. In either circumstance, we only have a few years on this earth to sow to an eternal harvest. We can't lose sight of how fast the days slip by. So even at our lowest point, let's resolve to grab the tissues and the *right* seed and keep on faithfully sowing to God's glory!

Graciousness When Others Are Blessed

In my first year as a Christian, I attended or participated in approximately twelve weddings, including those of my two younger sisters and two former flames. As a new believer, I perceived that God was making a *big* point to me—"rejoice with those who rejoice" (Rom. 12:15). The Greek word translated as "rejoice" is *chairo,* a primary verb that means to be full of cheer, calmly happy, or well-off.[14]

But it's impossible to be calmly happy if we're full of jealousy or resignation when others are blessed. Jealousy is a poison that simmers in indwelling sin and corrodes our hearts from the inside out. Resignation is a begrudging existence, one based in not believing the best of God. Both operate out of a mind-set that God has finite resources—a God of scarcity and not abundance—as though if one person gets blessed, that diminishes our chances of being similarly blessed. That's just not true! If my best friend gets married, it doesn't mean the pool of blessings is now down by one. This isn't a game of musical chairs, in which I might be left standing with fewer and fewer chairs each time.

I think most Christian women have learned to either subdue or hide overt jealousy. It's an ugly sin, and more often than not it is easily detectable; so we don't get away with it for very long. Someone will usually point it out. As we saw in chapter 3, resignation is much more subtle. We can mask our unbelief by saying we're just accepting God's plan for our lives—and other mature-sounding statements. Jerry Bridges skillfully draws out the difference between acceptance and resignation:

> Trusting God in the midst of our pain and heartache means that we accept it from Him. There is a vast difference between acceptance and either resignation or submission. We can resign ourselves to a difficult situation, simply because we see no other alternative. Many people do that all the time. Or we can submit to the sovereignty of God in our circumstances with a certain amount of reluctance. But to truly accept our pain and heartache has the connotation of willingness. An attitude of acceptance says that we trust God, that He loves us, and knows what is best for us.[15]

What do graciousness toward others and acceptance toward God look like on a daily basis? I think these attitudes are grounded in a biblical understanding of marriage. Marriage is a blessing, but it's also a lot of work. It's two sinners committing to love and forgive each other for the rest of their lives, to the glory and honor of God. They are no longer two, but one flesh (Matt. 19:5).

I do recognize how hard it is to see your friends get married. Not only did they receive something you'd like for yourself, but also most times it severely affects the original friendship. It is costly to rejoice with your newly married friends, knowing that you won't have the same access to them that you once did. You can no longer spend hours on the phone with them late at night or see them at every singles' ministry meeting or just hang out together over the weekend. What your married friends gain in intimacy, you sacrifice in many cases. But our Lord sees this. I've never had one friend get married without Him giving me another good friend in short order. I'm always amazed at His provision for friendship.

As women of noble character, we must be committed to the biblical model of marriage and its purpose within the local church. We should quickly relinquish our expectations and bless our newly married friends as they learn their new roles as wives (and even husbands—but we'll address that further in chapter 6). It's not easy to merge lives, households, schedules, and families, and we should endeavor to recognize the *work* that comes with establishing a marriage. In most cases, we'll have to be the ones to pursue the friendship after the wedding. That's just life. Our circumstances didn't change as radically; so we'll have to carry the ball for a while. But this is a wise investment, because after a year or two the friendship often settles comfortably into a new pattern if we've been faithful to maintain it. I've experienced this countless times, and I'm so grateful for it.

Another way we can serve our married friends is by always pointing them back to their husbands in times of conflict or disappointment. We should never allow ourselves to be the standard sounding board for complaints. (I'm not saying that our friends can't ask us for counsel or share their struggles, but we should not routinely be accepting sinful criticism and gossip about their spouses.) When one of my friends got married, she struggled with a part of her husband's personality that had never bothered her as a single woman. I told her that I was going to demonstrate godly love and care for her right then by pointing out her sinful judgment of her husband and reminding her that I was committed to doing whatever I could to strengthen her marriage. I would love her by caring for both her husband and her marriage, not just nod and tell her that her other half sure was idiotic.

Rejoicing with our married friends is something that lasts far longer than the engagement and wedding. Long after the ceremony, we have the opportunity to be "full of cheer, calmly happy, and well-off" in the ways we pursue friendship, protect the marriages of others, and trust God's love and wisdom for ourselves. The rewards are a wider circle of friends, seasoned friendships of many varieties, and the pleasure of honoring God by rejoicing with those who rejoice.

HUMILITY SEEKS TO *BE* A BLESSING

I've never wrestled with long-term chronic illness or pain, but I do understand how one can grow weary of the topic. When one of my good friends was dying of cancer, he told me that he got so tired of talking about it. He was grateful for visitors who would discuss other issues with him—especially those who would talk about what God was showing them during devotions or how He was leading or providing for them. Others with long-term illness have told me that they are reluctant to ask for prayer yet again for an ongoing condition or disease.

I understand how certain topics can seem to dominate one's life and reputation. At times I feel that way about singleness. I have been praying for a husband for so many years that *I'm* sick of hearing my own prayers! But humility forces me to keep praying. I have a desire that I can't fulfill on my own—I *must* pray to the One who can.

But here's an interesting question that someone once asked me: *How often do you pray to be a good wife?* My answer was truly eloquent: "Ummmm . . . well, up to now, I'd have to say, uh . . . never."

What a forehead-slapper! I've got a list of things I'm asking God for in a husband, but until that point, it had never occurred to me that I'd better be praying for the grace to be a good wife. Proverbs 19:14 says, "House and wealth are inherited from fathers, but a prudent wife is from the LORD." Prudent? Yikes! I'd better start praying for that quality!

It takes humility to realize we need to spend more time praying to be conformed to the image of Christ than we do petitioning God for blessings. At the moment of our conversion, the dominion of sin—the power of sin—was cancelled in our lives. But indwelling sin is with us until our final breath. Should God grant us the gifts of marriage and children, indwelling sin goes along for the ride. By the power of the Holy Spirit, we will grow a bit in this life, but we'll never attain perfection. Until we obtain that glorified body in a sinless heaven, we will need our Savior every day.

COUNT IT ALL JOY

At the beginning of this chapter, we left my friend Kristi in the coffee shop, pondering her future. Since that time she has become a teacher. And an accountant. And a married mother of two. And a childless, single woman celebrating her thirty-fifth birthday. And an artist. And the author of this book.

How can this be? Kristi is a composite. She is a composite of the dozens, if not hundreds, of conversations I've had with single women throughout the years. In some cases, I've been Kristi, too. My most recent Kristi conversation happened over e-mail. A thoughtful woman named Connie asked me these heartfelt questions:

• At what age do you start making long-term goals for singleness? I'm (*only*, I know) twenty-seven, and like all my friends expected I'd be married by now, or any day now. I'm still kind of expecting it before thirty, honestly. Why is it that singleness after thirty sounds so . . . second-rate?

• How do I plan for my future? Do I invest further in graduate school so that I can have a better-paying job? If I knew I'd be single for the next ten years, I'd be willing to invest the money (or go into debt) to get into a dream job with financial benefits. I'm hoping, of course, for a groom to appear in the next two years (or two months!), in which case it might be unwise. I'd willingly leave a career outside the home to pursue one inside the home upon marriage or the birth of children. Also, should I move to a career that would help with long-term savings? Sometimes it sounds like I'm gambling, betting that the (hopefully increased) financial security of a husband is a shoo-in. Not that I'd probably admit that out loud. And obviously I ultimately trust in God for provision. But these are the questions I ask myself.

• Why are there so many unmarried women in the church whose only goal in life is to be a wife/mom—and yet they are still unmarried?

• Are you sure that I'm not incomplete as a single woman? I surely could use spiritual leadership, close accountability, and somebody to handle my car questions. Sometimes I feel doomed to be less godly, less sanctified, and vulnerable to the auto mechanic.

• I agree with the teaching I've received that I should enjoy being a woman. I just think it would be more fun with a husband.

These are gut-level honest questions that real women ask themselves. These matters are confusing to consider at times. But with our fruitful Proverbs 31 role model, we have clarity. Why *are* there so many unmarried women in the church whose only goal in life is to be a wife and mother? I think for one reason—it's a godly, legitimate desire. But typically it's also the *only* model of femininity that is fleshed out for women in the church. I believe all women desire to be fruitful in their femininity. The Proverbs 31 woman shows us how to do that in any season of life. Thus, we don't have to be concerned about when to start planning for lifelong singleness—it's no different than planning for lifelong femininity.

For example, take Connie's question about investment in a career. The Proverbs 31 woman is financially savvy, and her shrewd dealings are a blessing to her family and enable her to care for the needy. We will explore this further in chapter 8, but I don't believe planning for our futures has to be an either/or proposition. With wise counsel and a good understanding of our goals as godly women, we should cultivate all the gifts and opportunities that God has given us. They could end up being the very skills our husbands need in a helpmate. If we don't marry, then we can enjoy more challenging work and professional opportunities. Either way, these skills could also benefit the ministries of our churches. For those reasons, anticipating marriage shouldn't be a justification to put our lives on hold.

Conversely, giving everything we have to our jobs and not creating a home life, investing in our churches, or taking time to care for others is equally wrong. (It's wrong for men, too.) In Proverbs 31, we find a woman whose home was a warm, richly appointed haven for her family and presumably her friends. Why wait for marriage to create that kind of appealing environment? We'll consider this further in chapter 7.

I empathize with Connie's question about being incomplete without a husband because I've held that perspective, too. During many weddings, I've heard it said that as these two people become one flesh, they will experience greater fruitfulness together than they would alone. There are things they couldn't do as individuals. They need to be joined together for this purpose. The groom couldn't complete the task that God has called him to do without the help of his bride, God's provision of a helpmate. The bride couldn't help without knowing her groom's task. Thus, they will be more fruitful married than they were previously as single individuals.

I don't find fault with this statement. It's true! But please note the purpose: *service in God's kingdom*. There is a level of fruitfulness that God wants from their lives that will come in being joined together. This does not imply that they were *un*fruitful as singles. They just have an assignment from God that requires them to work together for this kind of effectiveness. They are incomplete for this task until they are yoked together.

But in this sense they are not incomplete as *beings*. Their value as human beings remains the same the day after their wedding as the day before: Humans made equally in the image of God who are fallen sinners redeemed by God to worship and serve Him for all of eternity.

Married or single, our only contribution to our valuation is our sin. It is our sin that mars us as incomplete, causing us to fall short of the glory of God (Rom. 3:23). *This is important: A husband does not complete us. It is Christ who completes us.* When Jesus said to the Pharisees in John 10:9, "I am the door. If anyone enters by me, he will be saved and will go in and out and find pasture," the word He used for saved was *sozo*, which is used throughout the New Testament. It literally means to deliver, protect, heal, preserve, make whole.[16] Our salvation in Christ addresses every bit of our lack. A husband is a partner, a fellow heir in the grace of life. He has a specific role in marriage, which we'll look at later, but he can't complete anyone.

There is an aspect of *sozo* that is also produced over time, as God works in us and through the events of our lives. I'm not referring to our status before God as forgiven of our sins, but to our spiritual maturity. God uses an unusual tool for that purpose: trials. Is singleness a trial? In many ways, it can be. I don't dispute that. But marriage has trials, as does parenthood. Life is full of trials of various kinds. In those very trials, we find this perspective: "Count it all joy, my brothers, when you meet trials of various kinds, for you know that the testing of your faith produces steadfastness. And let steadfastness have its full effect, *that you may be perfect and complete, lacking in nothing*" (James 1:2-4, emphasis added). *Steadfastness* is not a common word today. It is a translation of *hupomone*, a Greek word that means cheerful or hopeful endurance.[17]

Is this sounding familiar yet? Where have we encountered endurance before? As we saw earlier in this chapter, it was in the "chain of hope" of Romans 5:3-6. "[W]e rejoice in our sufferings, knowing that suffering produces endurance, and endurance produces character, and character produces hope, and hope does not put us to shame, because God's love has been poured into our hearts through the Holy Spirit who has been given to us. For while we were still weak, at the right time Christ died for the ungodly."

So count it all joy, my dear sisters in the Lord. God is using any suffering and trials in your life to create a noble character that produces unashamed hope and is worth more than rare and precious jewels.

FOR FURTHER STUDY

❖ If you are in a season of struggle, I would highly recommend *When God Weeps: Why Our Sufferings Matter to the Almighty* by Joni Eareckson Tada and Steven Estes (Zondervan). It not only provides an outstanding, biblical perspective on suffering, but it also contains one of the finest chapters on the Crucifixion that I've read. If you can't afford to buy the book, at least borrow it long enough to read chapter 3, "The Suffering God." The last line will knock the wind out of you—if you can see it through your tears.

❖ If you want to be a blessing in your marriage, then I hope you will start studying this book immediately. *Feminine Appeal: Seven Virtues of a Godly Wife and Mother* (Crossway), by Carolyn Mahaney, is the training manual every woman needs. Many of us no longer have daily access to our mothers or never have been mentored by an older woman in the Titus 2 virtues. This book is full of the wisdom we seek, and it was written by a friend whose life and legacy meshes with her words.

❖ Do you want to study more about how to take your thoughts captive and not let them roam wild through the fields of self-pity? *Loving God with All Your Mind* by Elizabeth George (Harvest House) is an excellent resource. I highlighted nearly the entire first chapter. Here's a bite-sized morsel to enjoy:

> Like our relationship with God and our perspective on ourselves, our relationships with people need to be guided by the command of Philippians 4:8 (KJV)—'Whatsoever things are true [real] . . . think on these things.' Women who think on what is real do not spend time analyzing other people's words and actions or second-guessing what they say and do. Such negative thoughts damage relationships. When we focus on what is real, we experience sound and sincere relationships characterized by a genuine love for others.[18]

5

DO HIM GOOD ALL THE DAYS OF YOUR LIFE

The heart of her husband trusts in her, and he will have no lack of gain. She does him good, and not harm, all the days of her life.

PROVERBS 31:11-12

In the early '80s, any man who wore all black, had spiky hair, and liked R.E.M and Elvis Costello was the height of new wave cool. In my eyes few were cooler than my friend Michael. He got me backstage to meet Bono after a U2 concert, and he took me to the Mostly Mozart festival at the Kennedy Center. He introduced me to popular punk dance clubs and also brought me to his home for my first Passover seder. He was adventurous and loved new experiences but never got drunk. I don't ever recall him using drugs either. He soaked up the culture, but never seemed to be overcome by it.

He also asked me one of the most important questions of my young adult life. Sitting on campus one afternoon, we were talking all around the issue of our friendship. As in many male-female friendships, the tension of "what if" always tugged at the edges of our relationship. Turning to look at me, he regarded me kindly but spoke with quiet resolve.

"You know . . . I'm not going to ask you out," he said, pausing momentarily to allow his statement to sink in. "I don't believe in dating anyone that I couldn't consider marrying. And I would only marry a Jewish woman because my religion is important to me."

I met his gaze with a small smile. "I understand that, Michael."

"Good," he said. "Well, what are you looking for in a husband?"

"Oh, I guess I would look for a sense of humor, a sharp dresser, someone who is into music," I mused. "Definitely someone who likes to dance."

After a diplomatic pause to let the shallowness of my answer register, he asked, "What about trust? Isn't that important?"

I blinked, considering the implications of his question. At twenty I was not a Christian, and I was thoroughly indoctrinated in the random, uncommitted dating culture. Trust was neither expected nor given. I wasn't even considering issues of character (mine or his)—just entertainment. "Yeah, that's important," I mumbled, mildly embarrassed. But even then I didn't fully comprehend what was being asked.

THE HEART OF THE MATTER

Proverbs 31:11-12 says, "The heart of her husband trusts in her, and he will have no lack of gain. She does him good, and not harm, all the days of her life." I believe the area that requires the greatest wisdom for single women is knowing what's "good" when interacting with men, both single and married. In our friendships with single men, we can't presume that any man is "the one." We might *hope* that he will be "the one," but only time will unfold God's plan for us. It could be that our future husbands are watching us at this time, evaluating how we interact with them and other men. One certainty is that the vast majority of single men we know now will be someone *else's* husband in the future. The woman of noble character, therefore, doesn't live just in the present, but carefully considers her interactions from the perspective of an entire lifetime—and thereby earns the trust of her husband (should God provide), as well as the numerous men who will be her friends and brothers in the Lord.

That's simple to say but harder to live. There are two challenges with this concept: 1) There's more than one heart involved, and 2) Our culture is entirely at odds with the biblical standards that we will look at in this chapter.

So how do we break it down? Let's go to the end of this verse and work backwards. "All the days of her life" is a translation of a Hebrew idiom that means "constantly, all the time," similar to our modern phrase "24/7." But to be that constant *after* the wedding means that we are building on the foundation of the days *before*. So in these days before, we have to evaluate our actions and plans in the context of what will ensure good, not harm, for our future husbands. We have to consider what will bring him gain, or as the New International Version translates it, that he lacks nothing of value. This is the bedrock of trust.

I think the key here is found in the first noun, *heart.* The Hebrew for this word is *leb,* also used figuratively for the feelings, the will, and even the intellect.[1] The biblical view of the heart is not the intense intoxication of romantic passion as we view it today. *Leb* means more than subjective attraction or ardor. Our feelings are only one-third of the package; the other parts are the will and the mind, which are usually far more objective. As much as our culture is currently concerned with how we feel about various things, Scripture is more concerned with how our feelings should be governed by what we know to be truth about God. (Isn't it amazing that the psalms so consistently end with praise to God no matter where they begin?) So if you find matters of the heart to be confusing and arbitrary, this is actually good news! The Bible is telling us that we have more tools to work with in romance and friendship than our culture would tell us.

In the middle of a series of articles about beauty and fitness in a women's magazine, I once found this important nugget:

> Despite the conventional wisdom, being married boosts happiness only one-tenth of a point on an 11-point scale, and most people are no more satisfied with life after marriage than they were before, says Richard Lucas, Ph.D., a psychologist at Michigan State University in East Lansing who analyzed 15 years' worth of data on 24,000 people. Although happiness rises after exchanging vows, most people return to their pre-marriage level within two years. (The same is true for people who win the lottery.) "People need to have realistic expectations," Lucas says. "But if your marriage does not bring everlasting happiness," he adds, "it does not mean it's not a good one."[2]

Only *two* years of wedded bliss after all that fuss and scheming to get there? We shouldn't be surprised; this mainstream study confirms what we read throughout the Bible. God has designed us to find our ultimate fulfillment in Him, not in anything He's created. Therefore, it's not surprising to read that the author of this study found out that "people are no more satisfied with life after marriage than they were before," and that he cautions readers to "have realistic expectations." A realistic expectation of what or whom is merely left to the reader's inference.

Our culture uses this phrase a lot—"realistic expectations." But really what's a "realistic" expectation? In some ways, I think that's the secular counterpart to the Christian phrase, "guard your heart." We casually toss those phrases around, and we freely give them as advice to one another. But they have a way of stopping a meaningful conversation short, as though everyone involved knows exactly what it means to have realistic expectations or to guard the heart. If we did know, the lucrative self-help publishing industry wouldn't exist. The truth is, relationships are messy. They require risk. But the Bible doesn't leave us in the dark here. In matters of the heart (whether or not we get married) there are at least four perspectives to consider:

- Ourselves
- Our husbands
- Our "brothers"
- Our unions

When we examine romance through these four perspectives, I think we'll see how we can live wisely all the days of our lives and earn the trust of our future husbands. In this chapter, we'll look at the first point, and in the next chapter we'll explore the last three points. (By the way, this topic is a tough one for me. I've learned a lot in recent years—mostly the hard way. So I need to rely on a "multitude of counselors" for their wisdom and their pithy quotes. The good news is that I've done all the reading for you!)

GUARD YOUR HEART

Proverbs 4:23 says, "Keep your heart with all vigilance, for from it flow the springs of life." The King James Version translates it as, "Keep thy heart with all diligence; for out of it are the issues of life." Here, "issues" doesn't mean the disparaging way we use the word now—"He's got issues!" Rather, this phrase in Hebrew alludes to geographic boundaries or the source, as for water.[3] Like the mountain spring that's the source of a mighty river, the heart is the source for all the operations of human life, and we're commanded to "keep it" (guard, protect, maintain it) with all vigilance (watchfulness). In the area of romance, this means we have some work to do—or we *will* end up with some issues!

I remember talking to my pastor as a new believer, wondering why everyone always talked about guarding the heart. This was an intriguing phrase to me. I didn't know why it mattered to anyone if I was or wasn't guarding my heart. I'd already survived several broken romances by the time I became a Christian; so I wasn't concerned about handing my heart to someone new. I was a seasoned dating veteran. But my pastor wisely pointed out that with each dashed relationship, I was dinging my heart. By the time I got married, I would be handing my husband a fairly scarred, dented heart, complete with the bitter memories of how each injury occurred. This was his elementary advice for a new convert, but there was still much more for me to learn.

Sometime later I actually noticed that phrase in the Bible: "And the peace of God, which surpasses all understanding, will *guard your hearts* and your minds in Christ Jesus" (Philip. 4:7, emphasis added). Backing up one sentence, I read, "The Lord is at hand; do not be anxious about anything, but in everything by prayer and supplication with thanksgiving let your requests be made known to God." Fact one: The Lord is at hand. Fact two: Prayer, supplication, and thanksgiving are the ways to let our requests be known to God, who is at hand. Fact three: Because we've made our requests to a Lord who is at hand, we can know peace. Fact four: Peace guards our hearts in Christ Jesus, who is at hand and has heard our requests.

What makes us anxious about romance? It's our speculations. Does anyone like me? Does *this* man like me? Will he call me? Will he introduce me to his family? Does he think we have potential for the future? Will he propose? Will we get married? Will we stay married? Will he commit adultery? Will he die first and leave me alone? And on and on and on. When we do this, we are way out in the future all by ourselves, churning in sinful anxiety.

Meditating upon imaginary future circumstances is a futile exercise. There isn't grace for our speculations. That's why God tells us, "do not be anxious about anything." We can try our best to control all of our circumstances to ensure we won't be hurt or that we'll get what we want, but it will never produce anything more than anxiety. We have to learn to keep from getting ahead of God and the man who has attracted our attention. What that looks like can vary, but I like this description of guarding your heart:

> The moment we meet a man, we snatch our heart out of God's hand, toss it at this new guy we've gotten all excited about, and say, "Here!" Small wonder the poor little thing is so banged up. I think it's time to get a clue, don't you? How about trying this approach—you meet a man, he's *re-e-al* cute, you like him. Your little heart is all aflutter, revving up to leap out of your chest and at the poor unsuspecting guy. Place your hand over your heart, whisper to it: "Calm down," and put it back in its secret place. And then say this: "God, I think I really like this one. What do you know about him? What is the purpose of his being in my life? Is he the one for me? Should I proceed, or should I not waste my time on him?"[4]

In due time, I believe the Lord will always answer those questions and provide peace to the woman who first talks to God before she talks to the man.

RIPPED OFF BY OUR CULTURE

Let's talk about that habit of tossing our hearts at men. Practically speaking, our generation is completely clueless about romance. I believe that the women of almost any other era were much better equipped. But women today are told that we can just go get whatever we want; so we have no idea of the power of being reserved, the joy of being pursued, or the security of being cherished. As a result, we've arguably gained a dubious "equality," but we have forsaken feminine value. This shift has been widely documented in several recent mainstream studies, including the *Hooking Up, Hanging Out, and Hoping for Mr. Right* report released in 2001 by the Independent Women's Forum. The executive summary reported:

> There are few widely recognized social norms on college campuses that help guide and support young women in thinking about sex, love, commitment, and marriage. College women say they want to be married someday, and many would like to meet a future husband at college. Yet it seems that virtually no one even attempts to help them consider how their present social experience might or might not lead to a successful marriage, or how marriage might fit with other life goals.
>
> As a result, the culture of courtship, a set of social norms and expectations that once helped young people find the pathway to marriage, has largely become a hook up culture with almost no shared norms or expectations. Hooking up, hanging out, and fast-moving ("joined at the hip") commitments are logical, though we believe seriously flawed, responses to this disappearance of a culture of courtship. The options available to college women are obviously strongly influenced by choices that other young men and women make, but each young woman today tends to see her choices as wholly private and individual. For example, while most college women expect to marry for life and 88 percent would not personally consider having a child outside of marriage, 87 percent agree that "I should not judge anyone's sexual conduct except my own." Consequently, when women are hurt or disappointed by the hook up culture, they typically blame themselves.[5]

We blame ourselves because we traded in the control our culture had provided us in being able to say yea or nay to a suitor. This happened during one turbulent decade of the twentieth century. If you think I'm going to say the sixties, you're wrong. The Roaring Twenties did far more damage on most fronts to our culture than we generally acknowledge.

> Young women of the middle and upper classes did set the course of relationships prior to the 1920s, according to Beth Bailey, professor of American studies at the University of New Mexico. A young man would arrive at the home of a young woman and offer his card. She might see him or she might not. If the courting progressed, the couple might advance to the front porch, always under the eye of watchful parents.
>
> Then came the automobile and the invention of dating. Bailey writes in her book *From Front Porch to Back Seat: Courtship in Twentieth-Century America*, that when men took women out in a car and spent money on them, they expected something in return: a woman's full attention, submissiveness, even sex. Men, and not the women they dated, were now in control. This equation held straight through to the last third of the 20th century, when feminism and the sexual revolution started to shake things up.[6]

I believe Ms. Bailey and I would take a vastly different view on whether or not the sexual revolution was an improvement, not to mention the definition and value of submission. I also hope that in Christian circles we are all in agreement with and holding to Scripture's commands against sexual immorality. By citing these secular publications, I'm painting a wider picture of the cultural confusion about romance, courtship, and sexuality that exists today, confusion that no doubt has also wafted through the doors of our churches.

But did you know that purity is broader than sexuality? Purity is also part of our emotions and affections. One Rutgers University study addressed the impact of our culture's relationship trends on women's emotions:

> Since breaking up is a painful and distressing experience for young lovers, it is desirable for such breakups to be relatively few and far between in the course of seeking a mate. However, today, a young single woman may experience several breakups during her late teens and twenties, and these breakups seem to have a cumulative negative impact on subsequent relationships. The women in this study say they feel burned, angry, betrayed when they are dumped. They say they are more mistrustful of the next guy who comes along. Moreover, the experience of multiple breakups can lead to a global mistrust and antagonism toward men. Women say they become more suspicious and wary of all men over time.[7]

THE RULES

What a mess! By now you may be tempted to read ahead, looking for the solution. What *are* we supposed to be doing? Several years ago a book came out trying to fill that need. It was called *The Rules: Time-Tested Secrets for Capturing the Heart of Mr. Right.* This secular book caused quite a firestorm in the mainstream press and earned the disdain of feminists everywhere. Right at the beginning of the book the authors addressed this anticipated backlash for their embrace and promotion of traditional roles:

> *Men are different from women.* Women who call men, ask them out, conveniently have two tickets to a show, or offer sex on the first date destroy male ambition and animal drive. Men are born to respond to challenge. Take away challenge and their interest wanes. That, in a nutshell, is the premise of *The Rules.* . . .
>
> We understand why modern, career-oriented women have sometimes scoffed at our suggestions. They've been MBA-trained to "make things happen" and to take charge of their careers. However, a relationship with a man is different from a job. In a relationship, the man must take charge. He must propose. We are not making this up—biologically, he's the aggressor.[8]

When I first read this book, I felt that hot flush of shame as I encountered "rules" I never knew existed—*always end phone calls first, rarely return his calls*—and considered how many times I had done the opposite and reaped exactly what the authors warned I would. While I couldn't recommend this book because the authors' premise and motivations aren't biblical, I did find that its legalistic rules and specific illustrations were helpful to challenge my ingrained forward behavior and thinking. As I read, I recalled a friend of mine from high school who was always being pursued and that she seemed instinctively to know these "rules." She was big on Rule 7: "Don't accept a Saturday night date after Wednesday." Men learned to book her early or not at all. As a result, she was rarely home alone on a Saturday night.

The point is, these women resurrected a timeless truth: "Men are born to respond to challenge." Even as I wrote this book, I told a friend of mine who is an established Christian author that I was getting consistent social invitations from male friends that I had to decline to be alone and write. Where were these guys a few months ago? He wrote back an encouraging short note: "About those guys . . . A little 'unavailability' can make the unattainable all that more attractive!" Confirmation! As one author wrote in a Christian perspective on *The Rules*:

> The bottom line is this: if a man doesn't make the first move toward you—even if you do manage to capture his attention for awhile—he will inevitably go off in pursuit of someone who catches his eye and gives him a good challenge. In short, you've become temporary filler because he had nothing better to do at the time. . . . Therefore, if you're in a room full of people and your eyeballs land on some guy who you think is awfully cute, you need to keep that comment to yourself and keep right on stepping if he doesn't approach you. Why? Because if he doesn't approach you, he wasn't moved enough by what he saw when he looked at you. "Well, maybe he didn't notice me," you say. Well, if he didn't notice you, all the more reason to leave him where you found him! If you have to make him notice you, you're starting off on the wrong foot already.[9]

One problem with *The Rules* is that it tempts women to be manipulative and self-centered. It was no surprise then to read several years later that one of the authors had filed for divorce.[10] As Christian women, we are called to "look not only to [our] own interests, but also to the interests of others" (Philip. 2:4). A second problem with *The Rules* is that it doesn't address what to do with the vast number of men we know whom we'll never date or marry—a topic we will explore in the next chapter.

There is one rule, however, for single Christian women, and it must be honored diligently: We are not to marry unbelievers. The testimony of Scripture is clear from first to last about this. Though it mostly speaks to men marrying foreign women and the consequences of that union (see Solomon and how far he fell from a good start because of his unbelieving wives), there is one New Testament passage addressed to women that can't be argued: "A woman is bound to her husband as long as he lives. But if her husband dies, she is free to marry anyone she wishes, but he must belong to the Lord" (1 Cor. 7:39 NIV). When women then were given a choice about a mate, it was generally as widows. It was still common during this time for most first marriages to be negotiated by the families. So though we might be tempted to think this command doesn't apply if we're not widows, it does, as it speaks to our choices.

I think that by extension this command also applies to dating unbelievers. Why should we engage our emotions, invest our time, and possibly stir up another's heart if we can't move forward to marriage? Dating is an exploration of commitment, and if we know from the start that we can't commit to someone, we shouldn't string him along or create a stumbling block for ourselves. (I used the word *dating* here because it's a more widely used term. I won't be addressing the dating/courtship model in this book because there are better resources already published on this topic, one of which I've listed at the end of this chapter.)

DATING IN OUR MINDS

I have a friend who once observed that our interactions with men should be like a peanut butter sandwich. No one likes to eat a sandwich where the peanut butter is all clumped up in one corner. We like our peanut butter to be evenly spread around. "So, honey, don't get all clumped up in one corner, distracted by one guy," she advised. "Spread yourself around! Let him get clumped up around you!" We had a good laugh at that, but there's much truth in this homespun advice.

I think one of the big distractions of Christians singles is "dating in your mind" (again, a great phrase coined by another friend). Because our churches often provide the context to get to know single men as friends, we women can start investing more significance in these interactions than is wise. We get all "clumped up" around one guy—until he says something or does something to make us realize he's not going to pursue. Then comes the disappointment.

In our defense, I have observed men going through all the motions of dating without declaring their intentions. I've seen men "try on" certain women and then fade away if there wasn't enough spark to attract them to pursue. I've seen men hang out with women for *years* as extremely good friends, seemingly oblivious to the potential there, while the women struggle to guard their emotions and expectations. While I think we can become wiser about evaluating the men in these situations (which we'll look at next), all things start with our own "spring of life"—our hearts. Because I've been "clumped up" far more often than I'd like to admit, I've learned to discern the symptoms of this tendency in my life. Here are some questions I ask myself whenever I think I'm starting to "date someone in my mind":

• Do I talk about him a lot to other people?

• If these other people don't share my enthusiasm and even caution me to avoid cultivating expectations, do I feel deflated and resent their input?

• Am I going to this event or meeting primarily because he will be there?

• Am I distracted in church or small group meetings because of his presence?

• Do I break other commitments because he's invited me to do something spontaneously?

• If he doesn't talk to me or single me out at events, do I go home disappointed?

• Am I jealous of the women he does talk to or serve?

• If he declines one of my invitations, am I tempted to feel rejected?

• When he does pay attention to me, am I so oriented to him in a group setting that I don't consider the needs of others around me?

This "dating someone in your mind" concept might seem to be a harmless distraction, but I've found that's rarely the case. (In fact, I've seen some serious consequences from it.) When we do this, typically we're laying claims and forming attachments that are deadly to our spiritual growth and witness. Because these attachments are one-sided, when the relationship doesn't occur in the way or time that we want, we usually respond sinfully.

Author and counselor Paul Tripp explains the pitfalls of this continuum in this way: Desire leads to demand, which re-labels itself as a "need" and leads to expectation of fulfillment, which, when unmet, leads to disappointment, and thus ends in punishment. As he writes:

> The objects of most of our desires are not evil. The problem is the way they tend to *grow*, and the control they come to exercise over our hearts. Desires are a part of human existence, but they must be held with an open hand. . . . The problem with desire is that in sinners it very quickly morphs into *demand* ('I must'). Demand is the closing of my fists over a desire. Even though I may be unaware that I have done it, I have left my proper position of submission to God. I have decided that I must have what I have set my heart on and nothing can stand in the way. I am no longer comforted by God's desire for me; I am threatened by it, because God's will potentially stands in the way of my demand. . . . There is a direct relationship between expectation and disappointment, and much of our disappointment in relationships is not because people have actually wronged us, but because they have failed to meet our expectations.[11]

When I first read that passage, I was stunned. That's exactly what happens when I "date someone in my mind"! One sentence in particular screamed from the page: "There is a direct relationship between expectation and disappointment, and much of our disappointment in relationships is not because people have actually wronged us, but because they have failed to meet our expectations." These are self-induced dings to our hearts! Even more seriously, these acts are seeds we are sowing to future conflict in our own marriages. No husband will meet all of our desires; so we should learn to protect our own hearts and minds in Christ Jesus by *not* indulging this cycle of idolatry.

So how do we change? Here's something I've been meditating on over the past year. The secret is in the worth of a woman with noble character. The Bible says she is "more precious than jewels." Jewels aren't out on the store's front counter for every passerby to carelessly handle. Precious jewels are guarded in the vault and are only brought out for consideration by a buyer who has demonstrated serious intentions and the wherewithal to purchase. Costume jewelry attracts casual inspection—and lots of it—by its cheap presentation. But because it's not seen as valuable, it's not treated as such.

Dear friends, we don't have to put our affections and ourselves on display. We can trust our heavenly Father to ward off the casual shoppers and only bring those with serious intentions to consider us. But know that this will mean some "vault time." While you're in the dark, wondering when—and *if*—you will have a chance to sparkle for an appreciative buyer, you'll be tested. During this time, keep in mind these three reminders:

• Pray: Take your petitions to God, for He's the only one who can change a man's heart, and this brings His peace to guard our own hearts.

• Pursuit: It's not our job as women. Instead, we should have the joy of *being* pursued.

• Prevent   Disappointment: Check yourself before you head

A Personal Postscript . . .
There's nothing like the discussion of wisdom in relationships to make every one of us feel like we've fallen short. This wasn't an easy chapter for me to write, either. I found myself grieving over the time I've wasted in foolishness and sin. For this reason, I'm so grateful to know my Savior redeemed my past and has a purpose for my future. Every time I have closed my fist over a desire and made it a demand, I have received grace to repent and change. Every time I have suffered a broken heart, I've received grace to offer it to the Lord for His healing. When it comes to relationships, I will never "do it right" in friendship or romance because I'm a sinner. Jesus alone "did it right"! Robert Murray McCheyne, a single man and Scottish pastor in the 1800s, wrote memorable advice for us all: "The four Gospels are a narrative of the heart of Christ. They show His compassion to sinners, and His glorious work in their stead. If you only knew that heart as it is, you would lay your weary head with John on His bosom. Do not take up your time so much with studying your own heart as with studying Christ's heart. For one look at yourself, take ten looks at Christ!"[12]

down the slippery slope of desires, demands, and expectations that Paul Tripp outlined. When you find your fist closing over good desires and making them demands, stop. Open that clenched fist and hold that desire up in prayer (see point one again).

To do our future husbands good and not harm, we have to be very careful about guarding our own hearts. This is a wisdom issue. More importantly, it's a worship issue. The real motivation for guarding our hearts is *not* to be able to hand our husbands a relatively unscathed heart on our wedding day, as important as that is. The real motivation is to preserve our trusting dependence on God with a peaceful spirit, whether we get married or not. It's to keep a scriptural imperative: "Keep your heart with all vigilance, for from it flow the springs of life" (Prov. 4:23).

FOR FURTHER STUDY

❖ *Boy Meets Girl* by Joshua Harris (Multnomah) is an invaluable guide for developing biblical standards for our relationships. But even if you aren't persuaded to "kiss dating goodbye," please beg, borrow, or buy this book to read chapter 10, "When Your Past Comes Knocking." This chapter will help you look at your past (especially past sexual sin) in the light of the cross.

❖ *Instruments in the Redeemer's Hands: People in Need of Change Helping People in Need of Change* by Paul David Tripp (P&R Publishing) is a great resource to learn how to wisely counsel others for true biblical change. But you don't have to serve on the counseling ministry or be in that profession to benefit from this book. Each of us gives counsel or advice to others, and that's why we should all read this gracious book and apply its wisdom.

RESPECTED AT THE CITY GATE

Her husband is known in the gates when he sits among the elders of the land.

PROVERBS 31:23

Several years ago I volunteered as a big sister/mentor at a local pregnancy center. My job was to befriend one pregnant woman at a time and to be a helpful resource to her throughout her pregnancy (and usually beyond). Though their pregnancies were the reason they sought help, typically there were many other problems in their lives that made their pregnancies a complication on top of a heap o' troubles. In all but one case, the fathers of these children had bolted, but the one who stuck around was in and out of jail.

What troubled me was that in each instance, the character of these men had been revealed early in the relationship, but the women had been seemingly unable to discern the large gaps between their promises and their subsequent actions. I remember one man who was unearthed through the legal system and forced to make child-support payments. His payments weren't withheld from his salary, unfortunately, and so each month he'd tell my friend some elaborate story about why the payment was delayed and that he'd bring it with him during a visit to his child. Each month her hopes would soar. And each month he failed to come through. Not the money. Not the visit. It was as though his mere words were sufficient for both of them even if they were never backed up by his actions.

If that sounds like I'm putting self-righteous distance between these women and myself, I'm not. It's just that in their cases, it was easier for me to clearly assess what was happening because my emotions weren't involved. I've often displayed the same lack of discernment in my life when it comes to evaluating men. In fact, we are all susceptible, or else we wouldn't find the following observation in Proverbs 20:6: "Many a man proclaims his own steadfast love, but a faithful man who can find?" One of the valuable benefits of guarding our hearts by waiting on God and on the initiative of a man is that we avoid rushing into foolish relationships. We gain the time to observe what a man *does* rather than just hear his romantic promises.

The verse that we studied in the last chapter says, "she does him good"—not "she does *them* good." I don't believe God wants us to have relationship after relationship in order to practice serial rejection. Honestly, I think I've been through some relationships simply because I was not wise about evaluating a man's heart and character. If I'd been looking soberly for the evidence of a faithful man, I would not have dated a number of the men I did before I became a believer.

THE TESTED MAN

The Proverbs 31 woman is the wife of a godly husband, whose character is commendable to the community at large. Proverbs 31:23 says, "Her husband is known in the gates when he sits among the elders of the land."

Here is the second point I raised about heart issues in the last chapter—a husband's heart. We're exploring this verse because to say someone "sits at the gates" was shorthand for saying he was a man of influence, a community leader who was worthy of respect. This phrase was derived from the architecture of Israelite cities:

> City gates played a significant role in ancient life. Because openings in city walls created a weak place, ancient people strengthened their gates to prevent their city from being easily invaded. Building a gatehouse inside the city wall became a customary practice. Also, the sewer channel under the main street could run out below the city gate.
>
> During peacetime, city gates became the focal point for social and commercial activity. The chambers operated as a city hall where legal matters and business transactions were conducted. The room above the chambers served as a guardhouse (2 Sam. 18:33); the towers provided added protection and a lookout point (2 Sam. 18:24); and the area outside the gate became a marketplace.

The city gate became a gathering place for prophets, kings, judges, and other officials. These leaders would "sit in the gate." For example, Jehoshaphat (king of Judah) and Ahab (king of Israel) sat on their thrones in the gate of Samaria (1 Kings 22:10).[1]

Today, those whom God has given to lead the church are pastors and elders. Because Scripture lists character requirements for those leaders—which are required of all believers—those requirements can be trustworthy standards by which we evaluate men.

> *The saying is trustworthy: If anyone aspires to the office of overseer, he desires a noble task. Therefore an overseer must be above reproach, the husband of one wife,* sober-minded, self-controlled, respectable, hospitable, *able to teach,* not a drunkard, *not violent but* gentle, not quarrelsome, not a lover of money. *He must manage his own household well, with all dignity keeping his children submissive, for if someone does not know how to manage his own household, how will he care for God's church? He must not be a recent convert, or he may become puffed up with conceit and fall into the condemnation of the devil. Moreover, he must be* well thought of by outsiders, *so that he may not fall into disgrace, into a snare of the devil. Deacons likewise must be* dignified, not double-tongued, *not addicted to much wine,* not greedy *for dishonest gain. They must* hold the mystery of the faith *with a clear conscience. And let them also be* tested *first; then let them serve as deacons if they prove themselves blameless.* (1 Tim. 3:1-10, emphasis added)

Are the men you relate to seeking to pursue and grow in these character traits? Are they trying to be purposeful or vigilant (as the King James translates "sober-minded")? Are they cultivating self-control? Are they respectable? Are they hospitable? (I don't mean that they throw ten-course dinner parties. I mean, do they make people feel welcome? Are they observant of the needs of those around them?) And so on, right until the last point: *Have they been tested*? Testing doesn't mean that these men have performed flawlessly on each and every character trait listed above, but that they have allowed examination and have gained the approval of others around them for their commitment to spiritual growth.

Ladies, this is where we can find protection in our local churches. Watching a man's commitment to the bride of Christ is going to help us discern how he will interact with an earthly bride. We can evaluate many things about a man's character through serving together in church before we invest any of our emotions in a relationship with him. We really want to marry men who love one person more than they love us—Jesus. And if they love Jesus, they are going to love His bride. Does the bride of Christ get consistent attention and time from this man? Does the bride of Christ receive his financial support? Does the bride of Christ benefit from a consistent relationship, or does this man only show up in church sporadically? Does he want to sacrifice his leisure time to serve the bride of Christ through participating in her ministries? Does he love the body of Christ by caring for a wide variety of her members—or is he only interested in meeting the more attractive eligible members? Is he faithful to the bride of Christ, or does he hop from church to church and meeting to meeting? (And can the same be said of us?)

We should also note how a man treats his family, even when he is no longer living at home. Does he honor his parents in the way he speaks about them? Does he make an effort to serve them or visit them? Douglas Wilson has written that you can often foretell how a man will treat his wife by the way he treats his mother: "If a girl wants to be impressed with a young man, she needs to see how he speaks to his own mother at home, and not how nice he can be across the dinner table from a cute girl in a restaurant. If she wants to know how he will speak to her as a wife in ten or fifteen years (and if she is taught well by her father, she *should* want to know), she should look very closely at how he talks to his mother."[2] This is not a new caution. In commenting on the union of Isaac and Rebekah in Genesis 24, Matthew Henry makes the same observation from the perspective of the seventeenth century. "Observe what an affectionate son Isaac was: it was about three years since his mother died, and yet he was not, till now, comforted. See also what an affectionate husband he was to his wife. Dutiful sons promise fair to be affectionate husbands; *he that fills up his first station in life with honour, is likely to do the same in those that follow*"[3] (emphasis added).

THE NOBLE MAN

Once when I was praying about a man I liked, the Lord brought to mind the Scripture address of Isaiah 32:8. I looked it up eagerly and read, "But the noble man makes noble plans, and by noble deeds he stands" (NIV). I had no idea how to apply this Scripture to my prayers; so I waited and watched. Over the course of time, I came to see that this man was not being purposeful in our friendship, that noble plans were not being made, and the deeds I observed were careless, not intentional. However, as I later studied this passage, I saw several ways to evaluate whether a man would be commended by the Lord as a noble man. This verse concludes a passage about the kingdom of righteousness that reads:

> *See, a king will reign in righteousness*
> *and rulers will rule with justice.*
> *Each man will be like a shelter from the wind*
> *and a refuge from the storm,*
> *like streams of water in the desert*
> *and the shadow of a great rock in a thirsty land.*
> *Then the eyes of those who see will no longer be closed,*
> *and the ears of those who hear will listen.*
> *The mind of the rash will know and understand,*
> *and the stammering tongue will be fluent and clear.*
> *No longer will the fool be called noble*
> *nor the scoundrel be highly respected.*
> *For the fool speaks folly,*
> *his mind is busy with evil:*
> *He practices ungodliness*
> *and spreads error concerning the* LORD;
> *the hungry he leaves empty*
> *and from the thirsty he withholds water.*
> *The scoundrel's methods are wicked,*
> *he makes up evil schemes*
> *to destroy the poor with lies,*
> *even when the plea of the needy is just.*
> *But the noble man makes noble plans,*
> *and by noble deeds he stands.* (Isa. 32:1-8 NIV)

I realize this is a prophetic passage about the Messiah, and not anyone's husband. But because here in Scripture we find the characteristics of a noble, godly man contrasted with those of a scoundrel, this is a useful passage for women to study to understand what God calls godly.

A Noble Man	The Scoundrel
Is a shelter from the wind	Speaks folly
Is a refuge from the storm	Mind is busy with evil
Is streams of water in the desert	Practices ungodliness
The shadow of a great rock in a thirsty land	Spreads error concerning the LORD
Makes noble plans	Makes up evil schemes
Does noble deeds	Does nothing for the hungry, thirsty

A noble man is a hiding place from the rough elements of life, a man who offers protection and shelter. He does not leave you exposed—either to ridicule or to harm. He is refreshment in a dry place, bringing much encouragement. He flows with streams of living water because he is a man of the Word. He is shade in weariness—reflecting the strength of the Rock, Christ. When a man is making noble plans toward you, he wants to offer you covering. He will offer to serve you, help carry your burdens, and pour the Word into your dry soul. His deeds will be noble, not common. He will show evidences of cherishing you, protecting your boundaries and standards. He won't touch you like a common object, and he will exert himself to care for you and to notice your needs.

Most importantly, a noble man is a submitted man himself. He serves his King wholeheartedly and makes himself accountable to other men. In my opinion, this should be one of the first characteristics we look for in any man who pursues us. In the happiest marriages I've seen, the husbands have other men in their lives who observe them, offer correction, and ask them how they are doing serving their wives and children. Without that community of accountability and authority, a couple has no one outside themselves to appeal to for help in unresolved conflict. Author and pastor Andrew Farmer writes:

> A woman should evaluate a man's respect for authority. In our society, the godly man is most distinct from the worldly man in the way he has put away prideful independence and pursued humble submissiveness. A man who is independent in his faith and does not seek the counsel and oversight of pastors and other mature men, will be a failure as a leader (and therefore as a husband) as defined by Scripture. See the story of Abigail and Nabal for a sad example of an arrogant man not worthy of his virtuous wife (1 Sam. 25).[4]

THE INTENTIONAL MAN

If you are fortunate, you know a few tested noble men. What remains is whether or not they are being intentional toward *you*. The "problem" with godly men is that they are so markedly different—gentlemanly, kind, attentive—from most men in our culture that it's hard *not* to receive it personally. I see that over and over again in my church as new women join. Inevitably, one of the guys will offer to walk a woman to her car after a meeting. These women usually have one of two reactions. Either they will refuse the offer because they think the guy is interested, or they will light up like Times Square because they think he is interested. What they don't know is that there is a third option: He's not interested—just extending gentlemanly care. Because they don't know the culture, it's easy to be confused.

The point is, an intentional man makes his purposes known. He tells you what he's doing and where he's leading. He is clear about where he wants the relationship to go. When he's not clear, when he's not saying anything, when he's enjoying the friendship but not moving forward—he's not being intentional. Period. You don't see noble deeds because he's not making those noble plans. You may have the greatest friendship in the world, but he's just hanging out in it. In fact, one man (a Christian) called this half-hearted testing of the water "the buddy approach," which he indulged for a number of years with the woman he eventually married:

> I crafted what I thought was an ingenious approach to women: the "buddy approach." . . . I saw it as a safe way to take a chance—to see if a relationship could grow without the pressure of formal dating and terms like "boyfriend" or "girlfriend." If the friendship began to disappoint, I could always just say, "Oh, maybe you misunderstood me, we're just friends." . . . To make matters worse, my expectations for women were set by movies and magazine covers that caused me to fantasize about perfection and to overlook the real and available women right in front of me.
>
> I realized that honesty about the deep friendship I enjoyed with Candice meant I had to quit looking out of the corner of my eye for other options. She deserved my full attention. Traditional wedding vows often include the phrase, "forsaking all others as long as you both shall live." I knew I needed to start practicing the art of "forsaking."[5]

I know how tempting it is to hang out in these undefined friendships where the best you can get is a blurry, part-time boyfriend. At least some attention is better than none, right? Nope, sorry, I'm no longer convinced of that. For one, I find it challenging to guard my heart and keep my peace before God in these "hopeful friendships." I'm always in danger of closing my fist-of-demand over the friendship. Second, it tempts the men to passivity, in my opinion. It provides them with the out of "Oh, maybe you misunderstood me, we're just friends." If we women would be better about guarding the amount of time and attention invested in these close friendships, we might see our reserve rewarded with pursuit instead of passivity. After all, we don't want to manipulate the situation and then live under one of the three things the Bible says makes the earth tremble: "an unloved woman when she gets a husband" (Prov. 30:23). I like this direct counsel:

> I know that the temptation to give a man a preview of life with you is great, but it's a very bad idea. Remember when your mom said, "Why buy

the cow if you can get the milk for free?" Mmm, hmm, I thought you knew! Don't behave like you're his wife if you're only his girlfriend, and don't behave like his girlfriend if you're only his friend. Got it? It's never smart to move ahead of the man's—or God's—agenda. Moving ahead only leaves you open to experience the pain of rejection. . . . On the other hand, don't be his mother or his nurse if you want to be his woman. Be kind, be nice, be supportive, but leave some room for him to keep coming toward you. Men are naturally independent beings. Remember who first noticed that Adam was alone? God did, not Adam! . . . [You] can't make life so comfortable for him that he doesn't understand that he needs to commit to marriage in order to enjoy the full benefits of life with you.[6]

When is a man interested? *When he says so and his actions back up his words*. Anything less is at best merely friendly and possibly even uncertain or inconsiderate. If he's a noble man who's made noble plans, one of his noble deeds is letting *you* know about it!

ALL THE MEN YOU DON'T MARRY

I was once told—by a man—that if a man didn't treat me like a queen, I should kick him to the curb. As well meaning as this advice was, not every man *is* going to treat me like a queen. Most men are going to treat me like a sister and a friend. So either I kick a lot of men to the curb, or I had better come up with a plan for how I treat all the men I *don't* marry—the third point in the heart issue list.

Ironically, it was a man who showed me how. Years ago I was critically evaluating another man in a conversation with my friend and small group leader, Doug. I explained the cryptic actions of this other man, which I then pronounced as "creeping me out." I thoroughly expected Doug to agree and even to laugh with me. But when I finished my long tale, there was a customary pause on the other end of the telephone. I waited, my smile fading.

"I'm wondering," he said kindly, "how you would define 'creeping me out' in biblical terms."

"Ummm," I replied cautiously, "I guess I mean I'm irritated by him. I don't understand his actions or his motives."

"Uh, huh," he said, waiting for me to put two and two together.

"I'm not the only one who feels this way though," I added. "A lot of other women feel this pressure from him, too."

Hellloooo! Now you've added gossip to self-righteous criticism!

"Uh, huh," he repeated.

I had better shut up.

I was digging myself into a hole in this conversation. As always happens whenever we sinfully judge others, we end up condemning ourselves. After Doug patiently revealed to me my self-righteous attitude (and I repented of it), he asked me another memorable question.

"One more thing—I'm not hearing where you are concerned about this brother being conformed to the image of Christ," he said gently. "Have you thought about that? If he is offending you or these other women, why hasn't anyone kindly brought that to his attention so that he can grow and change?"

Doug has always been good at asking me the tough questions! During our conversation, he not only helped me see my sinful, critical attitude, but he also revealed to me my worldly way of thinking about single men. His question ultimately revealed that I was thinking of single men in three categories: Potentials, Just Buddies, and No Ways, with each meriting different treatment. That's too many categories. There's just one for believing single men: Brothers, and consequently they all deserve the same treatment. Maybe one day a Brother will initiate a relationship to find out if the Lord would be moving him into the Husband slot. But until the words "I do" ring out from the wedding altar, he's still my Brother and potentially someone else's Husband.

My job as their sister in the Lord is to encourage and support these men, not to categorize them and treat them accordingly. James 2:2-4 reveals our tendency to show partiality:

> For if a man wearing a gold ring and fine clothing comes into your assembly, and a poor man in shabby clothing also comes in, and if you pay attention to the one who wears the fine clothing and say, "You sit here in a good place," while you say to the poor man, "You stand over there," or, "Sit down at my feet," have you not then made distinctions among yourselves and become judges with evil thoughts?

My paraphrase is, "For if a fine-looking man without a wedding ring comes into your assembly, and an awkward, plainer man in outdated clothing also comes in, and if you pay attention to the good-looking man and say, 'You sit here in a good place, right here by me, sweetie,' while you say nothing to or cut short the conversation with the less attractive man, have you not then made distinctions among them and become proud women with self-centered ambitions?"

We will stand out from our culture if we are consistently kind to everyone we meet, not just the Potentials. Not only that, we will stand out to a truly godly man who observes this impartial kindness in us. In doing so, we reflect our Savior. As J. C. Ryle once wrote in 1873:

> "Jesus loved Martha, Mary, and Lazarus" (John 11:5). This verse teaches us that Christ loves all who are true Christians. The characters of these three people seem to have been somewhat different. Of Martha, we are told in a certain place, that she was "anxious and troubled about many things," while Mary "sat at Jesus' feet, and heard His word." Of Lazarus we are told nothing distinctive at all. Yet all these were loved by the Lord Jesus. They all belonged to His family, and He loved them all.
>
> We must carefully bear this in mind in forming our estimate of Christians. We must never forget that there are varieties in character, and that the grace of God does not cast all believers into one and the same mold. Admitting fully that the "foundations" of Christian character are always the same, and that all God's children repent, believe, are holy, prayerful, and Scripture loving; we must make allowances for wide varieties in their temperaments and habits of mind. We must not undervalue others because they are not exactly like ourselves.[7]

This generosity is not easy to cultivate, in my opinion. To grow in our sisterly affections, we must purposefully examine how we interact with our brothers. I didn't grow up with natural brothers; so I've always thought of myself as hindered in this area. But I don't have to rely on my experience to shape this concept, for there is a Scripture passage that's concise and helpful for me. Matthew 12:46-50 says:

> While he was still speaking to the people, behold, his mother and his brothers stood outside, asking to speak to him. But he replied to the man who told him, "Who is my mother, and who are my brothers?" And stretching out his hand toward his disciples, he said, "Here are my mother and my brothers! For whoever does the will of my Father in heaven is my brother and sister and mother." (emphasis added)

The first concept I note here is the humility of Jesus in calling a broad range of sinful people His family. We have been adopted into His family because we are fellow sinners reconciled to God through what Jesus accomplished for us on the cross. Thus, by grace we are enabled to do the will of our Father in heaven. The second concept I take away from this passage is that this is how I can relate to each of my brothers. I can point them back to the will of our Father, thereby helping them bear fruit that glorifies God. I've found I can apply this concept in three ways:

• Observe them. In order to be intentional as a sister, I must take note of the men the Father has put in my life, from colleagues to Bible study members to church friends. It's fun to observe the men we're interested in, but it takes more effort to study and take note of other men. If we resolve to observe all of our brothers, then we easily can do the next two steps.

• Encourage them. It's not always effortless to do the will of the Father, especially in our current culture. But how refreshing to the soul it is to receive a timely word of "well done." There's a fine line between encouragement and flattery. If you are faithful to encourage many men, especially in the hearing of others, you will not confuse anyone about your intentions. For me, these two steps require that I shut my mouth in group contexts and sit back to study what God is doing at that moment in the men around me. Often I will find many things to comment on later—from hearing a more reserved man bringing up a good point in a Bible study, to seeing a busy man offer to help someone move. Encouragement keeps people from growing weary in doing good deeds. Let's be faithful to *look* for these reflections of God's grace in these men's lives and to *comment* on them as we see them doing the will of the Father.

• Seek to see them conformed—not to your preferences but to the image of Christ. This is what Doug was encouraging me to do. It's not so much an active process but an active concern. Our motivation should be care and concern when someone is not doing the will of the *Father* and to humbly bring what we've observed and our questions about it (not judgments) to our brothers. (We'll look at this in greater detail in chapter 11, "Wise Speech.")

It's tempting as singles to simply avoid those people who irritate us or whose sin or weaknesses always seem to spill out whenever we're around. But that's not carrying a concern to see our brothers (and sisters) in the Lord grow and mature in Christ. If there's something we don't understand or that offends us, we should ask kindly about it, motivated by an understanding that we don't know or see everything related to the situation. We should also trust that the Holy Spirit is the one who brings conviction for change; so our observations should initially and continually be in our prayers. Galatians 6:1 says, "Brothers, if anyone is caught in any transgression, you who are spiritual should restore him in a spirit of gentleness. Keep watch on yourself, lest you too be tempted." We are called to restore one another gently, not to *ignore* one another. Let's not excuse ourselves from the family just because we're single!

PREPARING FOR A "HAPPY WE"

I once attended a performance of Handel's *Acis and Galatea*, an English opera of love and rejection taken from classical mythology. In one scene when the lovers are united, they burst into an exuberant song of praise with primarily two words throughout the entire duet: "Happy we!" It's an engaging song of celebration, one I secretly noted in case I ever needed a wedding recessional song.

Here's the fourth point about heart issues that I first mentioned in chapter 5: our union. We can guard our hearts, evaluate men's hearts, and kindly deal with our brothers, but we must also remember to build a right foundation for the day when two people become one. "Happy we" should be a theme song for marriage, not just a song to end a wedding ceremony. This is not possible without a clear view of the third person in any Christian union: God. Knowing His standards and goals for marriage helps two individuals live together for a greater common goal than their own pleasure and preferences.

A good place to start developing the right foundation is with our expectations for marriage. I have a married friend who observed once that most of the single women she knows want a companion, not a husband. That's the kind of statement that hangs in the air for a moment as its meaning sinks in. So . . . what *is* the difference? Carolyn Mahaney summarizes it this way:

> In the Garden, God made man and woman fellow stewards of creation but with different, divinely assigned roles. The Lord said, "It is not good for the man to be alone. I will make a helper suitable for him" (Gen. 2:18 NIV). This is why God created Eve from Adam. She was created to be a helper suitable to him, to complement him, to nourish him, and to help him in the task that God had given him. Paul summarizes the creation plan by saying: "For man did not come from woman, but woman from man; neither was man created for woman, but woman for man" (1 Cor. 11:8-9 NIV). . . . Wives, we all have the same job description: We are our husbands' helpers. If you are wondering whether or not to pursue some particular endeavor, ask yourself this important question: *Does this help my husband?* Usually that one simple question will make your decision clear.[8]

At most weddings one Scripture is often read, from Ephesians 5:22-33. It says:

> *Wives, submit to your own husbands, as to the Lord. For the husband is the head of the wife even as Christ is the head of the church, his body, and is himself its Savior. Now as the church submits to Christ, so also wives should submit in everything to their husbands. Husbands, love your wives, as Christ loved the church and gave himself up for her, that he might sanctify her, having cleansed her by the washing of water with the word, so that he might present the church to himself in splendor, without spot or wrinkle or any such thing, that she might be holy and without blemish. In the same way husbands should love their wives as their own bodies. He who loves his wife loves himself. For no one ever hated his own flesh, but nourishes and cherishes it, just as Christ does the church, because we are members of his body. "Therefore a man shall leave his father and mother and hold fast to his wife, and the two shall become one flesh." This mystery is profound, and I am saying that it refers to Christ and the church. However, let each one of you love his wife as himself, and let the wife see that she respects her husband.*

Point one: *Submit?* Yes, submit. And respect. This passage starts with one concept and ends with another, but they are bound up in each other. You won't submit easily if you don't respect his leadership. But we ladies have an easier charge by far. We are to submit to our husbands by following his lead, trusting God to be leading him. All of that is expressed through respect. But look at what the husbands are charged to do—love sacrificially as Christ has loved the church. What woman wouldn't submit to that kind of loving leadership? It's not surprising that with the charge to be a servant leader comes a greater responsibility from God.

When I was little, I was fascinated by the Dr. Dolittle character called a "Push-Me, Pull-You." This creature had a head on both ends, and it was often at odds with itself in deciding where to go. That's what happens in many marriages. You can't have two heads if you really want to get any-where. *Someone* has to lead, and God has assigned that task to men. But that doesn't mean that the followers have less worth. It's a *role*, not a valu-ation. And the purpose of these roles is much greater than a worldly idea of self-fulfillment—it is to create a harmonious relationship that glorifies God.

One of the clearest Scripture passages on the topic of submission is 1 Peter 3:1-6, which begins with the charge of "wives, be subject to your own husbands." As Carolyn Mahaney writes:

First of all, note to whom this command is addressed: to *wives*. Submission was not our husbands' idea, and neither are they responsible to enforce it. This command is *not* divine permission for husbands to assert authoritarian leadership. Nowhere in Scripture does it say, "Husbands, see to it that your wives submit."

The requirement to submit to our husbands comes straight from God, to us as wives. And we are answerable to *Him* for our obedience. We cannot blame our husbands for our lack of submission. This responsibility is entirely ours!

Secondly, we ascertain to whom we are to submit. As married women, we are not to submit to *all* men, but rather to our husbands. Conversely, we should not seek leadership from *other* men, apart from our husbands, no matter how worthy they are of honor or respect. We are to be subject to *our own* husbands.[9]

When I first became a Christian, my church was going through the book of Ephesians. I read along, eager to learn what I could. Then I came to the stumbling block—that "antiquated verse" about submission. I immediately dismissed it as irrelevant. Shortly thereafter I had a meeting with Gene and Liz Emerson, my senior pastor and his wife. After graciously answering all my other abrupt, direct questions that newcomers can ask ("What are you doing with my money?" and the like), Gene asked me if I had any questions about what I was reading in the Bible.

"No, not that I can think of," I replied too quickly.

"What are you reading?" he asked.

"I'm going through Ephesians. It's a great book—except for that submission stuff!" I said with a dismissive laugh.

No one else laughed (not a good sign), but Gene did lean forward with a kind expression.

"Do you like to read?" he asked.

"Yes," I responded, somewhat warily.

"Then you may be interested in a book called *Recovering Biblical Manhood and Womanhood*," he said.

I bought that weighty theological book within the month, but I can't say I warmed up to this valuable resource right away. There was still much to be done in my heart. By resisting that concept and maintaining my proud independence, however, I was missing the boat on many other aspects of my new faith. I soon became convinced that God's plan is right (as if He needs my affirmation!) because of what I saw in the peaceful marriages around me in church. So I continued to study the topic, and I soon came to see that submission is commanded by God (Eph. 5:22, 24; Col. 3:18) and based on the created order (1 Cor. 11:8-12) because it is part of God's design to reflect the relationship between Christ and the church (Eph. 5:22-33). For these reasons, submission is not degrading. It is God-glorifying.

I also came to understand a profound principle that has been extremely helpful to me: Submission is a principle we see in the very nature of God Himself in the Trinity. As theologian Wayne Grudem writes, "the Father and the Son relate to one another as a father and a son relate to one another in a human family: the father directs and has authority over the son, and the son obeys and is responsive to the directions of the father. The Holy Spirit is obedient to the directives of both the Father and the Son."[10]

The most important act of submission ever was what redeemed my sinful soul—when Jesus submitted to the Father in the Garden of Gethsemane with the powerful prayer, saying, "Father, if you are willing, remove this cup from me. Nevertheless, not my will, but yours, be done" (Luke 22:42).

The relationship between a man and woman in marriage is supposed to reflect this aspect of the Trinity. As Wayne Grudem notes:

> Here, just as the Father has authority over the Son in the Trinity, so the husband has authority over the wife in marriage. The husband's role is parallel to that of God the Father and the wife's role is parallel to that of God the Son. Moreover, just as Father and Son are equal in deity and importance and personhood, so the husband and wife are equal in humanity and importance and personhood.[11]

What a privilege—to model the role of the Son in the Trinity! But submission runs against the grain of our stubborn independence, and so Titus 2:3-5 says that older women should teach younger women how to love and be submitted to their husbands. As single women, we can practice a little now by evaluating how well we do respecting, supporting, and following the authorities God has put over us in this season. We can cultivate godly submission by:

• Seeking the counsel of our pastors and following their leadership. To follow their leadership means making their task a joy by cheerfully accepting their priorities and participating in the meetings they deem essential, encouraging them, praying for them, and avoiding slander and gossip about them.

• Whether we live with them or not, seeking the counsel of our parents and honoring their preferences, where appropriate.

• Serving and supporting our bosses. (We'll look at this more in-depth in chapter 8.)

We can even practice this with our single men friends. Instead of *defaulting* to taking the initiative to plan something (planning is fine to do—don't misunderstand me), we can instead invite our men friends to lead a particular event. I've been told on several occasions how much this encourages the guys. (But it can't be a dictate to do something. It really has to be a question and invitation for their leadership, which they should feel free to accept or decline.) Here's something I'm learning to do as well—ask questions. "Is this something you'd like to lead? What would serve you in doing this? How can I help you in this? Do you have preferences about how this would be done?" Then when these men do lead, guess what? We should follow! That means when they initiate an event and do it differently from the way we prefer, we get to enthusiastically support them, not sit it out. Nothing squelches initiative faster, ladies, than a lack of participation.

Should God call you to marriage, your joyful submission and respect for your husband is one of the ways he will be qualified to "sit in the gates." A man who can lead and manage his family well is one who is qualified to lead the church (1 Tim. 3:4-5). Let's not forget this is a team effort, and should God call him to that task, any lack of submission on our part disqualifies our husbands from serving in this way.

A second way we can develop a biblical perspective of marriage is to understand the importance of confessing sin. Did you know that confession of sin builds intimacy? I've used this word—*sin*—freely in this book, and you might not truly understand why. We often hear those in the church called "saints" and those outside called "sinners," which is an unbalanced picture. We're all sinners, from toddlers throwing tantrums to adults in road rage. Sin is rebellion against God—His laws, His provision, His Word. Sin is shaking our fist in God's face, telling Him we don't want to be told what to do. But for believers the power or rule of sin in our lives has been broken at the cross. We are justified at the cross—meaning that the penalty for our sin has been removed—but we continue to grow in our Christian maturity through the progressive sanctifying work of the Holy Spirit. Which means we still wrestle with sin—and our sin is not hidden from anyone, except maybe ourselves. Everyone else can see our sin clearly! This is why confession builds intimacy. It tears down the walls of pride that separate us from one another.

When I became a Christian, I had this faulty idea that the cross was a monument in time, a marker sitting on the calendar date of the day I became a Christian. I thought somehow I could motor on to maturity in my own strength, only casting a glance at the cross in the rearview mirror of my life. How surprised I was, then, to start working for a ministry and be confronted with evidences of my sin on a daily basis! At first I was ashamed and defeated. But eventually I realized how immature and proud that reaction was. Because these circumstances revealed my faulty thinking, I saw how the cross actually loomed large over the entire landscape of my life—and I was *so* grateful! I found out that I need my Savior on a daily basis because I sin on a daily basis (though hopefully less over time). This isn't to say I need to be justified on a daily basis, but I surely do need to repent and rejoice in God's provision of the cross on a daily basis. I slowly became less self-sufficient and more dependent each day on grace.

As single adults, it's easier to be oblivious to our sins and so be cavalier about confession. It's also easy to withdraw when we're offended and not seek reconciliation. In effect, singleness seemingly provides the "option" of avoiding the hard work of self-examination, repentance, confession, and reconciliation that is required in a godly marriage. This is deceptive. Unconfessed sin has a destructive effect on a single adult's life, as well as upon the relationships within the church. So while we may have to work harder to practice this spiritual discipline, it's possible. One sure way to grow is to invite people to *ask* you questions about possible sins they observe. Another is have an accountability partner with whom you meet regularly to reflect on your life and to confess sin.

During the time the Holy Spirit was taking off my blinders regarding sin, I heard about a couple who had ended their courtship because the man was concerned about the lack of confession of sin from his girlfriend. I remember being truly puzzled about this. *Why in the world would you confess sin? Wouldn't it kill the courtship?* How merciful of the Lord to reveal this theological hole in my life. This man was right in being concerned, and it revealed that he was leading in the right way. The Lord honored his concern, and this couple is now married and presumably skilled in confessing sin to one another.

From my observation, a good marriage requires good confessors. Our future husbands are going to be able to experience and view our sin up close and personal. The fact that we sin won't be any surprise. The fact that we can humble ourselves, repent, and ask for forgiveness on a regular basis might be an agreeable surprise. So let's not wait until marriage to grow in this spiritual discipline.

A third point is understanding that marriage is a union, not a fifty-fifty proposition. Because I've never been married, I'm going to lean heavily on one godly woman who has been widowed three times. As Elisabeth Elliot says, there's no competition or scorekeeping in a union. She writes:

> Your equalities have been delineated: equally sinners, equally responsible, equally in need of grace, and equally the objects of that grace. That's where the fifty-fifty matter ends. You take up life as husband and wife and you start laying down your lives—not as martyrs, not as doormats or ascetics making a special bid for sainthood, but as two lovers who have needed and received grace, and who know very well that they are going to keep on needing and receiving it every day that they live together.[12]

In marriage the *I* is submerged into the *We*. Each part of the We should be pulling for the other, not pulling away. It is an interdependent entity, much like the members of our physical bodies. Again Elisabeth Elliot provides wise counsel:

> There is union in the physical body—all the members joined together in harmony and for the good of the whole, all subject to the head. So there is union in marriage, two separate persons made one in the flesh, and, if they are Christians, one in Christ, subject to His leadership. If they are one in Christ, they have not only union but communion, and this is a priceless thing.[13]

NO LACK OF GAIN

These four perspectives on heart issues covered two chapters. Many pages later, I hope you remember the initial question from chapter 5 that my friend Michael asked me: "What about trust? Isn't that important?" Yes, it is! Years later I found my answer in the Bible. "The heart of her husband trusts in her, and he will have no lack of gain. She does him good, and not harm, all the days of her life" (Prov. 31:11-12).

Trust is the result of many wise choices made over the years as we guard our hearts, discern, serve those around us, and develop a biblical understanding and expectation of marriage. Those daily choices are the deposits that will bring a good return in marriage, ensuring "no lack of gain." Those wise investments will benefit our churches, too, as we preserve the high value of the brother-sister relationships in our churches and guard the institution of marriage.

In matters of the heart, it's so easy to take the short-term, self-centered view. Dear friends, let's take the long-term perspective—committed to being trustworthy all the days of our lives.

FOR FURTHER STUDY

❖ There are two extremely useful chapters for single women written by Nancy Leigh DeMoss in the collection titled *Biblical Womanhood in the Home* (Crossway Books). These chapters are titled "Portrait of a Woman Used by God" and "Portrait of a Foolish Woman." I recommend the whole book, but these two chapters (especially the one on a foolish woman) are outstanding resources for cultivating wisdom in our relationships with men. I wish I could have quoted from "Portrait of a Foolish Woman," but I wouldn't be able to include the whole chapter, and it's better for you to read it in its entirety.

❖ *Sacred Marriage* by Gary Thomas (Zondervan) carries an intriguing subtitle: "What if God Designed Marriage to Make Us Holy More Than to Make Us Happy?" Gary's premise is that marriage is more than a covenant with another person. It's also a spiritual discipline designed to help people know God better, trust Him more fully, and love Him more deeply. If you want to make sure you are anticipating marriage in the right light, I recommend this book.

❖ *Recovering Biblical Manhood and Womanhood*, edited by John Piper and Wayne Grudem (Crossway), is a collection of theological essays on various topics of debate between those who hold to complementarian (the view of the authors) and egalitarian views on the roles of men and women. The foreword by John Piper, titled "For Single Men and Women (and the Rest of Us)," is full of empathetic but sound counsel to single adults.

❖ I didn't address the issue of sexual temptation in this chapter because a better resource has been written—*Not Even a Hint: Guarding Your Heart Against Lust* by Joshua Harris (Multnomah). This book is for both men and women, but it won't embarrass you to read it. Josh's honesty is breathtaking, but he's not saying anything that isn't common to us all.

❖ I could only briefly skim the surface of sin, justification, and progressive sanctification in this chapter. A much better resource is *The Cross-Centered Life* by C. J. Mahaney (Multnomah). This small book packs a

wallop, and I highly recommend it—especially if you are trying to earn
God's approval or if you fear losing His favor.

❖ *Her Hand in Marriage: Biblical Courtship in the Modern World* by
Douglas Wilson (Canon Press) is aimed at fathers of young women, but I
found much value in reading this book myself.

PART THREE

Finding a Guide for
Daily Life in the
Proverbs 31 Woman

7

FOOD FROM AFAR

She is like the ships of the merchant; she brings her food from afar. She rises while it is yet night and provides food for her household and portions for her maidens.

PROVERBS 31:14-15

The dining table was draped with a festive Christmas tablecloth and set with fine china and crystal, but my kitchen was a wreck. Potato peels were strewn all over the floor, the butternut squash puree decorated uncharted realms of my kitchen counters, and dirty dishes were piled precariously in the sink. I stood in the midst of it all in my stained sweatshirt and with partially applied makeup. With one eye on the clock, I was cleaning at a feverish pace. I had thirty minutes to go—those critical last moments when the kitchen slave heroically morphs into a gracious hostess.

That's when the doorbell rang. Like a deer caught in the headlights, I surveyed my options. There was no way to pretend I was ready. "Who in the world shows up half an hour early to a formal dinner?" I complained aloud.

Opening the door, I saw two of my smiling guests, their breath evident in the chilly night air. Incredulous, I announced shrilly, "You're *early*!"

Their eyes widened with surprise as their smiles shrank. "I'm sorry," the man began abjectly. "I, um, thought you said—or, um, I at least heard you say—that it started at six o'clock."

"No, I said six *thirty*!" I replied anxiously, before looking back to the living room. "I suppose you could come in now, but I'd probably put you to work first."

"No, no—that's okay," he said quickly, backing down the sidewalk. "We'll just drive around and come back in thirty minutes."

When this couple returned (a safe forty minutes later), they were greeted by a calm, smiling hostess in clean clothes and immediately ushered into a candlelit room to enjoy the fire by the twinkling Christmas tree. "I'm so sorry about my cranky kitchen maid. She was completely out of line," I told them. "You just can't get good help these days!"

Here's the moral of the story: Don't make your guests feel guilty when they show up at your door. That's the opposite of hospitable. (But I bet you guessed that by now.)

If you've ever tried entertaining as a single woman, you've no doubt felt that same wave of panic moments before your guests arrive. I have yet to successfully balance mingling with my guests and getting a warm, edible meal on the table in a timely way. We often eat at the late hour that fashionable Europeans do. I keep fine-tuning the process, but there's only so much advance prep I can do with the *Bon Appetit* recipes I love to cook. I'll start the cleaning and prep a day ahead even and still rush around at the last moment. Over the years, however, I've learned that my priorities needed to be corrected. When push comes to shove, we're always better off to be gracious to the guests and cut corners on the food.

This chapter starts a new section in this book—finding a guide for daily life in the Proverbs 31 woman. Even though we might prefer to be married now, there's much living to do as single women! In the words of Jim Elliot's memorable quote, "Let not our longing slay the appetite of our living."[1] We've seen that we can trust God to provide a husband (should that be His will) in His timing and that there is much joy in being pursued by a godly man. But let's not forget that our singleness is a gift to the church and that we have a wonderful, vibrant, purposeful life to lead until the day the Lord chooses to change our circumstances. Our wise Proverbs 31 woman provides much instruction for daily life. In this chapter, we'll start at home.

THE FREE-RANGE GOURMET

In fact, we'll start in the kitchen. Our verses for this chapter are Proverbs 31:14-15: "She is like the ships of the merchant; she brings her food from afar. She rises while it is yet night and provides food for her household and portions for her maidens." We see that the Proverbs 31 woman ministers to many others from her home. She "is like the ships of the merchant"—ranging far and wide to obtain what she needs, but her focus is on her home and those who live and even serve there. It is a priority for her, and so she rises while it is still dark to feed everyone.

Do you think "food from afar" is a pizza delivery? Do you ever range far and wide to find interesting items to cook—even for yourself? What does your kitchen pantry hold? A few cans of tuna and some cereal perhaps? You may eat TV dinners when you are alone, but do you ever cook for others? If you were to get married in just a few months, would you have the skills to cook three meals a day every day for your family? Can you cook intuitively, or do you have to rely on a recipe for most dishes?

In our microwave society, you can easily feed yourself without much effort. People eat in their cars and at their desks but rarely at home. It's not hard to find *something* to put down your throat as you run from event to event, but that's not what we see in our wonderful role model. She's not rummaging in the freezer looking for something to nuke and consume. She's making an *effort* because the kitchen table is the heart of the home.

We shouldn't wait until marriage is on the horizon to cultivate domesticity. In Titus 2:5 we find that older women are to train younger women to be "working at home." This is one of Scripture's commands to *women*. Period. Granted, this passage does assume that most women will be wives, but it also assumes that we need instruction to prepare for that role. We need training to love our husbands and love our children. We need to be taught how to be self-controlled, pure, working at home, and kind, as well as how to be submissive to our husbands. Single women are included in that training. We are to be trained in all aspects even though we may not be called by God to fill those roles, immediately or ever. In that light, we're no less exempt from the charge to be working at home than we are from the commands to be self-controlled, pure, or kind.

HOME, SWEET MISSION FIELD

Why does Scripture put this emphasis on the home for women? Why does the paragon of feminine virtue in Proverbs 31 invest so much of her time and resources into her home and its residents? *Because our homes are a mission field.* As the author of *The Hospitality Commands* notes:

> Lacking sacred temples or a special class of priests, the first-century Christians naturally made the home their base of operations. . . . Indeed, the first Christian congregations conducted all or most of their meetings

in homes because they did not own buildings. This necessitated that some members of the congregation open their homes to provide places in which the church could meet. The home thus became a hub for evangelism and teaching. . . . For the early Christians, the home was the most natural setting for proclaiming Christ to their families, neighbors, and friends. The same is true today. If you and/or your local church are looking for ways to evangelize, opening your home is one of the best methods for reaching the lost. Most of us, however, are not using our homes as we should to reach our neighbors, friends, and relatives. Tragically, many of us don't even know our neighbors. Yet through hospitality, we can meet our neighbors and be a lighthouse in spiritually dark neighborhoods.[2]

In fact, our ministry through our homes is so important that women are included in all four of the major "hospitality commands" in the New Testament:

• Romans 12:13, written to all in the church at Rome, says: "Contribute to the needs of the saints and seek to show hospitality."

• First Timothy 5:9-10 is specifically written about widows who seek the charitable support of the church: "Let a widow be enrolled if she is not less than sixty years of age, having been the wife of one husband, and having a reputation for good works: if she has brought up children, has shown hospitality, has washed the feet of the saints, has cared for the afflicted, and has devoted herself to every good work."

• Hebrews 13:2 commands all believers, "Do not neglect to show hospitality to strangers, for thereby some have entertained angels unawares."

• First Peter 4:9 was written to persecuted Christians scattered throughout Asia Minor: "Show hospitality to one another without grumbling."

Dear friends, did you ever think of your home as an outpost for your church? You can use your home for a variety of ministry purposes—from inviting newcomers to lunch after the church service, to inviting your neighbors over for a Bible study, to celebrating milestones with your friends over dinner. Though it might be a little more work to do this as a single woman, it's quite possible to do—and let's not forget, it's *fun*. There's an immediate reward for hospitality in the relaxed smiles of our guests and their appreciation of our generosity.

PEOPLE, NOT PRESENTATION

The Greek word in 1 Peter 4:9 for "hospitality" is *philoxenos*, which means "fond of guests."[3] Not fond of Martha Stewart-type ambition, a *Town &*

Country room, or a gourmet meal. Fond of *guests*—even those who arrive half an hour early! Though home design shows are everywhere on cable TV now, and our houses are getting bigger while the occupants are getting fewer, our culture is about *entertainment*, not hospitality. That's why I selected the opening illustration and mentioned the panicky moments before the guests arrived. I suspect this feeling is universal, but my anxiety is not due to my concern for the people coming. It's because I'm worried about my *presentation*. I want the kitchen to be spotless, the candles to be lit, the flatware to be gleaming, the music to be inviting, and the aromas to be enticing. The reason I shooed my guests away that cold December evening was because I wasn't ready for the *inspection of my presentation*. I wanted to impress them with an elaborate four-course meal from *Bon Appetit*. I wanted to entertain them, but I wasn't acting like I was fond of them.

Cultivating a love for the home means acquiring practical skills and training so that you can intentionally make your home a mission field, not a museum. If you're single and live by yourself, this means all your ministry will be to those who live outside your house. If you're single and have roommates, this means you minister to your roommates and to those outside your home. If you're a parent, this means your mission field is first in your home to your children and then to those outside your home. It takes some effort and forethought to do this, especially if you're only home a few hours out of every day. Romans 12:13 tells us to "seek to show hospitality." The NIV translates it as "practice hospitality." But the original Greek is better rendered "strive for" or "pursue" hospitality. Again as the author of *The Hospitality Commands* writes:

> Thus we are to actively pursue, promote, and aspire to hospitality. We are to think about it, plan for it, prepare for it, pray about it, and seek opportunities to do it. In short, the Romans 12 passage teaches that all Christians are to pursue the practice of hospitality. . . . Brothers and sisters, allow me to ask you the following questions. Do you eagerly pursue opportunities to practice hospitality, or is it something that you do only on holidays and during special events? Do you understand the important role that hospitality has within the Christian community? Do you see the relationship between brotherly love and hospitality? Beloved, only when we understand that the Spirit of God commands us to practice hospitality will we be adequately motivated to sacrificially open our homes to others.[4]

If that sounds overwhelming, perhaps this little thought will encourage you: Some of the most hospitable women in Scripture were single. Consider the example of Martha and Mary. Their home in the modest village of Bethany was the site of several Bible accounts. We know of at least three occasions when Jesus visited their home—the famous account where Martha is frazzled, the time Jesus raised Lazarus from the dead, and when He ate at their home just six days before His final Passover. As one commentator notes: " . . . after Jesus left His natural home at the age of thirty to enter upon His public ministry we do not read of Him returning to it for rest and relaxation. It was the warm, hospitable home at Bethany to which He retired, for He loved the three who lived in it, Martha, Mary and Lazarus—in this order—which is something we do not read concerning His own brothers and sisters according to the flesh."[5]

Another outstanding example was Lydia (Acts 16:14). She was the first European convert to Christianity, and her home was presumably the gateway to the rest of the continent. Let's look at her example.

LYDIA: A PORTRAIT OF HOSPITALITY

Everyone agreed that the doors to preaching the gospel in Asia clearly seemed to be closed to the small band of missionaries. Then Paul had this unusual night vision of a man begging them to come to Macedonia. The confirmation came in the wind-assisted crossing that provided smooth sailing right into the port near Philippi, a leading Roman city in that province. But they found no synagogue in Philippi. Were there not even ten male Jews in this significant city to form the quorum of a synagogue? Perhaps if any Jews existed, they would be praying by the riverside like the Jews did in the days of the exile in Babylon.

As might be expected with the lack of a synagogue, there was only a small group of women praying that day by the river. But these were women the Lord had prepared. The first convert in the group—the first in all of Europe, to be exact—was a woman named Lydia. She was a successful businesswoman, trading in the luxury item of purple cloth. Upon her conversion, she insisted that Paul and his apostolic missionaries share her home and receive her hospitality, evidence of her faithfulness to the Lord (Acts 16:15).

It appears that Lydia was also a single woman, head of a household consisting mainly of servants. It was probably in her house that the first church in Philippi began to meet. Perhaps it was in her house that the church gathered to take up a collection to send to Paul as he endured house arrest in

Rome. Maybe church members were there to hear the letter from Paul that contained his effusive thanks for their generosity and shared his secret for being content in all circumstances. It's hard to know precisely what happened in Lydia's home, except for two facts: Her first act of ministry as a believer was to offer her home and hospitality, and it was in her home that Paul and Silas sought refuge after their release from jail. They had been beaten, put in stocks, and imprisoned; they had survived an earthquake, evangelized and baptized their jailer and his entire household, and faced down the magistrates who wanted to brush their mistreatment under the rug. After such a night, where do they turn for refreshment? Acts 16:40 simply says that "they went to Lydia's house, where they met with the brothers and encouraged them. Then they left."

CARING FOR GOD'S PEOPLE

What an incredible ministry Mary, Martha, and Lydia had! To be able to host and refresh our Lord and Paul, His chosen instrument to carry His name before the Gentiles! These were no small acts of service. These women applied themselves to making their homes a refuge and a center of ministry, and that affected their *communities*.

Throughout history Christian women have continued to follow their example. One of my favorite examples was Katherina von Bora, who became Mrs. Martin Luther. She lived from 1499 to 1552, during a time of tremendous upheaval in Europe. At nine years old, she was placed in the Cistercian convent of Nimbschen in Saxony (now part of modern Germany). At sixteen she became a nun. Seven years later, at age twenty-three, she renounced her vows because of the influence of Dr. Luther's writings. Having nowhere else to go, she and eight other nuns were smuggled to the Augustinian monastery at Wittenberg where Luther was still a monk. He arranged to place these ex-nuns in good homes or in suitable marriages. But, as one historian writes, "Katherina spent two years in Wittenberg, learning domestic economy and keeping her eye open for a suitable match."[6]

When those two years were up, Katherina, now twenty-five, married Martin Luther, forty-two, and became mistress of the former monastery—no small feat.

From the start, she took over the management of her home with a determined will. The Augustinian monastery, first loaned to Luther by the

Elektor Frederick and then given to him as a wedding present by the new Elektor, had forty rooms on the first floor with cells above. In time it would house Katherina's and Luther's six children (one of whom died in infancy), six or seven orphaned nephews and nieces, the four children of one of Luther's widowed friends, Katherina's aunt Magdalene, tutors for the children, male and female servants, student boarders, guests, and refugees. Katherina was not just a good *Hausfrau*; she became a remarkable manager of an oversized boardinghouse.

For the sake of cleanliness, she installed an indoor bathroom, which probably also served as a laundry. For the sake of economy, she created a brewery, planted a vegetable garden, and developed an orchard that produced apples, pears, grapes, peaches, and nuts. She herded, milked, slaughtered, and sold the cows, and made butter and cheese. No one has ever accused Katherina of laziness, though her critics—and there have been many—found her bossy and overbearing. . . . "In domestic affairs," [Luther] said, "I defer to Katie. Otherwise, I am led by the Holy Ghost."[7]

Practical Issues

While I was working on this chapter, I traveled to a conference where I was working independently of the rest of the group. I ate all but two meals alone in restaurants. I made the best of it, but it feels much more forlorn to eat alone in a public place than it does to eat alone while standing at your own kitchen counter. As I ate dinner one evening in an upscale Mexican restaurant, I noticed that I was an island in a sea of humanity that flowed and swirled around me, but didn't interact with me.

Picking at a burrito, I thought to myself: *This is the difference between twenty and forty. At twenty I would have been mortified, sure that everyone was staring at me and pitying me for having no friends. At forty I'm sure that everyone is too absorbed with themselves to notice or care about the woman dining alone.*

Eating alone in public places is a stark reminder of why table fellowship is so important even in these drive-thru days. There is a sense of shared community over a meal. As uncomfortable as it is to ask for a table for one, these lonely moments prod me to think about others—to consider who else may desire company.

A restaurant, however, is not really the solution. It's too easy to let all our table fellowship occur in restaurants, which can short-circuit real fellowship. Who hasn't been interrupted during a great punch line or a blessing over the meal by a rushed waiter? Who has been able to ignore the waiters circling like sharks to clear the table while someone is sharing a moving testimony? Who can even *hear* in the din of the open kitchen designs that are so popular now? Instead, our homes can provide an oasis in many a busy life to demonstrate interest in and care for those around us.

If you need encouragement to cultivate your domestic skills, let me assure you that I was no *Bon Appetit* aficionado in my early single years! I lived on happy hour appetizers and fast food. My cooking was so bad that my family called it "fish wads and pudding lumps"—a nickname earned after a spectacularly bad Mother's Day meal. My apartment looked like New York City when the sanitation engineers go on strike. My home decor was Early Goodwill with a touch of Target. No one around me ever talked about home and hearth; so I didn't give it any particular thought.

When I became a Christian, I noticed how much effort the women I knew put into their homes. *Candles in the bathrooms! Real linen napkins! Matching dinner dishes!* I felt like an anthropologist in a foreign culture. But it inspired me to do the same. In short order, I was buying furniture and clipping recipes. After a few years, I was bold enough to even throw elegant dinner parties for my pastors and their wives, which I enjoyed doing immensely.

If you want to grow in your hospitality or domesticity skills, here are a number of practical issues you can consider:

• This is a great opportunity to pursue an "older woman" in the Titus 2 mentoring model. Consider the women around you. Whose homes do you enjoy visiting? Whose hospitality has blessed you? Ask these women to show you how they do it! Don't be too shy to ask for training. It's honoring to these women that you want to emulate their examples.

• Start small. Have friends over for coffee or tea and conversation. It's not the meal you provide that makes a memory; it's the focus on your guests. Sometimes it's a lot easier to do that when you don't have an elaborate meal planned.

• If you're not a great cook, practice. I bet you'll find many supportive friends who would willingly consume your experiments. A great basic cookbook to have is *The Joy of Cooking*. It removes the mystery from this topic. I like *The New Basics Cookbook* for the same reason. It's also fun to take cooking classes with your friends, especially classes on international cuisine.

• Don't be afraid to select patterns for your daily dishes or fine china. It's not a jinx! If the Lord gives you a husband, he might like what you already have. If not, you'll have fun selecting a pattern together. I chose a china pattern years ago, and my friends generously gave me select pieces at various times. Now I have place settings for ten. People enjoy knowing what you collect, and it sure beats another bottle of fragrant lotion!

• If you live with roommates, consider cooking for your household on a rotating basis. I have a set of friends who live in a townhouse they've nicknamed The Abbey. Each week one of the women cooks for the rest. Though their different work schedules often prevent them from eating together, they've agreed to set aside Monday Family Nights as a household priority—a time when they eat together and catch up on the news of the week. They also regularly plan for hospitality to others.

• If you live with your family, offer to be responsible for the family meals on certain days. My friend Mindy makes dinner once a week for her family—a blessing to her mother.

• If you've moved around a lot and feel like no place is home, consider buying a home. Again it's not a jinx! You can always sell it if you get married, and your profits will certainly bless your husband. Owning a home is usually a wise financial investment, and it allows you to put down some roots and combat that lonely tumbleweed feeling. Often it is the only way you'll be able to create a guestroom, too. (There are many things you should consider before purchasing a home, though. We'll consider this idea further in the next chapter.)

• Create a memento of your guests. Some people use guest books; I take photographs. I have photo displays of most of the people who have been at my home. They are a useful diversion for my current guests when I'm busy in the kitchen!

• Let your pastors know that you are willing to host visitors. I know a single woman in Wales who has had numerous people from the States (and possibly other countries) in her home. Allyson cheerfully tours the same Welsh landmarks and tourist hotspots with most of her guests, cooks for them, and laughs lots with them. She seemingly knows everyone in my international church network because of her hospitality.

• Team up to pull off larger events. My former roommate and I used to trade off being the "kitchen slave" (our joking term) for each other's dinner parties. Or share your resources. I once threw a formal New Year's Eve party at one single man's house because it was large enough to accommodate everyone. He supplied the house, and I supplied the party.

• Finally, don't forget to show hospitality to those who cannot repay you, for in this way you will be emulating your Lord and following His command (Luke 14:12-14).

When I hosted that Christmas dinner party, I invited three couples to thank them for their friendship and investment in my life. All three couples were members of my church and were greatly involved in the church's ministry. Two of the men were my pastors. All three of the women were busy mothers with children ranging from preschool to high school. Each of them was notable for the amount of time and service they poured into other people. So I counted it a great privilege that I could invite them all over for an evening where *they* were served. If any of them thought it was odd to be invited to the home of a single woman, there was no evidence of it. All of them accepted eagerly and remarked repeatedly that they had a great time. If any thought it was uncomfortable to seat seven people, and not an even six, at the table, they gave no indication. Instead, they all seemed delighted to receive hospitality—even when one couple encountered the "cranky kitchen maid." What a joy it was to use my home to gather together these friends and friends in the kingdom for a holiday dinner.

Ladies, may we never fear odd numbers around our tables, for our Lord is always with us. And may He richly reward us as we "contribute to the needs of the saints and seek to show hospitality" (Rom. 12:13).

FOR FURTHER STUDY

❖ It's really a booklet, but *The Hospitality Commands* by Alexander Strauch is a "meaty" read (bad pun intended). I recommend you read this before you get sucked into the vortex of gourmet and home decor publications. The booklet will provide the right perspective!

8

OUT OF HER EARNINGS

*She considers a field and buys it; out of her earnings she plants
a vineyard. She sets about her work vigorously; her arms are
strong for her tasks. She sees that her trading is profitable, and
her lamp does not go out at night. In her hand she holds the
distaff and grasps the spindle with her fingers.*
PROVERBS 31:16-19 (NIV)

We'd agreed to meet early for breakfast, but it seemed that Erin was
already pumped up even before she got her coffee. We placed our
orders, and I sat back, motioning her to start the download.

"Okay, so I've got some good news," she began. "I've been accepted to
graduate school—at Harvard's Kennedy School of Government. A master's
degree in public policy from Harvard could really get me into the White
House."

"That's great!" I replied. "I'm really proud of you."

"Well, the bad news is that this would put me about $200,000 in debt,"
she added.

"Oh." I sipped my coffee in silence, sobered by the numbers.

"That's not all," she continued. "My pastor also asked me to consider
working as his assistant. I didn't even consider this when I came on this
church-planting team, but now I find myself rather intrigued by it."

"That's quite a range of career possibilities!" I said, amused.

"I know! Some of my friends and family can't understand why I'd even
entertain the idea of being a pastor's administrative assistant—and it's not
even full time," she replied. "Some thought I was nuts just to move to
Boston for a new church, much less to work for it."

Our food arrived, but Erin didn't seem interested in breakfast. Pushing her scrambled eggs around the plate, she let the conversation drift for a moment.

"So where's your heart, Erin?" I asked.

"In both places, to be honest," she replied.

"I understand," I replied. "How about faith for marriage? Would you like to get married? Is it something you are praying about?"

"Yes, of course!"

"Well, I wonder how your decisions today might affect your husband in the future. To take on $200,000 of debt would be a serious ball and chain for any man—as it would be for you," I offered. "Whether or not you get married, you would have to be making decisions about your future based on your debt obligation."

"I know," she said quietly. "This will definitely be a prayerful decision."

That conversation was more than two years ago, and today Erin is working as her pastor's part-time assistant. While she postponed attending Harvard, Erin has added an array of interesting part-time assignments to her work at her church, including an unpaid government internship writing for a healthy marriage initiative, as well as freelance jobs writing for various magazines and editing children's books. As interesting as those jobs are, she considers the most important one to be what she's doing to build a local church. She is still single, but should she get married, she is building a track record of serving her husband with the decisions she's making now.

CAREER CONFUSION

For single women, a job can sometimes feel like a statement. If they have other priorities outside of the job—such as serving family members or a church ministry—their colleagues may question them. This is the case for my hospitable friend Allyson. "One challenge that I constantly find in work is not meeting up to people's expectations," she says. "Most of my colleagues assume that I have chosen to be single so that I can focus on my career, and as I don't take opportunities to move on and further my career, they are surprised."

Or if a single woman decides to pursue a demanding career, others can wrongly assume she is pursuing this for her personal glory. They may conclude she has no interest in getting married and raising a family—and may even discourage her from pursuing her studies or career. Yet marketable skills can often benefit a family in many ways throughout the seasons of a growing family. I've known many women who have fluidly moved in and out of full-time and part-time work or started their own home-based businesses, drawing upon the skills and experience they acquired when single. I know of a woman, for example, whose part-time nursing work provided for the family while her husband studied to become a pastor. What she had invested in her education and training as a single woman paid off for her family's goals once she was married and a mother.

Alternatively, some women find they've invested many years into what they assumed would be short-term jobs—springboards into marriage. Still single as their twenties wind down, they begin to panic that they didn't pursue a "real" career when they should have done so, and they worry that they won't be able to make ends meet in the future. (I did the opposite in my early thirties. I transitioned to part-time work and built a freelance writing business in anticipation of working from home when I got married. Years later, with no husband on the horizon, I went back to full-time work.)

Even Erin's story might confuse or challenge some readers. Why should the potential concerns of some unknown man in the future be a factor now? And why would she trade a Harvard-credentialed career track for working in her church?

What these situations have in common is that they are all decisions requiring godly wisdom. There aren't any definitive rules or cookie-cutter answers here.

Cutting through the confusion, the Proverbs 31 woman once again offers us clarity. "She considers a field and buys it; out of her earnings she plants a vineyard. She sets about her work vigorously; her arms are strong for her tasks. She sees that her trading is profitable, and her lamp does not go out at night. In her hand she holds the distaff and grasps the spindle with her fingers" (Prov. 31:16-19 NIV). Here we see this enterprising woman doing four specific tasks:

- Working vigorously and profitably
- Saving and investing
- Buying property
- Cultivating her strength

These aren't typically regarded as feminine skills, but our wise woman is certainly praised for developing business skills that are now a blessing to her family. In this chapter, we will tag along with her and see how her example helps us set a course for wisdom today.

THE DISTAFF AND SPINDLE

First, let's address the obvious. Did you notice what was in her hands? She holds the instruments necessary for spinning cloth. Yes, our Proverbs 31 woman was a . . . *spinster!*

According to a book on the history of single women, spinsters originally appeared in thirteenth-century France and later in Germany and England as spinners of cotton and wool. As the author writes, "They were not yet spinsters but *femmes seules*—unwed young girls, orphaned relatives, and widows of the Crusades who performed their tasks within the self-sustained family home."[1] The author adds:

> Long before the industrial revolution—and before the implementation of a restrictive British common law—single women worked on their own in other ways. Town and city records, portions of which have been published in academic papers, indicate that unwed women in medieval France, England, and Germany traded in raw wool, silk, and rare spices. Some engaged in foreign trading and owned their own ships, and a few are said to have managed large estates and breweries.
>
> On into the seventeenth century, spinster was used to identify a respectable employment category. When later that century the French began using spinster to indicate an unwed woman, the term was understood to be descriptive: a woman on her own, for any number of reasons, and in need of an income.[2]

It was the industrial revolution that introduced a new shade of meaning to that word. With 405,000 more women than men in Britain by 1851, the surplus of women were negotiating alongside the men for a place in the new economy. This was quickly recognized as a social problem. One British member of Parliament even labeled the growing number of unwed women as "a tragical redundant class."[3]

Ever since, single women largely have viewed their jobs with a mixture of gratitude and apprehension. But it doesn't have to be that way if you take God's point of view. After all, the best description for our current circumstances is simply "a woman on her own, for any number of reasons, and in need of an income." No woman is tragically redundant in God's economy. Let's shake off the stereotypes from all sides, and instead let's look at each of these four tasks from the Proverbs 31 woman's example.

WORKING PROFITABLY (FOR THE REAL BOSS)

"If you want to have a career here," Julie's boss told her one day, "you'll need to get your Ph.D. Without that, you might not be taken seriously and could be shuffled to the side."

Julie already has her master's degree and has spent many years as a hard-working, successful research analyst. She travels frequently, balancing her responsibilities at work with her responsibilities on various church ministry teams. She's also making a significant investment in her sister's family, especially her two nieces. Her life is full to the brim, and the thought of returning to school for a demanding degree program on top of these commitments isn't enticing. Yet she wonders if she's being foolish for not aggressively developing her career.

Ann teaches at a very small Christian school, with a commensurately very small salary. Her income curtails the amount of socializing she can do. Her job curtails the amount of free time she has. She feels this is where she should be, and she is glad to make the investment in these children. But her decision to take a $50,000 pay cut puzzles some people, who periodically suggest that she has put in enough time as a teacher, and she should find a better-paying career. Sometimes Ann is tempted to think the same thing herself.

What is the unspoken worldview here? *You are defined by your career, and it should be your ultimate priority.* Though that idea may be especially pronounced for women today, it's not new thinking. At the turn of the twentieth century, as women were moving from the factory to the office, advice guides for the working single woman multiplied. One example, written by Florence Wenderoth Saunders in 1906, is titled *Letters to a Business Girl: The Personal Letters of a Business Woman to Her Daughter, Replete with Practical Information Regarding the Perplexing Problems . . . By One Who Knows the Inside Facts of Business and the Office Routine and the Relations of Employer to Employee.* The author had strong views on how a working girl should conduct herself:

> I never saw a businessman's desk that was loaded with the trifles that some of the girls in my office used to have on theirs; photographs, flowers. . . . like knickknacks they kept because they were cute. . . . Remember, men have the advantage in business; they have been accustomed to work for generations. . . . if [a girl] expects to take her place by [his] side and eventually command the same salary, she must profit from

his example. . . . keep [your] desk cleared of every article *which is not absolutely essential in the performance of your work.*[4]

We are fortunate to have the career choices available today, but we may be even more distracted by the siren call of "success." When we receive counsel from those who don't know the Lord, that counsel is wholly unmindful of Him and His rule in our lives. While it's not wrong to consider the input of those around us, we have to consider the limited perspective of unbelievers—they have no higher authority, and their advice will clearly reflect that. In the case of Mrs. Saunders, her goal was that women command the same salary as men. That's it. But there's a much larger goal for our lives.

Erin, Allyson, Julie, and Ann are all friends of mine. Each has a different role in the marketplace, but each has the same definition of success: Am I pleasing my Father? Am I doing today what He's called me to do? Am I making sure that God's priorities are being met? Am I pouring my time, talent, and treasure into the eternal purpose of the gospel and the building of the local church? Are these activities I'm pursuing cultivating biblical femininity or detracting from it?

The choices they've made about their jobs probably can't be fully understood by someone with a different definition of success. But that doesn't mean that the work they've chosen to do is meaningless or that God can't be glorified in what they do on the job. In a chapter titled "Making Much of Christ from 8 to 5" from his book *Don't Waste Your Life*, John Piper writes:

> According to Genesis 2:2, God himself rested from his work of creation, implying that work is a good, God-like thing. And the capstone of that divine work was man, a creature in God's own image designed to carry on the work of ruling and shaping and designing creation. Therefore, at the heart of the meaning of work is *creativity*. If you are God, your work is to create out of nothing. If you are not God, but like God—that is, if you are human—your work is to take what God has made and shape it and use it to make him look great.[5]

We can make God look great at our jobs through two simple principles:
1) Do your work with integrity, humility, and gratitude.
2) Identify and avoid the snares of sin.

While each point merits a chapter of its own, I will only be able to give an overview here. With regard to the first point, I think each of us knows where we are tempted to cut corners at work. Are we punctual? Do we give our employers a full day? Are we lazy, or do we spend too much time socializing or attending to personal business? Do we surf the Internet instead of working? Do we send out personal e-mails on the job? Would our colleagues say we are open to correction or defensive? Would we be identified as team players or lone rangers? Are we working to make others successful or drawing attention to ourselves? Are we grateful for the position God has given us, or do we complain about office policies? As John Piper writes:

> In 1 Thessalonians 4:11 [Paul] tells the church, "Aspire to live quietly, and to mind your own affairs, and to work with your hands, as we instructed you, *so that you may live properly before outsiders and be dependent on no one.*" The point here is not that our work will save anyone. The point is that if we live and work well, obstacles will be removed. In other words, good, honest work is not the saving Gospel of God, but a crooked Christian car salesman is a blemish on the Gospel and puts a roadblock in the way of seeing the beauty of Christ. And sloth may be a greater stumbling block than crime. Should Christians be known in their offices as the ones you go to if you have a problem, but not the ones to go to with a complex professional issue? It doesn't have to be either-or. The biblical mandate is: "Whatever you do, work heartily, as for the Lord and not for men" (Colossians 3:23; cf. Ephesians 6:7).[6]

SEXUAL SNARES AT WORK

Our office settings or the functions of our jobs can also present specific temptations to sin—snares that we *must* identify and work hard to avoid. I think the most common is the temptation of sexual sin. Whether it's pornography in our hotel rooms while we travel on business or the allure of our married colleague's attentions, our jobs can be minefields.

Before I became a Christian, the majority of my dating relationships were connected to my job. When I became a Christian, I had to make some swift, radical changes. I'm sad to say, the most serious change was required with a married colleague who had often engaged me in banter ranging from flirtatious to vulgar. A few weeks after my conversion, I invited him to my office and explained my new beliefs. I then informed him that I would no longer entertain his attentions because I had been sinfully and selfishly drawing his affections away from his wife. But I wanted him to understand my new convictions and why I saw this as stealing from his wife, and I asked his forgiveness. He was stunned—but unfortunately he never seemed to entirely understand the boundaries I had redrawn that day. Over the years (even after I left this job), he would periodically ask me to lunch, and I would always decline, citing that as his wife wouldn't be present, I didn't think our lunch would honor her. Maybe he was testing my convictions, but I'm glad to say by God's grace I didn't waver.

As single women, we must be savvy about the emotional connections that can be made on the job. We were designed by God to be helpers and to make men successful. We can't be oblivious to the fact that our encouragement, support, and promotion of our male colleagues can sometimes misfire in our own hearts—not to mention theirs. I've known many Christian single women who have wrestled with their attraction to unbelieving single coworkers or even married colleagues. We can help each other here by listening carefully as our friends talk about their colleagues. Do our friends light up when talking about one particular person at work? If so, ask questions. It's better to be labeled a little nosy now than later to walk with your friend through the fallout of an immoral relationship or adulterous affair. It's not easy to do this, I know.

I remember one friend who seemed a little too delighted when her married male boss called her at home or asked her to work late. She talked about him a lot; so I finally asked her if she was sliding down that slippery slope of adultery. She was shocked when I asked, but I told her that the top of the slope is innocent attraction—and that's where she seemed to be. I wanted her to be aware of gravity's pull. She dismissed my concern then, but a few months later she did come back to confess that it was more serious. Though she did not overtly sin, she was poised for a spectacular crash-and-burn, and she was glad I had asked her about it in time.

Sexual sin isn't always a subtle, slippery slope. Sometimes it's just blatantly there. Another friend of mine recently confessed her temptation in a situation she never thought would appeal to her. While attending a political hearing in another town, she ended up talking to the immensely attractive man next to her. Their discussion made it clear he wasn't a Christian (strike one), but she wasn't sure about his marital status. He had no ring. During the lunch break he invited her to join him in the building's cafeteria. She accepted and found herself enjoying his attentions. She knew this wasn't a good idea, but she dismissed her conscience by telling herself it was just lunch. After the hearing concluded, he asked her to return to his hotel with him. By then the warning bells were going off, but she was still slow to flee sin—tempted by the idea that "no one would know." Except God, of course, who mercifully sent a coworker along from this man's office at that very moment. In the course of that conversation with his coworker, this man revealed that he had invited my friend to his hotel room. His coworker asked how this man's wife might react, and the man said his wife wouldn't care because they had an "open marriage." Upon hearing those words, the fear of God entered my friend's heart, and she immediately declined any further contact and left. Later she said she was appalled by how tempted she was to respond to this man's blatant sexual overtures, and she asked for ongoing accountability in this area.

None of us is immune at work. Just read the newspaper. How many of the accounts of adulterous affairs noted there began on the job? It's a classic story, and we must be mindful that we are not above the same temptations. The enemy of our souls studies us and knows our weaknesses, and the hunger for a relationship leaves us vulnerable unless we guard against sin and ask God for His grace to overcome. There are some practical steps we can take, however, to avoid sin. Here are a few questions we can ask ourselves to evaluate a temptation:

• Am I avoiding the appearance of evil on the job? Is it necessary for me to have exclusive lunch meetings alone with a married colleague? Or am I conducting business alone in a hotel room with him instead of in a public area?

• Am I looking forward to Monday morning because of the attention I might receive from an "off-limits man"—a married man or a single but unbelieving coworker? Or do I "swing by" his office with a question instead of using the telephone or e-mail just so I can engage his attention?

• Am I offering my male boss or colleagues the kind of sympathy or emotional support that is more appropriate from a wife?

• Have I allowed myself to become an outlet for the personal troubles of my married boss or colleague? (Warning! Do *not* discuss his marital woes!)

• Do I crave attention and encouragement from an "off-limits" coworker?

• Am I fantasizing about these "off-limits" men? If so, have I confessed this to the appropriate person and asked for accountability?

• Am I taking steps to avoid other sexual temptation, such as canceling the pornography channels in hotel rooms or refusing to buy trashy women's magazines when traveling?

You may be thinking that I'm being overly dramatic. Unfortunately, I've learned these warning signs from my own life and the lives of my friends.

Our little fantasies and mild crushes are sowing seeds to a craving that demands to be satisfied, and that satisfaction is not honorable before the Lord. But don't forget it's not our sexuality that is dishonorable—our lust is. As Joshua Harris writes:

> Keep this radical but liberating idea in mind: God *wants* you to embrace your sexuality. And battling lust is part of how you do that. Does the idea of embracing sexuality and fighting lust sound contradictory? That's probably because today's culture offers a very narrow definition of what it means to embrace your sexuality. It equates embracing your sexuality with doing whatever feels good. So according to our culture, to deny a sexual impulse at any point is to be untrue to yourself. . . . As Christians, embracing our sexuality looks radically different. We don't obey every sexual impulse—nor do we deny that we have sexual desires. Instead, we choose both restraint and gratefulness. For us, sexual desire joins every other part of our lives—our appetite for food, our use of money, our friendship, our dreams, our careers, our possessions, our abilities, our families—in bowing before the one true God.[7]

TIME AND TRAINING

Before we conclude point one (working vigorously and profitably), I want to highlight two useful assets of any job: time and training.

Let's start with training first. Our single years are an exciting time to pursue many opportunities that challenge us to grow and learn. But we need to carefully consider the influences shaping our decisions. Are they biblical standards or the world's? Women who choose the priorities of their relationship with God, investment in the local church, and cultivation of biblical femininity should be applauded. I think we should be unabashed in saying that marriage and motherhood are high callings for women, and we should prepare for them as we can. To put marriage and motherhood at the head of our personal goals list is to bravely swim against this culture's tide, and I believe it honors the Lord. This career requires as much, and sometimes more, training for excellence than many other professions.

But I would also gently suggest that no one should presume what's going to happen in the future. If you ask most single women in their thirties, forties, and beyond, we thought we'd be wives and mothers by now, too. But life throws us curveballs, so to speak. I know women who never got married, women whose husbands died young and left them as widows with children to rear, women whose husbands abandoned them, women whose husbands contracted debilitating illnesses and couldn't work, and so forth.

Unfortunately, in a fallen world, being married is no guarantee that you won't need education, training, and skills to one day support your family.

So I definitely encourage women to seek training. But I would say that the area where we should *first* seek training is the Titus 2 virtues—to be mentored by godly, mature women in the local church. *Then*, as the Lord leads, we can seek the professional skills and education we may need for a career. Professional training for women is neither automatically good (as our culture assumes) nor automatically bad (as some might reflexively assume). It's a wisdom issue that needs to be considered in light of the impact on a woman's relationship with the Lord and her church.

Personally, I'm thankful for the sacrifice my parents made in saving and paying for my college education. I've enjoyed many interesting jobs because my degree opened the door for them. But my college degree and most of my work experience have absolutely no bearing on eternity. My fruitfulness as a godly woman does have an eternal impact. So while we should not presume about our futures, our consideration should not be whether attending a top-flight school or getting graduate degrees would advance our careers. We need to determine whether the time demands and the campus culture might adversely affect our spiritual fruitfulness or undermine our commitment to biblical standards.

The second point is about time. As single women juggling jobs and home and church responsibilities, it can seem like we never have enough time. I think it must get worse when you add a husband and children to the picture though. So now is a good time to curb the tendency to burn the candle at both ends. Though I know some single women who have time to burn, most women I know—myself included—are running ragged.

There are a gazillion time management programs available, and like many people, I have my favorite method. But secular time management methods fail to recognize that we can't manage time as though it's our own resource—one we can invest, hoard, or spend. Time is a finite resource. Our days have been determined by God; so our job is to manage them wisely as a gift from God. As Moses wrote in Psalm 90:12, "So teach us to number our days that we may get a heart of wisdom."

We have many opportunities and few limitations as single women. Our resources seemingly can be stretched very far—but that also means *we* are stretched thin. Think of time as a piece of Play-Doh. You can't go both deep *and* wide at the same time. There's only so much to go around. Having wide borders means we can only invest so much in the depth of our relationships.

Marriage and motherhood pulls in our borders because we are required to use our resources to go deeper with a defined set of human beings. Being single means we have to work harder at defining our borders, but we do have them—and we should be pursuing in-depth relationships with at least a few people.

When I was a new Christian, a wise woman in my church sized me up and gave me some solid advice. Sandy suggested that it might be a good idea if I had someone as a sounding board to help me sort through any requests for my time. She was happy to help in this way, to counsel me as I sorted through my priorities. At first I hesitated, wondering if that would be really useful. Then I realized the wonderful gift she had given me: time to consider a request. Being married, Sandy knew the value of postponing a decision or request until she could talk to her husband—and she knew I lacked this protection. So as my small group leader's wife, she provided that accountability and covering to me. I believe her exact words were: "Carolyn, you are a very capable woman, and many people in this church would like to have you join their ministry teams, baby-sit their children, and help with their pet projects. I've observed that you tend to overcommit yourself, possibly because you like to please people. So I'd like to help you set priorities and learn to say no. If you'd like, you can postpone making any decisions by saying you'd like to discuss it with me first, as I'm helping you with your schedule. That way you don't have to feel pressured to give an answer right away." Sad to say, I often was unwisely independent and didn't take advantage of her kind offer when it was available.

Over the years, I've learned to prayerfully spend time at the beginning of the year and ask the Lord during a personal retreat what His priorities for me might be at this time. I often revise them throughout the year, but I've found that the new year is a good time for annual review. I look at job commitments, church commitments, ministry teams, outreach opportunities, personal goals (finances, health, etc.), and family responsibilities. I identify one thing to cultivate at a time in each of those areas. For example, as my sisters have gotten married and had children, I've shifted my childcare commitments from other families to theirs. As I've said yes to caring for my nieces and nephews, it makes it easier for me to say no to requests from other families. As I've learned, you can only say no without guilt when you can clearly articulate what you've already committed to. That's a reasonable limitation. Just because I'm single doesn't mean I have a forty-eight-hour day. I have the same amount of time as everyone else.

Another hard-learned lesson is about being a creature, not the Creator. God created me to need certain things for physical sustenance—nourishing food, quality sleep, physical exercise. When I was young, I thought I could cut corners on these things with seemingly no consequences so that I could pursue what I wanted to do. But that wasn't true. I was sowing to an unhealthy future. Now I realize that I won't get everything done on today's To Do list. As a matter of fact, I will *never* be able to say my work is finished. Only Christ could say that. I live with piles of undone things because I am a finite creature.

So I must stop and get to bed for the sleep that my Creator has deemed necessary for my physical well-being. And I must plan, shop for, and cook nourishing food. And I must drag myself out of bed in the morning and go to the gym to exercise muscles that aren't used in front of the computer all day. And so on. Once I put those nonnegotiable items in my schedule, including church commitments and services, my private devotions, and my job, I was able to see that I didn't really have that much time for a lot of outside commitments and social opportunities. I had to seek my Father to find out what He wanted me to commit to and trust that He would provide for the requests I had to decline.

Now let's look at the second aspect of what we see our Proverbs 31 woman doing in these verses: saving and investing.

A Man Is No Plan for Saving and Investing

When you're single, you learn to do a lot of things by yourself—from traveling independently to making home and automotive repairs. Or paying your taxes and investing in a 401(k) retirement account. Or buying disability and life insurance. Or handling your parents' estates after their deaths—or your husband's estate when you become a widow.

Most of these things aren't fun to learn, but they have to be mastered. How well I know the temptation to yearn for a husband to handle what I don't want to. But as one women's financial organization reminds us, "A man is no plan." Even marriage doesn't guarantee we can be blissfully ignorant about financial matters because women generally have to carry on alone—more than 75 percent of all women are eventually widowed, and at an average age of fifty-six.[8] Statistically, we also live longer than men; so we have to be especially wise about saving for our futures.

Now it may seem like a sweeping generalization to say that women don't want to learn about financial issues. I know that for many women, this isn't true. But for lots of us, it isn't a natural inclination. We may enjoy spending money more than we do saving and investing it. However, this is both unwise and unbiblical. Throughout the Scriptures, we can read many verses about God's perspective on our money. Our money is God's, and He has laid out a very specific plan for how we are to use what He provides for us. As Randy Alcorn writes in *Money, Possessions & Eternity,* the Bible has "a staggering amount to say about money, how we are to view it, and what we are to do with it." In fact, he notes, a full 15 percent of Jesus' recorded words concerned money and possessions, more than He spoke on any other single topic.[9]

The first principle of money is that we should not consume all we receive. When I was a child, my father tried to train me in the discipline and wisdom of saving money. My allowance was twenty-five cents a week (not much even then!), but I only received fifteen cents. He put the other ten cents in a savings account that I couldn't access until I was an adult. What he was trying to show me flew over my greedy little head. All I remember was that with only fifteen cents each week, it took forever to buy the model horse I wanted. But over time, those dimes in my savings account earned a lot of interest. When I graduated from college, I had a little more than $2,000—which I promptly emptied out as I looked for a job and treated myself to side vacations. I had to learn Dad's lesson the hard way as an adult instead—and this still years after I started working. Because I didn't save at all in my early working years, I lost the most valuable commodity in saving and investing: time. The dollars I could have saved then would have earned more return than the hundreds of dollars I am saving now. I didn't believe it when people told me that principle. I didn't heed the warning of the numerous articles I read.

Now I try that (usually) futile method of impressing my hard-won wisdom on younger women. Whenever I meet a girl just starting her first job or a young woman at the beginning of her career, I give her the "Two 'S' Lesson." The first "S" is for saving. The second "S" is for sunscreen. If you ignore both, I say, you will wake up thirty years old before you know it—having lost the best years of your life for the impact of compound interest and with leathery skin and crow's feet that make you look older than you are. (Generally, these young women just smile and nod—probably wondering if that's the extent of my life's wisdom for them.)

I know it's hard to save. I know that you are probably earning less than your male friends. I know that it simply costs more to be a woman—from dry cleaning to personal grooming and feminine hygiene products. I know that it's tempting to spend more than you have to be as attractive as possible to the single men around you. (We'll explore this topic more in chapter 10.) I know that singles tend to eat out more than their married counterparts. But the simple fact is that American women on the whole earn vastly more money than millions of women around the world. How much more do we need? Dear friends, we really have no excuse for spending beyond our means. If we don't plan to save and invest, Proverbs calls us foolish— and I've been foolish more often than I'd like to admit.

> *The sluggard does not plow in the autumn;*
> *he will seek at harvest and have nothing.* (Prov. 20:4)

> *The plans of the diligent lead surely to abundance,*
> *but everyone who is hasty comes only to poverty.* (Prov. 21:5)

> *In the house of the wise are stores of choice food and oil,*
> *but a foolish man devours all he has.* (Prov. 21:20 NIV)

> *The rich rules over the poor,*
> *and the borrower is the slave of the lender.* (Prov. 22:7)

I once read an article stating that our personal finances are the last frontier of privacy in American culture. Emotional trauma, graphic discussion of sexual immorality, family secrets, and conflicts—these topics dominate our airwaves and conversations. Even in Christian culture, we will candidly confess our sins in these areas. But rarely, if ever, do we know the details of our neighbors' or friends' incomes and spending patterns, even in the church. In my observation, this is especially true for single adults. As we don't have to answer to anyone else for the way we spend our money, we usually lack financial accountability. No wonder money and finances are such tough topics for newly married couples!

The way we manage our money is one discipline that *definitely* will bless our husbands before and after marriage. To be debt-free is the modern dowry; to bring financial assets to a marriage is even better. This discipline is also attractive to men. I remember one man telling me that when he first met his wife, the topic of the group conversation was finances. He hadn't taken particular notice of this woman until she began to talk about money. As she described her plans and efforts, he realized how financially savvy she was—and his interest bloomed!

Practically speaking, if this hasn't been your conviction or you are mired in debt, you will need help. Please take advantage of resources in your church or among your friends. Does your church have a financial counseling team, or do you know a skilled person who could review your income and spending patterns? It's humbling to bare your finances, true. I know a woman who invited her parents over to her house to review her income, spending, and saving, and to help her set up a budget *because* she knew they would follow up with her.

Not only will you need sound advice about budgeting and saving, but you will also need to study God's Word about money and repent of any self-centered habits. That sounds harsh in black and white, but sadly I can tell you from tough personal experience that it's true. We can set up all the budgets we want, but we will blow them every time if we are not convicted about being a poor steward of what God has given us. Because I still struggle with this, I've arranged to have 10 percent of my salary withheld from my paycheck for my retirement account. I don't even get it; so it's not a temptation to justify spending it.

The second principle of money is that the best investment plan is to give it away to God's purposes. There was a single man in my church years ago whom I wish I had met. He died before I moved to the area, but his legacy lives on. Richard Moore was a generous, hospitable man, and his giving was legendary in our church—even as he tried to be anonymous with his gifts. After he died, one of his friends cleared out his house and was amazed to see how much effort Richard put into his giving—both materially and financially. The most telling was his checkbook. The record left there was of a man who purposed to bless others, who lived modestly, and who faithfully supported his church. Richard didn't keep what he had when he died. But what he sowed financially is bearing fruit beyond his own lifetime. I've never forgotten that witness of Richard's checkbook, and nearly every time I open mine, I wonder what it says about me.

The reason we shouldn't consume all we have is not so we will have a comfortable retirement. Yes, we should save for our future needs. That's evident in several places in Scripture. *But our actions don't secure our futures. Our Father has promised to provide for us, and that's our security.* If we are in the habit of living below our income, we will have money to invest in the kingdom—an investment that promises a huge return. Author Randy

Alcorn says that once we understand God's incentive program, our attitude toward generous living will never be the same. While the Bible makes it clear that our faith determines our eternal destination, our actions—including what we do with our money—determine our eternal rewards. He writes:

> What's the biggest misconception Christians have about giving? That when we give our money away to a church or ministry, or to help the needy, it's gone. While we hope others will benefit from it, we're quite sure *we* won't. We think we're *divesting* ourselves of money, disassociating from it. Once it leaves our hands, we imagine, it has no connection to us, no future implications relevant to our lives.
>
> We couldn't be more wrong.
>
> What we think we own will be rudely taken from us—some of it before we die, and anything that's left the moment we die. But now is our window of opportunity not to *divest* ourselves of money but to *invest* it in heaven. We don't have to have everything taken from us. We can give it before disaster or death strike. Now's our chance to give what we can't keep to gain what we can't lose.
>
> We are God's money managers. He wants us to invest his money in his kingdom. He tells us he's keeping track of every cup of cold water we give the needy in his name. He promises us he will reward us in heaven because we help the poor and needy who cannot pay us back for what we do for them.
>
> We can buy up shares in God's kingdom. We can invest in eternity.[10]

Because of recent financial scandals, some Christians are wary of giving to their churches and other ministries. In my view, instead of being wary, we should rejoice that the sin was brought to light (a sobering thought when we consider our own sins). Other people's sins do not negate the biblical commands to give, however, and there are plenty of these commands.

In the Old Testament, God's people were to give a tithe, or the first tenth, of their income to God. This practice predated the giving of the Law (Gen. 14:20; Gen. 28:22) and was later formalized in the Law of Moses for the maintenance of the temple and provision for the priests and Levites who served there (Lev. 27:30-32; Deut. 14:22-24). Malachi 3:10 says: "Bring the full tithes into the storehouse, that there may be food in my house. And thereby put me to the test, says the LORD of hosts, if I will not open the windows of heaven for you and pour down for you a blessing until there is no more need."

In the New Testament, giving to support the work of the church remains an expectation of believers. We see this in 1 Corinthians 9:13-14:

"Do you not know that those who are employed in the temple service get their food from the temple, and those who serve at the altar share in the sacrificial offerings? In the same way, the Lord commanded that those who proclaim the gospel should get their living by the gospel." And in Galatians 6:6: "One who is taught the word must share all good things with the one who teaches." More importantly, we are to willingly invest in the kingdom, as 2 Corinthians 9:7 commands: "Each one must give as he has made up his mind, not reluctantly or under compulsion, for God loves a cheerful giver."[11]

These commands are not about paltry, spare-change giving. How can the work of the Lord get done with nickels and dimes? Our first priority of giving should be tithing to our local church. When we see our Lord's own words, we see that He expects His followers to tithe: "But woe to you Pharisees! For you tithe mint and rue and every herb, and neglect justice and the love of God. These you ought to have done, *without neglecting the others*" (Luke 11:42, emphasis added).

I remember my first question about tithing as a new believer, which my brother-in-law, Fred, answered for me. I didn't understand why the church should have my money. Fred responded that if we didn't give to the church, the church wouldn't have the resources to be a blessing to the community. We would then have to resort to asking our community to underwrite our causes through events like bake sales and raffles. Our giving positions the church to be ready to serve those around us and to further the work of the gospel. I appreciated the simplicity of his answer and never struggled with tithing again, by God's grace. Furthermore, I have seen the Lord faithfully provide for me even when tithing didn't seem to make sense in human wisdom. His promise in Malachi 3:10 stands firm through time. Dear friends, the priority of giving to our local churches should be evident in a quick glance at our checkbooks.

Our Proverbs 31 woman obviously knew how to make money and to invest it. She is commended for that skill, and her example is worth emulating. This passage goes on to commend her generosity to the needy; so we will explore this further in the next chapter.

For now let's look at the third task we see our Proverbs 31 woman doing: buying property.

BUYING FOR THE FUTURE

I remember vividly the conversation I once had with an acquaintance at a conference. I was asking him about his family, and he told me that everyone was doing well. His oldest children were married—one was about to have his third grandchild. But his youngest child was his current concern.

"She just turned thirty, and she's still single," he said. "She's just been rattling around in a series of temporary living arrangements. So her mother and I told her, 'Well, it looks like you may not get married. You better make some adjustments. We think you should go ahead and buy your own home. It will at least bring *some* security.'"

As he proceeded with this story, my smile froze. Inside I cringed, sympathetic to this unknown woman. I listened without comment, but later I found that I was distracted by this conversation. I kept thinking about the underlying assumption in those remarks. Although I don't know the whole story in this situation, I realized that I'd heard variations of this conversation at other times. Home ownership is the usual domain of stable, married people. But it also can be the consolation prize for a woman when lifelong singleness is forecasted. I think this is why many of my single friends feel somewhat defeated in purchasing a home on their own, like it's a bad omen.

In these verses, we see that the Proverbs 31 woman "considers a field and buys it; out of her earnings she plants a vineyard." Planting a vineyard requires a long-term perspective. We see in Leviticus 19:23-25 that the Lord said not to harvest in the first three years of planting any kind of tree for food, to reserve the fruit in the fourth year as a praise offering to the Lord, and then the owners could eat the fruit in the fifth year. This is not unlike what modern vineyard owners have to do. After planting the vineyard, they must tend and train the vines and wait about three to four years before they get any significant production. It actually takes five or six years for full production. The point is that when one plants a vineyard, it's an investment for the future.

This is true for home ownership, too. Common real estate advice is that it takes about three to five years, depending on the market, to get a significant return on the purchase of a home. Our Proverbs 31 woman could have rented a vineyard—a common practice in both the Old and New Testaments—but she chose to buy.

I'd like to suggest that single women should think of home ownership as an investment for their futures—not as something conferred with matrimony or offered as a consolation prize. Home ownership is another way to save for the future, a good complement to other saving vehicles. I purchased my home five years ago and have encouraged many other single women to do the same. While my mutual funds plummeted when the technology bubble burst, at the same time my house more than doubled in sales value. It's an unusual time in the local real estate market, but this is an illustration of why investment diversity is good. I'm not alone. In 2000 twice as many single women as single men bought houses. Single women accounted for 18 percent of all homebuyers, compared with 1989 during which single women represented only 13 percent of homebuyers, according to the National Association of Realtors.

Many times singles are told not to tie themselves down with a home—as if we're fugitives needing to flee in the middle of the night. Do we have to go somewhere any faster than married people? If you need to sell your house for a job, you put it on the market—just like married couples. If you need to sell your house because you are getting married, you usually know about this in advance, too. Even if you have to sell your home quickly and at a loss, you probably won't lose any more money than you would have if you'd simply rented for the same period. (True, some local markets have had dramatic losses due to dependence on a single industry—like oil—that goes bust. These cases are in God's hands and shouldn't unnecessarily scare us away from this investment.) As with vineyards, the earlier you start, the longer you have to enjoy the fruit.

But can you afford a home? You may be pleasantly surprised. I qualified for my home based on a part-time ministry salary. The only way I could do that was through a first-time homeowners program sponsored by my county. Check out what your local government offers—there are some great programs out there. As for the costs of homeownership, a nationwide survey conducted by the Commerce Department's Census Bureau in 2001 found that overall the country's households spent a median of $658 monthly on housing costs. The respective medians for homeowners and renters were $686 and $633—not that great a difference.

If you buy a home, you will learn a great deal as you go along. I've learned how to search for carpenter ants, hire a contractor to finish a basement, install a gas fireplace, handle a faulty carbon monoxide alarm, repair minor toilet problems, paint a room, use a drill, identify and prevent Indian meal moths, un-jam a garbage disposal, and *much* more—but not all at one time and not by myself. The Lord has been faithful to provide friends and family members who have been generous with their time and advice. I've also enjoyed the company of several housemates, all of whom have contributed in various ways to the running of the household and the good cheer of its owner. (I've chosen, for now, not to live alone in order to remain as flexible as possible in accommodating other people's preferences.) And every year when I celebrate another year of making mortgage payments and keeping a roof over my head, I thank God for making it all possible.

If you have faith for homeownership, I would encourage you to seek the Father in prayer for His guidance. Then submit your ideas to others for counsel. Your pastors may know someone in your church who would be a great buyer's agent for you and wouldn't push a home purchase on you. I would also recommend that you take an experienced homeowner with you to ask the hard questions and to point out potential problems. If the timing isn't right to purchase a home now, don't worry and don't be pushed into it. I could fill a book with stories of people who resisted the arm-twisting and waited on God—only to have their dream house come on the market at an unusually low price in a matter of months. But not every woman wants to bear the responsibility of home ownership. If the Lord isn't leading you to make this investment, and you lack the faith to shoulder this responsibility now, that's fine! Either way, I believe single women can benefit from simply exploring the idea of home ownership.

Now for our last point.

Solo Strength

These verses from Proverbs 31 celebrate a woman of strength. This is seen in verse 17, which is also translated as "she dresses herself with strength and makes her arms strong" (ESV) or "she girdeth her loins with strength, and strengtheneth her arms" (KJV). To gird one's loins means to prepare for hard work, even battle.

It can also make us an old battleaxe if we're not careful.

"It is unavoidable that we single women develop independence and decisiveness, sometimes more than our married sisters who have husbands to decide for or with them," writes Ada Lum. "But what is avoidable is the defensive brittleness and strident voice that often accompany female independence."[12]

The key to understanding this reference to strength is to recognize the One for whom she is working. This is a capable woman, but she's not independent. Her husband is her earthly supervisor, but her master is the Lord. God sets her boundaries, and she works hard within them. The phrase "out of her earnings" doesn't stress independence but rather stewardship. Based on the whole of the Proverbs 31 passage, the emphasis is not on "her" but on "earnings." Her strength is shown at work, but it is for the benefit of others, not herself.

This is one of my biggest challenges, an area I've endeavored to change and grow in over the past five years. Even so, I can see how much further I have to go. For example, I've been learning to make my boss's priorities my own and to revolve around his preferences and practices—not my own. With a nod to Carolyn Mahaney's great question in *Feminine Appeal*—"Does this help my husband?"—I've learned to ask myself, "Does this help my boss?"

I could tell that historically I'd been cultivating quite a different atmosphere in my office when one day my boss came in with a quick question, assuring me he wouldn't take too long and waste my time. I looked at him and sweetly replied, "That's fine. My time is your time." He jerked his head up from what he was reading and studied me in mock shock—and both of us laughed. But I didn't laugh for too long because it was actually a bit sad that this had not been my attitude from day one.

The key to real strength is meekness, an unusual word in today's vocabulary. The world would not define strength as meekness. Strength is usually portrayed in some fit of violence or anger—standing up for oneself in a passionate rage against an outside force. But the greatest strength is needed to master and subdue our own sin. Every day I have to "gird my loins" for the battle against my pride (defensiveness, self-pity, critical judgments) and worldliness (selfish ambition, covetousness, materialism, and more). It takes all my resources to control my mouth! The apostle James is not surprised. James 1:26 says, "If anyone thinks he is religious and does not bridle his tongue but deceives his heart, this person's religion is worthless." There's much more from James about our speech, but we'll save it for chapter 11.

Meekness is the strength to govern our sin. As Matthew Henry writes in *The Quest for Meekness and Quietness of Spirit*, "the work and office of meekness is to enable us prudently to govern our own anger when at any time we are provoked, and patiently to bear out the anger of others that it may not be a provocation to us."[13] He says there is nothing said or done in passion that couldn't be better said and better done calmly later. "It is better by silence to yield to our brother, who is, or has been, or may be, our friend, than by angry speaking to yield to the devil, who has been, and is, and ever will be, our sworn enemy."[14]

Meekness will help us as single women to avoid that "defensive brittleness and a strident voice" and instead demonstrate true strength of character as we govern our passions and our tongues.

We've covered the four points of verses 16 through 19. Now I'd like to conclude this chapter with a portrait of two women of strength who invested their time, talent, and treasure to serve their Savior.

An Eternal Investment

When Jesus entered his public ministry, he went through the cities and villages of Galilee, proclaiming and bringing the good news of the kingdom of God. One day the Master's powerful words healed a woman of status and rank named Joanna—the wife of Chuza, Herod's administrator. Gratefully she dug into her worldly treasures to provide for the itinerant rabbi. She was not alone in her support, for Luke also records that at least two other women who had been healed of evil spirits and infirmities joined her in this effort—Mary, called Magdalene, and Susanna—among many others (Luke 8:1-3). Joanna's faithful support endured to the end, right to the cross. No doubt she was one of the unnamed women from Galilee who stood at a distance watching their Lord and Savior's crucifixion—and who watched to see where His body was laid so they could prepare spices and ointments.

Faithfully returning to His grave as soon as the Sabbath was over, Joanna and Mary Magdalene encountered the two angels at the empty tomb. It was their ears to first hear the incredible question, "Why do you seek the living among the dead?" (Luke 24:5). Such truth was too marvelous for the disciples to believe when the women told them, and all but Peter and John considered it "an idle tale."

What did Joanna and Mary Magdalene do with those spices and ointments—their last generous gift to the Lord? Scripture does not tell us. It only leaves us with a record of two women—one married, one single—whose gratitude overflowed from their lives and compelled them to invest their earthly treasure in an eternal cause. We don't know for sure what happened to them, but tradition has it that Chuza lost his position in Herod's palace because of his wife's conversion and courageous testimony among the servants.[15] We can be sure of this: Whatever they lost in this world is more than repaid in the next.

FOR FURTHER STUDY

❖ Randy Alcorn's books—any of them. His fiction books (especially *Safely Home*) will challenge you, too. But for the topic of finances and work, you can't beat the classic *Money, Possessions & Eternity* (originally published by Tyndale in 1989) or *The Law of Rewards* (an updated version of a few chapters found in the first book, published by Tyndale in 2003).

❖ *Don't Waste Your Life* (Crossway) by John Piper introduces the concept of "war-time mentality" for pampered Christians. This book warns us not to get caught up in a life that counts for nothing.

❖ *The Journal of Biblical Counseling* (published by the Christian Counseling & Educational Foundation) is a treasure trove of wisdom. One article I would highly recommend is "Putting Off Procrastination" from the journal's Fall 2001, Vol. 20, No. 1 edition. Whether you can easily identify procrastination in your life because you fit the classic mold, or whether you think you are too busy and productive to be a procrastinator (yet you're always in a panic to meet deadlines and pull off last-minute projects), this article's for you! You can order back issues from www.ccef.org/jbc.

The Blessing of
Children

Her children rise up and call her blessed.
PROVERBS 31:28

I hadn't touched a poopy diaper for more than fifteen years. I had never
heard of *Veggie Tales*, and I definitely could not remember the rules for
Freeze Tag. But somehow I was tapped to care for about a dozen children
ranging from toddlers to 'tweens. The parents in my small group had been
parents long enough to think that every adult was well-versed in kidspeak.
But it was a foreign language to me. I had quit baby-sitting when I hit high
school and hadn't hung around children since then. I was a thirty-year-old
woman who had just started coming to church; thus I had a high value as
a new childcare recruit.

The parents introduced me to the children, showed me the evening
snack, and told me they'd be meeting just down the street if I needed them.
Smiling cheerfully, they all waved goodbye and thanked me for serving
them. I, the Clueless Single Woman, waved back.

Sensing that there was no firm supervision, the children immediately
took over. Everyone made a mad dash for the doors. A toddler meandered
toward the street. Two eight-year-old boys began to charge and tackle each
other. A few girls tried without success to organize a game. Then a six-year-
old boy decided to dump his cup of water on the head of another girl. She
protested loudly, but the idea caught on. Soon everyone was running to
retrieve his or her own cups (thoughtfully labeled ahead of time by an
adult). A three-year-old was crying in the melee.

Then an idea I considered worthy of Solomon hit me.

"Stop!" I barked. Startled, the children actually stopped. I relished the power for a moment. "We all have to play *together*. If you want to have a water fight, everyone's got to want to play. We can't have children upset because they don't want to get wet. So does everyone want to play?"

The children looked at me, bug-eyed. After a moment's pause to consider the profundity of my wisdom, they all began chanting: "Water fight! Water fight! Water fight!" It was a warm October evening; so I didn't think anyone's health was in jeopardy, nor was anyone wearing fancy clothes.

"Then a water fight it is!" I smiled benevolently.

Two hours later the parents returned to find their children sitting quietly in the den watching a Veggie *Tales* video. Everyone was calm, cheerful . . . and sopping wet.

"What happened?" they asked, obviously concerned.

"Oh, well, one of the kids starting throwing his water on another child, and it started a water fight," I explained. "But not everyone was happy about this. So I said that there would be no water fights unless *everyone* wanted to play. They all agreed; so no one got upset."

I smiled. The parents frowned. The children were still locked onto the video. "Well, okay then," one father said. "Let's get them home and into dry clothes."

And that was my debut as an adult baby-sitter. Even though the word was out that I didn't know what I was doing, I was still asked to watch children—*after* some very detailed instructions and training.

For the next five years, I had the privilege of becoming an extended member of a number of families in that Richmond, Virginia, church. I was invited to family dinners, watched children during small group meetings and Sweetheart Banquets, had sleepovers at my house, and even went on vacation with a family. As I prepared to move to Maryland to my current job and church, I was invited to several goodbye dinners with those families. Inevitably the father of each family would prompt his children during the meal to share some of their favorite memories of our times together.

"My favorite time was when you let us play in the rain!"

"And eat dessert before dinner!"

"I liked staying up way past our bedtimes!"

"I liked the chocolate game!"

I could only smile sheepishly. What a portrait of discipline.

Those are some of my favorite memories of living in Richmond. When I moved, I assumed that time and distance would fray the bonds of those relationships. My assumption was, thankfully, wrong. Five years after I left, a young lady from Richmond came to visit her aunt, a friend of mine where I now live. I had known Katie—whoops, I mean *Kathryn*—when she was a young girl. Back then she had come for a sleepover when we wore our fanciest nightgowns and only ate pink food. I had taught her brothers how to shift the car's gears while I drove. We'd played flashlight tag on a late summer evening, brushing off the feasting mosquitoes. We ate crabs together during a beach vacation with her family.

But that was when she was young, and a trip to the mall was a big deal. Now that I'd moved away, I didn't expect she'd even remember me—much less want to visit. So what a pleasant surprise to receive the news that Kathryn would like the pleasure of my company at high tea with her Aunt Patti.

Over tea and scones we reminisced and laughed. Kathryn, now fourteen, was becoming a lovely young woman, with her blonde hair and crystal-blue eyes.

"My mother said I should ask you how I can encourage and support the guys in my teen group," she said.

I smiled and slowly sipped my tea, savoring the moment. All those little investments made over the years were not washed away with the passage of time. Here was an opportunity to grow into a new season, even with the impediments of many moons and many miles. Her question reminded me of the conversations about men and relationships I'd had with her own parents when I lived there.

"Your mother has a sense of humor, Kathryn, but what would you like to know?" I replied.

We soaked up the rest of that Sunday afternoon discussing the impact of feminine speech, the wisdom of feminine reserve, how to encourage young men as brothers without being flirtatious, which video version of *Pride & Prejudice* was the best, and much more. It was that special female bonding moment I'd always assumed was the exclusive domain of mothers and daughters, but God in His graciousness had provided it to two childless women. (How kind of Patti to share with me this time with her niece!)

From One Generation to Another

Until I interacted with those families in my church, I'd never fully considered whether or not I wanted children of my own. I wasn't against having children; they just weren't on my radar screen because I didn't know any.

Being with these children ignited a dormant affection in my heart. I found I actually enjoy them immensely, and I looked forward to spending time with them. I once even signed up to serve in the nursery during Sunday morning meetings just so I could hold dozens of babies in my arms. Even if every baby in the room was crying (those chain reactions in a nursery are always fun), I was content to have lots of babies nearby who needed to be held and soothed.

When my own nieces and nephews came along, I thought my heart would explode. How any of those children grew up without dents in their cheeks from my kisses is beyond me! I love each of them so very much. And through the years I began to wonder: If I can enjoy other people's children this much, and if I have such a deep love and affection for my nephews and nieces, *what would it be like to have children of my own*? That thought only grows more heart-wrenching with the passage of time.

FOR THOSE WITHOUT CHILDREN

If you are childless, you already may be in tears because your desire for children is overwhelming. Others may be tempted to skip this chapter and find a topic you can relate to. No matter your current opinion about children, I hope you'll keep reading because I believe the Lord wants childless single women to soberly consider how we are to make an investment in the next generation. My goal in writing this chapter is to give us a vision for investing in the children who are *already* in our lives and not to let that aspect of femininity atrophy due to singleness.

According to Christian pollster George Barna's research, the largest segment of American single adults currently is the never-married group.[1] Because of this trend (and my own experience) I have written this chapter primarily for single women without children. I believe we have a scriptural mandate for investing in the next generation. Psalm 145:4 says: "One generation shall commend your works to another, and shall declare your mighty acts. On the glorious splendor of your majesty, and on your wondrous works, I will meditate." In this chapter, we will see how this mandate can be fulfilled even when we don't (yet) have children of our own.

FOR SINGLE MOTHERS

If you're a single parent, you may be eagerly reading this chapter, hoping that I will have some advice for your unique position in life. You have my deep respect, but I regret that I am quite limited here. I believe your role as a mother is the most important and defining role in this season of your life, and those wise and fruitful parents in your own church will be your best resource for counsel and encouragement. I am praying for single parents as I write this chapter because I recognize that I have no experience in this area. I can't write a parenting chapter because, obviously, I've never been a parent.

Once during a question-and-answer session, a single mother asked me how she should address her child's questions about the lack of a father. "I really don't know," I said, stunned. "I have no parenting experience what-soever." I was in over my head with that question! Since that time, I've pondered this question. In hindsight I should have said that the truth is always best, when laced with biblical hope and conveyed appropriately for the age of the child. I later recalled these grace-filled words from pastor and author Andy Farmer, which I think will also encourage you:

> The overarching hope of the single parent is the Fatherhood of God. The psalmist expresses it this way:
>
> > Sing to God, sing praise to his name,
> > Extol him who rides on the clouds—
> > His name is the LORD—
> > and rejoice before him.
> > A father to the fatherless, a defender of widows,
> > is God in his holy dwelling. (Ps. 68:4-5 NIV)
>
> Notice two things. God the Father has a special place in his heart for the widows and the fatherless. His great heart beats with compassion for those who are his and are going it alone. But he is the Father "in His holy dwelling." He is not only willing, but fully able in his sovereignty to meet the needs of his loved ones. How does he do it?
> • He gives every one of his children a family large enough to fit in— the church.
> • He answers prayer—every promise given to parents is available to the single mom or dad.
> • He restores and protects. I have met so many single parents whose lives are a chaotic mess because of financial stress, poor choices, and iso-lation. And I have seen order and faith come to these seemingly hopeless situations as God's ways and means are embraced through faith.[2]

No matter how you became a single mother, I think the wisdom of one woman who is not only a biblical counselor but also a single parent herself would be beneficial to you. Though this advice is framed through the per-spective of divorce, it is full of godly truth:

> The question of all questions for a divorced woman, however, is this: What is my relationship to the father of my children now? The way she answers that question can have a profound effect on her children's rela-tionship with their father (and with her).
>
> Let's be more specific. A divorced woman's relationship with her ex-husband is that of a "co-parent" to their children. She doesn't have to like him or pretend that they are friends. She must, however, love him as a neighbor (Matthew 5:43-46; Mark 12:31; *see* 1 Corinthians 13:4-8 for a definition of love). She must respect him for his role as the children's father. Encourage her to bless him, pray for him, and live at peace with him as much as it is possible for her to do so. She should never take revenge. . . . As the mother lives out her faith, she should keep commu-nicating with her children. She can share with them scriptural principles and verses about the situations she faces. They will then learn how she approaches her problems and see that God is involved in all her deci-sions. This will help the children to think more biblically about their own situations and decisions.[3]

Because your most important role is being a mother, I hope I can encourage you by recommending good parenting resources. I have listed a number of materials at the end of this chapter that have been highly rec-ommended by my own pastors and that many friends and family members have used with great benefit. I've read them all—though some only in part—and I trust they will encourage you, too.

Finally, I suspect that if our roles were reversed, I'd want the help and support of my childless single friends. I pray that this chapter will inspire a few to do just that.

BUZZING BIOLOGICAL CLOCKS

Recently I stayed in a hotel where the alarm clocks started buzzing very softly but increased in decibels and irritation until they were turned off. I think my biological clock was designed by the same company. It was pretty faint several years ago, but now it's practically deafening. I think it's so loud other people can hear it, too, and probably want to slap me on the head to turn it off.

I encountered this alarm clock when I was attending a Christian con-ference. During that conference, one speaker urged the men to fulfill the biblical mandate to find the "wives of their youth," get married, and rear children. Wonderful advice. But it also provoked a number of women who have long desired marriage and who are no longer youthful nor possibly fertile. Would they—*we*—be passed over because the expiration dates on our eggs was dangerously close? Many women were in tears because of this perceived unfairness.

Ladies, you have my deepest sympathy. I truly understand how urgent this feels. But there's hope! Once when I was in utter despair about my childlessness, the Lord showed me an incredibly profound truth. *He simply reminded me that Christianity was founded on miraculous births by supposedly barren women.* He is the One who opens and closes wombs. Scripture is very clear about this (Gen. 16:2; 29:31; 30:22; 1 Sam. 1:5). Many of the matriarchs of our faith wrestled with childlessness: Sarah, Rebekah, Rachel, Hannah, and Elizabeth. But age is irrelevant to our everlasting God. Sarah was ninety-one when she conceived. Rebekah was young when she married (probably less than twenty), and Isaac was already forty. He prayed for her to conceive for twenty years, and was sixty when Rebekah finally gave birth—probably at around forty. Isaac married a young woman, but her youth didn't guarantee children any more than Sarah's old age prevented it. It is the Lord who gives life at His appointed time. In fact, I find a sweet sympathy in what the angel Gabriel said to Mary when he confirmed his message to her. Gabriel pointed to her family as a sign: "And behold, your relative Elizabeth in her old age has also conceived a son, and this is the sixth month with her who was called barren. For nothing will be impossible with God" (Luke 1:36-37).

For nothing will be impossible with God.

She who was called barren, Elizabeth, was a walking, breathing, expanding sign that nothing is impossible with God. I hope this strengthens your faith as you trustingly wait on the Lord for children. As we saw in chapter 3, what we know about our circumstances is not all there is in the lovingkindness of God's plan for our lives.

THE ULTIMATE GOAL OF PARENTING

Most of you reading this book will be parents one day. So if the Lord gave you children tomorrow, would you know what to do with them? Do you know what God's plan for parenting is? It's not about soccer, music lessons, regular naps, or feeding schedules. It's not only about rearing children who are successful in school or eventually on the job. What's clear throughout the Scriptures is that God's plan for parenting is discipleship.

"Gospel-centered parenting involves authentic example and scriptural instruction for ultimately the purpose of salvation—or the purpose of gospel proclamation," says C. J. Mahaney, himself a grandfather. "It is about impressing upon our children the authority and authenticity of the gospel."[4]

That's the message of the passage I highlighted at the beginning of this chapter, Psalm 145:4—how we are to commend God's mighty works from one generation to another. As the family of God, we all get to participate in this proclamation. Though parents bear a specific responsibility for their children, each of us has influence in relationships with the children that God has placed around us, especially within the church. (We should also consider that the authors of Scripture probably had a broader view of family and kin than the narrow American concept of the nuclear family.)

This is what I experienced when I became a believer. One of the joys of entering into a community where everyone is singing from the same page, so to speak, was that I was expected to participate in the training of the next generation, too—whether I had children of my own or not. Everyone in my church was in agreement about the basics of discipline and behavior because everyone was in agreement about the ultimate goal of parenting: evangelism. We were all trying to show these children their hearts and the sin contained therein so that they would understand their need for a Savior. When I baby-sat these children, I was told what character issues were being addressed, and I was invited to bring my observations to the parents and to encourage the children to respond properly. I was being trained for parenting by these parents—and I was able to practice on someone else's children. It was a sweet deal!

But, as they say on TV, don't try this at home. I once dated a man from another church, and during a visit when his young niece and nephew spoke disrespectfully to him, I reflexively (but kindly) encouraged them to make their requests again with the right attitudes. I overstepped my bounds on that one and embarrassed my date, who thought I was out of line for correcting someone else's children. I was. I forgot that I had not been invited to make this same investment in his family.

We might have to be invited or earn the privilege of relating to children like this, but when it is extended to us, we should accept it with joy. Part of our femininity is fulfilled in nurturing life, whether or not we ever actually bring life into this world through our own pregnancies and labor.

You may find it difficult to picture how you could do this. For that reason, I'd like to consider two ways we could invest in the children around us—the influence of an aunt and the impact of an *au pair* (more than just an occasional baby-sitter).

THE INFLUENCE OF AN AUNT

With all freshly bathed and wearing their best nightgowns, the fun of the sleepover was about to begin. I gathered all my nieces together (then ages four to seven) and asked if they wanted to see one of my favorite movies—about an English woman who lived in a big, fancy house.

"Is she a princess?" asked Stephanie. Every woman has to be a princess when you are four.

"Almost," I said. "But she gets a prince of a man, and that's the idea of this movie."

"Okay!" they chimed in unison.

So Natalie joined her cousins, Claire and Stephanie, on the sleeper sofa bed. Their baby sister, Abigail, was already asleep. I started the A&E production of *Emma* and held my breath. Would Jane Austen's witty dialogue captivate or lose them? They quietly watched, seemingly enjoying the video. Toward the end, I picked up the remote and stopped the scene.

"Mr. Knightley is the kind of man you want to marry, girls," I announced. They peered at me with wide eyes over their collection of dolls and stuffed animals on the bed. "Did you notice how he is concerned with Emma's character, her actions, her heart? When she was rude to that older woman, Mr. Knightley says something to her about it: 'Badly done, Emma, badly done.' He wants her to have a kind heart and to be as beautiful on the inside as she is on the outside."

"Ohhh," they said, nodding gravely.

"Now Mr. Churchill is *not* the kind of man you want to marry," I continued. "Did you notice how he only comments on the outer beauty of Miss Fairfax? But what's going to happen when she's older and no longer beautiful? And did you notice how often Mr. Churchill lies to people just so he can have his way? But Mr. Knightley is kind to everyone. This is important to find in a man you will marry."

Throughout the rest of the movie, the girls made sure they knew which man was "the good man" and which one was "the bad man." My sister Alice, who was also visiting, was intrigued at how I was interacting with her daughters and our niece.

"I never would have thought to make a Jane Austen movie into a lesson about a husband's character," she said with a knowing smile. "I guess that's the advantage of having a single woman as an aunt! I just don't think that way anymore."

I wonder if those girls will grow up and one day ask each other, "Do you remember how Aunt Carolyn was always talking about finding a good husband? But she was *single!*"

The role of an aunt might seem to be a very minor one, but it doesn't have to be. I believe it's what you invest into it. We do find an account in Scripture of one heroic aunt, Jehosheba (2 Kings 11:1; 2 Chron. 22:11). She rescued her nephew, Joash, from his murderous grandmother, Athaliah, and saved the sole remaining royal descendant of David. In the 2 Kings account, there is no mention of Jehosheba's husband, but in the parallel Chronicles account, her husband is named as Jehoiada, the priest. Though she wasn't a single woman, she still bravely intervened to spare the life of her nephew and to preserve the royal line of David. This was no short-lived heroic action either. Joash lived with his aunt and uncle for six years.

I believe Jehosheba's example is one we should emulate if the Lord has given our siblings children. Though few of us will be involved in royal intrigues, I do think the Lord has placed our nieces and nephews in our lives for a purpose. We have the opportunity to make an investment in these children through time, affection, counsel, and encouragement. We can amplify the training of their parents and encourage our nephews and nieces to respect and honor their parents.

We might be tempted to think this kind of relationship really can't make much difference, but that's not true. We can never know how our influence is being observed or our words are being considered. My sisters often tell me that their children repeat what I've told them. One of my most cherished presents is a three-inch crèche-style statue of a woman praying. My niece Natalie bought it for me with the money she earned for good behavior. Instead of getting something for herself, she chose to get this statue for me because, as she later said, it reminded her of me. It still makes me cry to think of it! I have that statue sitting on my bookshelf with my commentaries and Bible studies so that I will always be reminded of the importance of prayer for these precious children.

Occasionally I have the opportunity to invest extended time in my nieces and nephews, such as caring for them for several days while their parents travel. Whenever I do this, I return home marveling at the selflessness of my sisters and brothers-in-law. It takes a lot of energy to care for children, especially younger ones. I am always sobered (though not deterred!) about what I'm asking God for when I pray to be a mother.

Each of these children has gifts that need to be nurtured and encouraged, and each has selfish patterns that need to be highlighted and gently corrected. Even at this age, they have talents that I don't possess. My seven-year-old nephew, Patrick, will probably be a tremendous engineer. He can put together complicated Bionicle projects (without the instructions!) that confuse me even after he's shown me how to do them. I can't help him there, but I *can* encourage him in developing his merciful personality and also in what it means to be a young man. I once explained to him that being male means that God has designed him to care for and protect females. One small way he can demonstrate that is by opening the door for his sister. Now and then he rushes ahead to get the door. Even when I have to lean over him and give the door a shove from above, he always seems pleased to have remembered to do this.

Because I am the oldest child, I am attuned to the ways that oldest children often put down and discourage their younger siblings. (But, unfortunately, I didn't learn this until I was an adult. My two younger sisters are evidently resilient, and I'm fortunate to now count them among my best friends.) I am always reminding my two oldest nieces to be patient with their younger siblings and encourage them in their current capacities.

One day I received a call from Claire, who said she needed some advice about how to be a good oldest child. She felt that since her parents had been younger children in the family lineup, she had to talk to someone who knew what it was like. Claire reported that it was a big responsibility to have to watch out for her younger sister when her mother needed help and that those times didn't always go well. So we talked about how to be a servant even when you have a little authority and how this was good training for the day she would become a mommy, if that is God's plan for her. My sister Alice later reported to me that this conversation was timely because Claire had earlier expressed doubts that she would be a good mother. Though Alice had encouraged Claire, it was helpful for my niece to hear it from another adult.

My nieces and nephews are a source of enduring cherished memories. I'm glad they are willing to spend time with me. So far, our visits are eagerly anticipated. I hope it always remains this way (but it's going to keep me on my toes to make creative plans). I have an "Aunt's Journal" for each of them, in which I am writing to their future adult selves with observations and memories of our times together in their childhoods. I look forward to the day I give these faded, yellowed journals to them. I hope these books will kindle memories for them and reinforce my affection for each one.

THE IMPACT OF THE *AU PAIR*

In my church, I've met a number of women from other countries who have moved here to live with a family and care for their children for a specific period of time. But you don't have to move to be an *au pair* or to make a significant investment in someone else's family. One of my good friends has chosen to make a similar, though informal, investment in a family, and I have long admired the selfless choices she has made.

Theresa Wheeler, who is now forty, has lived with her friends, Marc and Terry Fortier, for fifteen years. Theresa met Terry when Terry was doing outreach to a halfway house where Theresa was then living. The Fortiers offered Theresa a place to live in their home, which she accepted.

"I didn't think I would stay there a long time—just until I was married," Theresa says, with her infectious laugh. "I wanted to be there primarily because I didn't have a family before."

Raised as an only child by her great-grandmother, Theresa had been estranged from her family and didn't know where her father was. The rest of her family was all over the place: Her brothers had been raised by her mother, her sister by her grandmother. "It took so much effort on my part to invest in my family because we were so different," she says. "I love and appreciate what my great-grandmother did for me, but I always wanted a family. With Marc and Terry, it was a two-way relationship."

The Fortiers, who are white, later adopted four children—two from Russia, one from Romania, and one from Washington, D.C. "But really I got adopted, too," says Theresa, who is black. "I tell people I'm the firstborn, the first adopted. We are truly an international family."

Theresa has lived in a single adult household, but she prefers living with a family. "I prefer it not only because I have the family that I didn't have before, but also—because I had my house-cleaning business for awhile—I simply saw the need for families to have help," she says. "I can baby-sit for them or give the mom an extended quiet time in the morning or help with the groceries and the chores. When Terry was working part time at one point, I saw that it was such a balancing act for her to handle her husband's priorities, do her job, and try to be home in time to cook dinner, and then do something to serve in the local church."

Right before the Fortiers adopted their first child, Theresa came across John 15:13, which says, "Greater love has no one than this, that someone lays down his life for his friends." She says that verse solidified her commitment to remain with the Fortiers even in their new season of parenting. When the Fortiers decided to homeschool their children and help them grow in fluency with their second language, Theresa made the investment right along with them. Marc reduced her rent, and Theresa cut back her work hours so that she could help with the schooling two mornings a week.

"Many people think I'm being heroic, but I'm not," she says. "I've received a real sense of purpose for the family. The Fortiers are my primary area of service right now, and through that I see the family unit as treasured by God. I also see how easily things can come in and twist what God has given to be such a rich gift. That conviction has led me to care for other families as well. I see that marriage and children take work and wisdom and dependence on God. There's really nothing romantic about it. The *wedding* is romantic. But even date nights can be really practical until the kids get older."

What kind of difference has Theresa, known affectionately as ReeRee, made in the lives of the Fortier children? On Mother's Day both Terry and ReeRee get flowers (though Terry gets the main appreciation). Megan Fortier often says she has three moms—her birth mom, Terry, and ReeRee. "It's such a neat thing to teach these children who have been adopted into a family that it's like being adopted into the family of God," Theresa says.

But what about her personal goals? Isn't this arrangement a little strange? Theresa acknowledges it is unusual, but it's been a blessing. "To the world, I'm sure, it would look like I'm not going anywhere," she admits.

But she cites how God has prompted different people in the church to bless her out of their financial abundance. One couple specifically sees a call on Theresa's life to serve the local church and the other families she's helped beyond the Fortiers. So they have done things for Theresa such as pay for her car repairs or contribute toward her vacations.

Over the years, Theresa's relationship with her mother has also been restored, and more importantly her mother has become a Christian. Her mother appreciates Theresa's relationship with the Fortiers. Theresa says that because her mom has been the recipient of the Fortiers' love and care, she's not threatened by Theresa's relationship with them. "She appreciates it; she honors Terry."

In addition to the Fortiers' children, Theresa estimates she has built relationships with approximately 100 children in her church over the years—which astounds her, given her own lack while growing up. "In my nothingness, in my not having a family, the Lord used that for my good. He not only gave me one family, He also gave me multiple families," she says with wonder. "I have this wealth of other families in my life as well—not only those I care for, but those who give right back to me. It's just been *rich*."

WHAT ABOUT ADOPTION?

Any time you talk about single women and children, the inevitable topic of adoption arises. I've known a number of single women who have reached their thirties and wondered, even if briefly, whether they should adopt. I've wrestled with that idea, too. (The plight of AIDS orphans, in particular, moves me. I've often wondered if God has a plan for the multitudes of child-less single adults in this nation and the multitude of orphans in other nations. That doesn't necessarily mean adoption is the solution, but I have wondered how God might use the desire for children in us to serve those needy orphans.)

One week of caring for my sick nieces when we were all suffering a stomach bug sobered me, however. Although I could barely lift my head off the bed, there were still two sick little girls who needed my help. After that ordeal, I wasn't sure if it was wise for me to voluntarily go it alone.

Before I proceed further, let me begin by saying that there isn't a clear set of rules here. This is a *wisdom* issue. My hope is that this section will provide single women and those who counsel them on this topic with a number of perspectives to consider.

On the one hand, there are real children existing now—some in hor-rendous conditions—who need someone to care for them. Scripture com-mands believers to care for widows and orphans as an evidence of authentic faith (James 1:27). For the childless woman who desires to be a mother, this verse can seem like a clarion call to action—but it needs to be tempered with clear-minded questions. The verse actually reads: "Religion that is pure and undefiled before God, the Father, is this: to visit orphans and widows in their affliction, and to keep oneself unstained from the world." The New

International Version translates it as "look after." To care for or look after is obviously not the same as adopt, and we must be honest in saying so.

There are also real, documented effects of fatherlessness in children. The National Fatherhood Initiative has been studying this social phenomenon for ten years now. Their research reveals one sad statistic: "Children who live absent their biological fathers are, on average, at least two to three times more likely to be poor, to use drugs, to experience educational, health, emotional and behavioral problems, to be victims of child abuse, and to engage in criminal behavior than their peers who live with their married, biological (or adoptive) parents."[5] (If you are already a single parent, please don't be unduly discouraged. Statistics never account for God's sovereign, loving, direct intervention in our lives. But I think this research is valid to consider with regard to adoption.)

If adoption is something you are currently considering, you may benefit from the experience of my friend Angela. The counsel she received as she considered adoption—and the five years she's given to this process—may be helpful for you to read. Here are some of the questions she was asked as she considered this step with her family, her small group leaders, and her pastor. These are great questions to help one recognize motives for adoption and potential lack of preparation:

• Are you wanting to adopt now because you aren't trusting God to bring a husband in time?

• What are your motives for adopting? Do you see any fear of man or selfish ambition?

• How do you see God at work in this decision? Is this being birthed of God or forced by you?

• Is this arising from a midlife crisis as you turn forty?

• Do you believe God is sovereign and can save these orphans without your help?

• How would you care for the child practically?

• How would you handle a prolonged illness, either yours or the child's?

• What would you do in the case of a job loss? What contingency plan do you have?

• What arrangements would you make to care for your child in case you are disabled or die prematurely?

• How would adoption affect your church life?

• Did you find yourself in the biblical description of a mother?

- What convictions do you have about parenting and discipline?
- Are you prepared for the possible increase in the intensity of your desire for marriage?
- How did you see God's grace preparing you for this ministry of motherhood?
- What would you do if in the future a man did pursue a relationship with you? How would that affect your child and vice versa? Are you thinking through the interests of a potential husband?
- How would you handle practical needs such as daycare?
- Who would agree to be your child's guardians in case something happened to you?
- How would you handle schooling, and could you afford it?
- Would you have any male role models for your child?

As you can see, adoption is a very serious step and needs to be guided by wisdom and much counsel. If adoption is something you are considering, please note how long Angela pursued this idea before going forward and how many people were involved. As one friend told me, "Adopting a child is not like getting a puppy from the pound—you can't take it back." You may want to get a reality check by first signing up to be a foster parent. There is an escape clause there.

I would also add a gentle caution that if you don't have a track record of serving other families and building relationships with those children, you *may* not perceive clearly your motives for pursuing adoption.

Practical Application

In presenting these topics, I'm not advocating any specific action—especially adoption—but I am advocating *action*. I trust that the Holy Spirit will quicken to us how we can invest in the children we already know, and that those in our churches to whom we are already accountable will confirm God's leading. But I'd like to challenge our thinking and the assumptions created by our culture.

For example, living with another family may sound weird to you. It certainly did to me at first. But as I watched, I realized there were great benefits for both the family and the single adult. Several years ago I lived with a family for a few months until I bought my own home. It was an honor to be part of this family. It also required change. I had lived in the single adult rhythm of life for so long that it was a small culture shock to adjust to the pace (and noise) of a large family! Until I moved into my own home, though, I didn't realize how quickly I'd adapted. I opened the door to silence. No little voices greeted me with, "Miss Carolyn's home!" No little girls were waiting to try on my jewelry. No toddler was trying generously to share his sticky sippy cup. The single adult rhythm was quiet, very quiet.

You may also think that as an adult, you are too old to be "baby-sitting." But, dear friends, consider the families in your church. The opportunities to befriend and invest in these children aren't mere childcare. The chance to bolster the marriages of your brothers and sisters in your church isn't just the job of teenagers. The strength and witness of your church is in large measure a result of strong relationships—relationships across all ages and seasons of life. You aren't simply providing an opportunity for a married couple to enjoy something you'd like to have—a date. You are serving them to preserve their marital harmony, which contributes to the harmony and longevity of your church. You aren't just watching their children if you see instead that time as an investment in the next generation. (Remember, these children are the people of your future. They will be the ones leading your church and maybe even the nation when you are in a nursing home somewhere. Now doesn't that inspire you to invest all you've got in them?)

Your church needs every adult participating in the discipleship of the next generation. Motherhood is a rewarding but sacrificial role. If that's something you desire, why not "warm up" by sacrificing a few hours of your weekend to give a couple a date night while you spend time with their children? Or take a child in a large family out for a special one-on-one date with you? Or serve in your church's children's ministry or the crisis pregnancy ministry? Or closer to home, help a single parent? I've known several single men in my church who have befriended the sons of single mothers, taken them on camping trips, coached them in sports, etc. My friend Dawn has done the same for a single father. For a year she "adopted" his preteen daughter and went with her to the mother-daughter ministry meetings and events.

The point is that the children of the Proverbs 31 woman "rise up and call her blessed" for the godly life she has modeled for them and for her care and faithful instruction. We, too, can be blessed when we pour our lives into the children around us instead of bemoaning the lack of our own. There are so many children already in this world who need the tender, feminine affection we have to give. Let's humble ourselves before our Maker and trust His wisdom and timing for our lives. Numerous children are already waiting to be blessed by the single woman who has put her trust and faith in the Lord.

FOR FURTHER STUDY

❖ *Shepherding a Child's Heart* by Tedd Tripp (Shepherd Press) is a biblical guide to caring for a child's heart and motivations, not just the outward behavior. The author also holds parents to a standard of authenticity and humility, requiring confession to their children when they sin against them. I remember first reading this book when I was baby-sitting a family of five—when no one was settling down for bed. I recall how irritated I was for being interrupted during my study of this great book to go upstairs one more time! *Mutter, mutter, mutter.* I wasn't five steps up before conviction hit: My heart needs this help, too!

❖ *Age of Opportunity: A Biblical Guide to Parenting Teens* by Paul David Tripp, who is Tedd's brother (P&R Publishing). Here's a novel idea: The teen years don't have to be rebellious. A follow-up to *Shepherding a Child's Heart.*

❖ Two encouraging from-the-heart audio messages are *Gospel-Centered Parenting* by C. J. Mahaney and *Mothers & Daughters* by Carolyn Mahaney and the Mahaneys' adult daughters (Sovereign Grace Ministries).

❖ After a number of years of helping single parents, Mark Mitchell, one of my pastors, has found that these articles are helpful: "Getting to the Heart of Your Worry," by Robert D. Jones, *Journal of Biblical Counseling*, Vol. 17, No. 13, Spring 1999. "Should We Get Married?" by David Powlison and John Yenchko, *Journal of Biblical Counseling*, Vol. 14, No. 3, Spring 1996. Both are available from the Christian Counseling and Educational Foundation's Web site, www.ccef.org. He would also recommend the chapter on counseling divorced women and single mothers from *Women Helping Women*, edited by Elyse Fitzpatrick and Carol W. Cornish (Harvest House). Finally, if divorce and remarriage are applicable issues, he would recommend Jay Adams's book, *Marriage, Divorce, and Remarriage in the Bible* (Zondervan).

10

DECEPTIVE CHARM

Charm is deceitful, and beauty is vain, but a woman who fears the LORD is to be praised.
PROVERBS 31:30

One of my initial childhood memories is my desire for long hair. I had the typical pageboy haircut of a preschool girl, but I wanted to feel my hair swish around my shoulders. One day while standing in the kitchen, I spotted my solution. One of those kitchen towels was just about the right length! So I put it on my head and swished it around my shoulders. My sisters thought this was cool, too (oh, the sad influence of the oldest child); so we now have many pictures of the three of us with satisfied grins and various shades of striped towels adorning our heads.

By sixth grade I was getting serious. I had developed a regimen that I recorded in my first diary as "Preparations for a Day of Beauty." As a seventh grader, I recorded my treasures of femininity: three bras, my *own* deodorant (to get my own deodorant was apparently a big deal, for earlier I'd written an entire page about this), Noxzema facial cleanser, makeup, fingernail polish, pantyhose, a purse, and—for some unknown reason—a radio. I also added a new resolution to my beauty routine: use a pogo stick daily. (If you're a child of the video age, you probably have no idea what I'm talking about. But apparently I thought that bouncing up and down on a stick with springs was going to do something for my quads and glutes.)

As a senior in high school, I took a job as a shampoo assistant in a local hair salon. My hair was then long and all one length. I had never colored it before. The very sight of my unsullied hair gave the stylists an itch to change it. For months I held them at bay like a pack of hungry wolves. But one day

I caved, and I fell hard. I got layers, a perm, and a henna color—all at the same time. I fried my hair to within an inch of its life. The results were far from glamorous. I wanted to look like pop icon Brooke Shields, but with the red henna tint and the frizzy layers, I actually resembled Little Orphan Annie.

Traumatized, I fled home in tears. I ran to my room, slammed the door, and heaved gushing sobs into my pillow. My mother tried to coax me out of the room so that she could see it. "I'm sure it's not that bad, honey," she said. "Come on out here. Let me see so that I can help you have some perspective."

For a long time, I refused. When I finally emerged, I called to her from the top of the steps. She appeared at the bottom of the steps, glanced up, and—no doubt against both her will and her better judgment—burst into laughter. I was horrified! *My own mother was laughing at my hair!*

There were many more bad haircuts to come. As an adult, I got talked into a short cut so severe that my stylist reminded me to always wear earrings and makeup with it. I didn't miss her implication of how mannish it looked, and I was steaming mad that *she* had done this to *me*. I cried all the way home, all through the night, and even harder as I tried to get ready to work the next day. With my face puffy, blotchy and red from the tears, I looked like a freak show. There was no way I could go to work. I called my supervisor (fortunately, a woman with her own history of bad hair days), still sobbing.

"I—I—I can't come to . . . *sniff* . . . work today," I said, hiccupping through my tears.

"Oh, no! What happened?" she asked with real concern. "Are you okay?"

"I—I got . . . I got . . . my hair . . . cuuuut!" I wailed.

From bad perms to orange self-tanning products to horrible shades of hair color ("Did you dump a bottle of shoe polish on your head?") to the thousands of nicks and cuts I've inflicted on my legs, you'd think I'd get wiser as I get older. But the Siren call of self-improvement simply can't be resisted.

Remember my twentieth-year high school reunion? I had another reason to dread going: I had waxed my eyebrows for the very first time that day. Now I had never waxed my eyebrows in my entire thirty-eight years (plucking was good enough for me), but when the nail stylist suggested I do my eyebrows, too, I was like a lamb going quietly to the slaughter. *Why, yes, let's do it! It's only hours before the Big Event, and since my skin is so pale*

and sensitive to sunlight and irritation, why not apply hot wax right now?
Within seconds my eyelids were burning. By the time I got home, they were
a puffy shade of magenta that had never before been captured in the
Crayola spectrum.

I panicked and called everyone I knew for advice. "Use witch hazel."
"Get Neosporin on it right away." "Did you try ice?" "Grind up aspirin,
make a paste out of it, and then wear it until it dries." Whatever they suggested, I did it—no doubt further irritating the skin. *You are an idiot,* I
berated myself as I troweled on the eye shadow. *What were you thinking?*

What woman hasn't experienced these "beauty trials"? That's why we're
exploring this verse: "Charm is deceitful, and beauty is vain, but a woman
who fears the LORD is to be praised" (Prov. 31:30). The New International
Version translates this verse as: "Charm is deceptive, and beauty is fleeting,"
emphasizing the transient nature of physical attractiveness. For the single
woman who is banking on her beauty for favor, this is a warning. For the
single woman who measures herself against other women and feels she falls
short, this verse offers encouragement. And for all of us, this verse helps us
to have the right perspective about beauty. As we consider this verse, we'll
look at six perspectives:

- The transient nature of beauty
- Avoiding the extremes
- The power of beauty
- How beauty is tarnished
- A beauty that is attractive to God and others
- Whose beauty will be worshiped?

RACING AGAINST DECAY

Each morning as I asphyxiate myself with my recommended daily
allowance of hairspray, I am reminded of Sisyphus. This mythical Greek figure was condemned to exist in the realm of the dead with the eternal, futile
task of rolling a stone up a steep hill, only to see it tumble back down when
he reached the top.

Every morning Sisyphus awaits me in the mirror. Each day I labor to
push that stone uphill to a good hair day, only to wake up in the morning
with the stone at the bottom of the hill—and with bed head. No matter how
much effort I put into my latest beauty regimen, it's always a race against
decay.

According to Greek mythology, Sisyphus was said to be the founder of Corinth. I find amusing irony in that idea because it was to the fleshly, contentious Corinthians that the apostle Paul writes with these words familiar to every aging Christian: "Therefore we do not lose heart. Though outwardly we are wasting away, yet inwardly we are being renewed day by day. For our light and momentary troubles are achieving for us an eternal glory that far outweighs them all. So we fix our eyes not on what is seen, but on what is unseen. For what is seen is temporary, but what is unseen is eternal" (2 Cor. 4:16-18 NIV).

For older women, especially those of us who are closer to retirement than to our high school graduations, each day we see the truth of Paul's words. Outwardly we *are* wasting away. A few gray hairs here, a few laugh lines there, an upper arm jiggling as we applaud, an aching back just from sleeping—these are the indignities of aging. And it's only going to get more undignified. My mother says that she, too, is startled to see the old lady in the mirror and to observe her grandmother's hands at the end of her own sleeves.

If you are young and still unlined, you may find this perspective alarming—and not as darkly humorous as the rest of us. If you are not prepared for the inevitability of aging, the day you discover that first gray hair or laugh line can be traumatic. I well remember grieving the loss of my youth, which I think is not atypical (especially as I did not yet have an eternal perspective). Just the other day I talked with a single woman ten years younger than I am who was reduced to tears after encountering her first batch of gray hairs. So I hope you will continue reading—as you will one day be there, and faster than you think! I trust the truths in this chapter will enable you to embrace that day and not mourn it.

One more consideration: I've recently thought that it's God's mercy that we fall apart as we get older. How humbling it is to end one's creaturely life dependent on others, unable to function as we once did, no longer as attractive as we were at our prime. It drives home the point that there is only One whose glory is unalterable. If that lesson didn't sink in when we were young adults, it will certainly sink in later. We might rail against it, we might work hard to hide the effects, but we won't change the immutable fact: "All flesh is like grass and all its glory like the flower of grass. The grass withers, and the flower falls, but the word of the Lord remains forever" (1 Peter 1:24-25).

BEAUTY IN THE BALANCE

Does that mean I need to put down my hairspray can and back away from the mirror? Not necessarily. God made women to be beautiful to men. There's nothing inherently wrong with seeking to be attractively feminine. The Bible certainly doesn't back away from celebrating feminine beauty: One quick read through Song of Solomon confirms this statement. "How beautiful and pleasant you are, O loved one, with all your delights!" (Song 7:6). My pastor's wife, Carolyn Mahaney, writes that women should want to be attractive, especially to their husbands: "We need to discover what makes us attractive to our husbands. What clothing, hairstyles, or makeup do they find most appealing? And we should strive to care for our appearance—not only when we go out, but also at home where only our husbands see us."[1] But as single women, we need to be mindful of the heart issues surrounding this topic. I think we can be tempted to swing from one extreme to the other when considering physical beauty. We either become a slave to the mirror, or else we disdain it. As in most things, wisdom is found in the balance.

First, let's consider something that can tempt older single women—giving up. I remember talking years ago to an older woman who had decided that her man was going to pursue her only for her character. But looking at her, I wondered if she might do something to make it a little easier for that man to *notice* her character. She had a prematurely dowdy look. I kept thinking, *Give the brother a break! Try to make a little effort here.*

In a show aimed at single women, radio host Nancy Leigh DeMoss addressed this temptation with her listeners: "I've noticed that frequently women who are single for a long time become less feminine, at least in ways that are visible. Now I'm not saying that's true of their heart, but I'm saying that in ways of appearance and manner, sometimes they become less feminine."[2]

I am not trying to be hard on anyone. Please don't get discouraged. I know what it's like to take on that "built for comfort, not for speed" look. I know what it's like to get older and find your own body thwarting your efforts to exercise or your metabolism flat-lining. But men appreciate *some* effort being made. They notice a woman who takes the right kind of pride in her appearance, who wants to be womanly. You don't have to be perfect, but feminine is good.

Philippians 2:4 tells us to look to the interests of others. Let's consider our potential husbands for a moment. Men are wired to notice beauty in women, but our culture is steeped in a standard of beauty that isn't even possible for the models themselves to have in real life. They are propped, styled, and digitized into otherworldly perfection. On top of that, godly men are negatively affected by the immorality of our culture. In real life and in the media, blatant sexuality and immorality are always but one averted gaze away. A godly man will do his best to avoid these pitfalls, of course, but consider how hard it must be for him *not* to be affected by our culture. In the midst of this barrage of flesh, we are asking Christian men to commit themselves to be faithful to one woman for the rest of their lives. Wouldn't it bless them if we were the best we could be, both spiritually *and* physically? That perspective has propelled me to the gym many a time—and not just for reasons of vanity. I'm sure our future husbands would also appreciate healthy wives.

Let's swing to the other side and consider vanity. It's not wrong for a woman to adorn herself, but the Bible does warn against the excess that results in immodest or ostentatious displays or becomes a life-consuming pursuit. The Hebrew word that is translated as "vain" in the phrase "beauty is vain" is *hebel,* which means "emptiness or vanity, something transitory and unsatisfactory."[3] This is the same word that permeates the book of Ecclesiastes. Ecclesiastes is an exploration of the meaning of life, but by the second chapter, the writer has concluded that pleasure, laughter, hard work, homes, gardens, herds, servants, gold and silver, and even wisdom are *hebel*! This overstatement is effective because the writer goes on to call *hebel* "striving after the wind." Many good things are called *hebel* because we can't grasp true satisfaction from these items any more than we can grasp the wind. There's nothing wrong with these activities, but they won't provide the fulfillment we often seek from them.

In the same way, beauty is *hebel*. There's nothing inherently wrong with beauty, but the meaning and fulfillment we seek in it will elude us like the wind through our fingers.

THE POWER OF BEAUTY

So then why do we care so much about being beautiful? Why aren't we content with the measure of attractiveness that God has given us? For one reason, because beauty has an effect on men. "In every man's heart there is a secret nerve that answers to the vibrations of beauty," wrote American journalist Christopher Morley. Men notice beauty. They fight for the favor of a beautiful woman. They memorialize beauty in art. They write lyrical poetry about beauty.

> *She walks in Beauty, like the night*
> *Of cloudless climes and starry skies;*
> *And all that's best of dark and bright*
> *Meet in her aspect and her eyes:*
> *Thus mellowed to that tender light*
> *Which Heaven to gaudy day denies.*
> George Gordon Byron[4]

Every woman wants to elicit this kind of rhapsodic response from a man. That's the second reason right there: "Every woman *wants*." Perhaps I would be more honest to say "craves" or "lusts after." As Joshua Harris writes:

> A man is created to pursue and finds even the pursuit stimulating; a woman is made to want to be pursued and finds even being pursued stimulating. . . . Lust blurs and bends true masculinity and femininity in harmful ways. It makes a man's good desire to pursue all about "capturing" and "using," and a woman's good desire to be beautiful all about "seduction" and "manipulation." In general it seems that men and women are tempted by lust in two unique ways: men are tempted by the *pleasure* that lust offers, while women are tempted by the *power* lust promises.[5]

Ladies, let's drive home that point by expanding that thought: "Women are tempted by the power lust promises *to attract other people's husbands*." You might say you don't want that kind of attention from married men. Good—I hope so! But let's face it: If we want lots of interest from *many* single men, we actually want to lure men who probably will be other women's husbands in the future. If these men were already married, I trust we would not want their attentions. So why do we want them now? Because we sinfully enjoy the self-centered power and attention of being attractive to others, even when we can't possibly follow through on the interest we've raised.

You may think from reading that statement that I have known this kind of allure personally. I have—in my heart and in my daydreams. If these are our desires, it doesn't matter whether or not we could *actually* attract hordes of men. I know a woman who honestly confessed one of her leading motives for losing a lot of weight was to be able to fit into slinkier, immodest clothes and draw lots of attention to herself. She is a godly woman, who repented and confessed this sin, but she was right to be concerned about her motives for being thin.

GILDING THE PIG

We see this every day in the popular media. Incredibly stunning women are stunning the rest of us with their scandalous behavior and jaw-dropping vulgarity. Sometimes it seems that the prettier they are, the trashier they live and speak. We live in a time when the power lust seemingly promises to women is not only tolerated, but it is celebrated. As I worked on this chapter, the nation was shocked by the crude and offensive actions of a female star on live television. There's no need to mention the details because, unfortunately, she probably will be upstaged by someone else in a few months, and this particular episode will become a footnote in history.

Why am I sure of this? Because an astute observation in Proverbs notes that this lack of good judgment and modesty is not uncommon to women of any age. Proverbs 11:22 drives home this point with comic hyperbole: "Like a gold ring in a pig's snout is a beautiful woman without discretion."

King Solomon wrote this proverb, and he, with his 700 wives and 300 concubines, had the demographic research to back up his observation—as well as the hard-learned lessons about the corrupting influence of indulging himself with so many women. "No man ever lived who has had as much experience with women as King Solomon, who 'loved many strange women,'" writes pastor and author Herbert Lockyer. "Solomon could be expected to say something about the vices and virtues of women, as he does, particularly in the Book of Proverbs. . . . In no other book in the Bible do we find so many references to loose women and grim warnings against any association with them, as in Proverbs."[6]

What does indiscretion look like? We may compare ourselves with the woman in the latest media scandal and think we're doing fine. But that's not the standard for a godly woman. I've found invaluable advice in the points that Nancy Leigh DeMoss raises in her "Portrait of a Foolish Woman," based upon the adulterous woman described in Proverbs 7:

> The foolish woman in this passage approaches her prey with a bold greeting. She throws herself on this man—physically and verbally. She evidences the lack of discretion and restraint that is so common between men and women today. Even in church it is not unusual to see women

casually, carelessly throw their arms around men. Such behavior may not have immoral intent, but it is foolish. At best, it pulls down appropriate restraints that ought to exist between men and women; at worst, it can lead to grave sins against God. . . .

The foolish woman is indiscreet—she talks freely about intimate subjects that should be reserved for conversation with her husband. One of the most disconcerting aspects of various highly publicized sex scandals in recent years is the open, candid talk about private matters that has been splashed throughout the news media. Explicit sexual language that was once considered inappropriate outside the bedroom has now become part of our everyday vocabulary. . . . We need to teach young women that there are things you don't talk about in mixed company. Indeed, there are personal matters between husbands and wives that should not be discussed even with other women.[7]

We will explore our speech further in the next chapter, but it is worthwhile to note here that what comes out of our mouths can truly diminish our appeal. Even in Lord Byron's famous poem, part of which I quoted above, we see how he goes on to praise both the fair lady's looks as well as her thoughts and words:

> One shade the more, one ray the less,
> Had half impaired the nameless grace
> Which waves in every raven tress,
> Or softly lightens o'er her face;
> Where thoughts serenely sweet express,
> How pure, how dear their dwelling-place.[8]

Just in case you're wondering, these ancient sentiments live on today because they are rooted in God's timeless truth. One of my single guy friends once made this comment, and I noted it immediately: "When I see an outwardly attractive woman do or say something that is foolish or worldly, it is like a slap in the face to me. I can't turn away fast enough. But when a godly woman does something to encourage someone else, I bless God for her and more than once such actions have caused me to consider her in prayer."

BEAUTY BLENDED WITH DISCRETION

Scripture provides us with a role model of beauty blended with discretion. We find her in 1 Samuel 25, and her name was Abigail. She was the wife of a very wealthy but foolish man named Nabal. Verse 3 says: "Now the name of the man was Nabal, and the name of his wife Abigail. The woman was discerning and beautiful, but the man was harsh and badly behaved."

In this account, David protected Nabal's shepherds and sheep when they were in the wilderness, and he expected that Nabal would reward him when David sent his greetings at the time of sheep shearing. But Nabal snubbed him, which raised David's ire. When Abigail heard this, she intervened quickly. She sent donkeys ahead loaded with gifts, and when she found David, she fell at his feet and begged him not to avenge himself. Her speech concluded with these words: "And when the LORD has done to my lord according to all the good that he has spoken concerning you and has appointed you prince over Israel, my lord shall have no cause of grief or pangs of conscience for having shed blood without cause or for my lord taking vengeance himself. And when the Lord has dealt well with my lord, then remember your servant" (1 Sam. 25:30-31).

David immediately recognized the wisdom in her words and exclaimed: "*Blessed be the* LORD, *the God of Israel, who sent you this day to meet me! Blessed be your discretion, and blessed be you,* who have kept me this day from bloodguilt and from avenging myself with my own hand! For as surely as the LORD the God of Israel lives, who has restrained me from hurting you, unless you had hurried and come to meet me, truly by morning there had not been left to Nabal so much as one male" (1 Sam. 25:32-34, emphasis added).

First, David blessed the Lord for His sovereignty in this encounter. Then he blessed Abigail for her discretion. But notice that David *did not* comment on Abigail's beauty. If she was striking enough for her beauty to have been noted in Scripture, David no doubt observed it. But that's not what he blessed her for. His focus was on how God used her in his life and how she wisely spoke to him. When her husband, Nabal, died ten days later, however, David was swift in asking this wise and beautiful woman to be his wife.

This is the kind of appeal we should have—beauty in visage *and* verbiage that makes a man say, "blessed be the Lord who sent you this day to meet me."

INWARD BEAUTY: PRECIOUS TO GOD

As attractive as that kind of appeal is to men, it is more important to consider how God views it. First Peter 3:3-4 says: "Do not let your adorning be external—the braiding of hair, the wearing of gold, or the putting on of clothing—but let your adorning be the hidden person of the heart with the imperishable beauty of a gentle and quiet spirit, which in God's sight is very precious." In this verse, we not only find a kind of imperishable beauty, but we also find how God values it—*precious*.

In examining this passage, Carolyn Mahaney writes:

> God's definition of beauty stands in stark contrast to the way our culture defines beauty. Our culture defines beauty by how we look on the outside. God defines beauty by what we are like on the inside.
>
> Our culture puts forth a standard of beauty that is unattainable by most. God puts forth a standard of beauty to which we can all attain if we just respond to His work of grace in our lives.
>
> Our culture encourages women to cultivate a beauty that is skin deep. God tells us to pursue an inner beauty of great worth.
>
> Our culture encourages women to cultivate a beauty that will only last for a brief time. God encourages women to cultivate a beauty that will never fade and that will only grow more attractive with the passing of time.
>
> Our culture calls us to cultivate a beauty that impresses others. God summons us to cultivate a beauty that is first and foremost for *His* eyes.
>
> Our culture entices us to aspire to the beauty of the latest glamorous model or this season's most popular actress. God bids us to aspire to the beauty of holy women in the past who put their hope in God.
>
> Do you see the difference? The beauty our culture esteems may turn some heads, but the beauty God calls us to cultivate will make a lasting impact. When a physically attractive woman walks by, we notice—men particularly! But that's the end of it. Her beauty makes a fleeting, momentary impression. But a woman who cultivates inner beauty, who fears God and lives to serve others, makes a difference in people's lives. Her beauty makes a lasting impact on the lives she touches. Godly, inner beauty makes an indelible mark on the lives of others and glorifies God.[9]

INWARD BEAUTY: ATTRACTIVE TO OTHERS

It may be hard to understand how a quiet and gentle spirit would make a woman beautiful. It sounds so mousy. At least that's what I thought when I first read that passage as a new Christian. My views had been shaped by the temperamental divas of popular culture—high-maintenance, self-centered, dramatic women who seem to drag men hooked by the nose in their wake. These divas commanded attention—but a quiet and gentle woman? How could she be beautiful?

I've since learned that a woman who is quiet and gentle is not contorted by stress, anger, or impatience. Her laughter, and not her frowning, is etched in the lines of her face. There is no turbulence in her air space from her agitation and distrust. She's not wound so tight that she vibrates with irritation and anxiety. Instead, this woman has learned, as the Countess of Blessington once said, "There is no cosmetic for beauty like happiness."

A quiet and gentle woman is like a weaned child. She trusts the Lord, and this lack of fear makes her radiant. Psalm 34:4-5 says:

> *I sought the Lord, and he answered me*
> *and delivered me from all my fears.*
> *Those who look to him are radiant,*
> *and their faces shall never be ashamed.*

If you are discouraged about growing older and losing beauty as the world defines it, then I hope you will be encouraged by this verse. You can cultivate radiant beauty simply from trusting the Lord in circumstances like your singleness. *You need never be ashamed when you are looking to Him!* When you seek the Lord as you are tempted by fear, and when you trust Him to work out your circumstances, the more radiant you will become.

Let me assure you that worthy single men *do* notice this kind of beauty. I have it on good (male) authority that men are intrigued by women whose satisfaction is in God. There's a mystery there that is captivating. They also understand and appreciate the concept of inner beauty. I once received a call from a friend who had obviously given a lot of thought to the "dining alone in a restaurant" dilemma I described in chapter 7. I had told him about the same trip and had laughed with him about how getting older makes it easier not to care what total strangers think about you. Weeks later he called me back. He said he'd been thinking about that scenario. He wanted me to know that though the other diners simply saw a forty-year-old woman eating dinner by herself, they couldn't see everything that's important about me. They could see me from the outside, but without talking to me or knowing me in other contexts, they could not know who I really was in terms of inner beauty. Then he went on to comment on some specific character traits that he considered glorifying to God.

I listened with some surprise. I hadn't been thinking of this event in this way, but I was humbled that *he* had. His encouragement was unexpected and meaningful. As I later pondered his words, they strengthened me for the never-ending task of governing my unruly passions and my restless tongue to obtain that gentle and quiet spirit. His observation was profound: "Inner beauty points to heaven. Outer beauty points to destruction."

WORSHIPING ETERNAL BEAUTY

Dear friend, you may have been reading this chapter with many misgivings. Perhaps you suffer from a physical limitation or a feature you consider a deformity. I pray that you have been encouraged by the perspective on everlasting inner beauty. I think you could be cheered also by the words of one woman who knows such challenges better than I.

"Suffering keeps swelling our feet so that earth's shoes won't fit," Joni Eareckson Tada writes. "My atrophied legs and swollen ankles, curled fingers and limp wrists are visual aids in a children's Sunday school lesson on Isaiah 40:6, 8: 'All flesh is grass . . . the grass withereth, the flower fadeth: but the word of our God shall stand for ever' (KJV)."

Joni is a woman who exudes inner beauty even though she is— wheelchair and all—a pretty woman on the outside. I've been to several dinners when she has blessed the participants with her fine singing, leading the group in resonant old hymns. She is fascinating to watch. Her joy commands your attention. But as a quadriplegic, Joni admits she is looking forward to the fulfillment of Isaiah 35:4-6:

> Say to those who have an anxious heart,
> "Be strong; fear not!
> Behold, your God
>   will come with vengeance,
>   with the recompense of God.
> He will come and save you."
> Then the eyes of the blind shall be opened,
>   and the ears of the deaf unstopped;
>   then shall the lame man leap like a deer,
>   and the tongue of the mute sing for joy.

"For me, verses like this are not cross-stitched promises nostalgic of a vague, nebulous and distant era," Joni writes. "It's part of the hope I'm already stepping into, the time when Jesus will 'transform our lowly bodies so that they will be like his glorious body,' (Philip. 3:21). I like that part about new bodies. But my hope isn't centered around a glorious body. It goes far beyond that."[10]

What awaits the Christian in that resurrected body is a mystery. We may have a few hints in Scripture. But as Randy Alcorn writes, it may be the inner man or woman that is recognizable—confirmation of the everlasting quality of inner beauty:

> Christ's resurrection body is the model and prototype for our own heavenly bodies (1 Corinthians 15:20, 48-49; Philippians 3:21; 1 John 3:2). Whatever was true of his resurrection body will presumably be true of ours.
>
> After his resurrection, Jesus emphasized that he was not a "ghost"—a disembodied spirit—but a physical body (Luke 24:37-39). A few times Jesus wasn't immediately recognized (John 20:15; Luke 24:15-16), suggesting there was some change in his appearance. (Most of us would welcome *some* change in our appearance, wouldn't we?) Then, after being with him awhile, his disciples suddenly recognized him (John 20:16; Luke 24:31). This suggests that despite any change in outward appearance, the inner identity of people may shine through.[11]

I'm fairly sure that no matter how glorious these new bodies will be or how brilliant our inner beauty will be when sin is completely absent, we will be utterly unaware of it all when we stand in heaven. Instead, I think our attention will be elsewhere. We will be utterly captivated by the beauty of the Lamb.

We have no description of what Jesus looked like when he lived on earth, but the prophet Isaiah had foretold that "He had no beauty or majesty to attract us to him; nothing in his appearance that we should desire him" (Isa. 53:2 NIV). The apostle John, however, had a vision of the ascended Lord, and He was both breathtakingly beautiful and terrifying in His grandeur:

> *I turned around to see the voice that was speaking to me. And when I turned I saw seven golden lampstands, and among the lampstands was someone "like a son of man," dressed in a robe reaching down to his feet and with a golden sash around his chest. His head and hair were white like wool, as white as snow, and his eyes were like blazing fire. His feet were like bronze glowing in a furnace, and his voice was like the sound of rushing waters. In his right hand he held seven stars, and out of his mouth came a sharp double-edged sword. His face was like the sun shining in all its brilliance. When I saw him, I fell at his feet as though dead. Then he placed his right hand on me and said: "Do not be afraid. I am the First and the Last. I am the Living One; I was dead, and behold I am alive for ever and ever! And I hold the keys of death and Hades." (Rev. 1:12-18 NIV)*

This is the One we will spend eternity worshiping. We will also be dwelling in otherworldly beauty. John described his vision of the holy city of Jerusalem coming down out of the heaven of God "having the glory of God, its radiance like a most rare jewel, like a jasper, clear as crystal" (Rev. 21:11). This city doesn't need sun or moon to shine on it, "for the glory of God gives it light, and its lamp is the Lamb" (v. 23).

As we consider this kind of beauty and majesty, it is right that our own physical glory should be *hebel*. The creature should be the lesser being; it is a reminder that we exist to glorify our Creator. Yes, dear friends, outwardly we are fading away, but that's not the end of the story. Scripture tells us we will spend eternity contemplating God's everlasting beauty.

May David's words be the banner over our mirrors:

> One thing have I asked of the Lord,
>   that will I seek after:
> that I may dwell in the house of the LORD
>   all the days of my life,
> to gaze upon the beauty of the LORD
>   and to inquire in his temple. (Ps. 27:4)

FOR FURTHER STUDY

❖ There is another facet to consider when the beauty of Christian women is discussed, and that's modesty. Because there are so many great resources already available about this topic, I didn't tackle it in this chapter. But I would highly recommend two resources for further study. The first is an audio message and an article derived from that message, both by Pastor C. J. Mahaney titled "The Soul of Modesty." They are available from Sovereign Grace Ministries (www.sovereigngraceministries.org). The second is Nancy Leigh DeMoss's booklet titled *The Look: Does God Really Care What I Wear?*, available from her Revive Our Hearts ministry (www.reviveourhearts.com).

❖ Modesty is a fruit of a commitment to purity. I've already recommended Joshua Harris's *Not Even a Hint: Guarding Your Heart Against Lust* in an earlier chapter, but now I would add Randy Alcorn's *The Purity Principle* (Multnomah). This little book is full of direct, candid teaching about how to prevent inching toward the edge until gravity takes over—and you fall.

❖ A great overview on the history of women torturing themselves for the sake of beauty was written by Robin Marantz Henig and reprinted in *The*

Journal of Biblical Counseling. The article was titled "The Price of Perfection" and was carried in the Volume 35, Number 2, Winter 1997 edition. Back copies of this magazine may be available through the Christian Counseling and Educational Foundation (www.ccef.org).

❖ There is a chapter titled "True Beauty" by Carolyn Mahaney in *Biblical Womanhood in the Home* (Crossway) that I also highly recommend. In it Carolyn provides this insightful "Heart Check" so that we can examine our personal pursuit of beauty. I close this chapter with this list because it is a great tool to help us practically apply the Proverbs 31 standard of beauty to our lives.

THE "HEART CHECK" ABOUT BEAUTY

1. Do I spend more time daily caring for my personal appearance than I do in Bible study, prayer, and worship?

2. Do I spend excessive money on clothes, hair, and makeup, or is it an amount that is God-honoring?

3. Do I want to lose weight to "feel better about myself," or do I desire to be self-disciplined for the glory of God?

4. Am I on a quest for thinness to impress others, or do I seek to cultivate eating habits that honor God?

5. Do I exercise to try to create or maintain a "good figure," or do I exercise to strengthen my body for God's service?

6. Is there anything about my appearance that I wish I could change, or am I fully grateful to God for the way He created me?

7. Am I jealous of the appearance of others, or am I truly glad when I observe other women who are more physically attractive than I?

8. Do I covet the wardrobe of others, or do I genuinely rejoice when other women are able to afford and purchase new clothing?

9. When I attend an event or activity, do I sinfully compare myself with others, or do I go asking God to show me whom to love and how to do it?

10. Do I ever dress immodestly or with the intent of drawing attention to myself, or do I always dress in a manner that pleases God?

11

WISE SPEECH

She opens her mouth with wisdom, and the teaching of kindness is on her tongue.

PROVERBS 31:26

I was tired, hungry, and hormonal. My day was jammed with deadlines, and I was on a caffeine-fueled drive to get everything done on my agenda. As I zipped from one meeting to the next, I rounded the corner and nearly ran over my boss, Bo.

"What's your schedule like this afternoon?" he asked.

Instead of answering this particular question, I proceeded with that maddening female habit of answering what I thought would be his next—or maybe fifth—question. In a split second, my thinking went like this: *He's asking about my schedule. He must want to interrupt it. I can't allow that—I've got too many deadlines. If I miss these deadlines, he's going to chastise me later. Just when I'm trying to get everything done—and now he wants to interrupt me! I just can't win.*

"There's no way I can squeeze anything else in this afternoon," I responded tersely. Then the overflow began to erupt. "I'm tired of always being told to make my deadlines, but always running into impediments to finishing them. It's a no-win situation, and (*insert name here*) isn't making anything easier—" (And so on. You get the idea.)

Bo listened patiently as I splattered him with my anger. He didn't say anything in return, except for this: "We'll talk about this later." Then he excused himself.

Within minutes, the conviction of the Holy Spirit settled on my soul like a lead weight. *What have I done? Why did I respond so sinfully to my boss?*

To top it off, I work for a ministry in a job I love, and the godly character of my colleagues is a daily example to me. But obviously that wonderful setting didn't constrain me in this case. So what in the world would cause me to react this way?

The Lord had my answer. Jesus said, "For out of the abundance *of the heart* the mouth speaks. The good person out of his good treasure brings forth good, and the evil person out of his evil treasure brings forth evil. I tell you, on the day of judgment people will give account for every careless word they speak, for by your words you will be justified, and by your words you will be condemned" (Matt. 12:34-37, emphasis added).

Every careless word. That promise is chilling. Especially when considered against the warning from Proverbs 10:19 (NIV)—"When words are many, sin is not absent, but he who holds his tongue is wise." This proverb is true in my life, and I have learned many lessons the hard way. I am a talkative woman; therefore, sin is not absent. Over the years, I've tried to prune my language like someone trimming an overgrown hedge: A little off the gossiping, a hard whack at the angry words, a snip off the boasting, and that should about do it . . . for a time. But while I'm batting around the branches, I'm completely missing the root of my problem—*my heart.* I can't simply prune my words. I need to uproot and replant everything.

"If we are going to understand our trouble with words, we must begin with the heart," writes author and biblical counselor Paul Tripp. "Our tongues are full of restless evil *because* the 'heart is deceitful above all things and beyond cure. Who can understand it?' (Jer. 17:9). Word problems *reveal* heart problems. The people and situations around us do not *make* us say what we say; they are only the *occasion* for our hearts to reveal themselves in words."[1]

As our Lord said, I need—we all need—an overhaul of the heart. I believe we find the model of a woman who has done this heart work in our Proverbs 31 woman. Verse 26 says, "She opens her mouth with wisdom, and the teaching of kindness is on her tongue." The overflow of her heart is wisdom and kindness. It's probably no coincidence that the account of the noble woman of Proverbs 31 concludes a collection of wisdom writings, much of which is concerned with the impact of speech. In this chapter, we will examine the impact of feminine speech and how to replace sinful words with godly ones. But if we started there, we would be batting around the branches again, simply exchanging one set of behaviors for another.

To overhaul our hearts and change our words, we must begin with the Word.

WORDS ARE IMPORTANT TO GOD

One of the first actions we find in the Bible is that of speaking. When God created, He *spoke*. "And God said, 'Let there be light,' and there was light" (Gen. 1:3). God's creative power was found in His words, and by His words the world was created. Can you imagine the sound of His creative might at work?

> By the word of the LORD the heavens were made,
>   and by the breath of his mouth all their host.
> He gathers the waters of the sea as a heap;
>   he puts the deeps in storehouses.
> Let all the earth fear the LORD;
>   let all the inhabitants of the world stand in awe of him!
> For he spoke, and it came to be;
>   he commanded, and it stood firm. (Ps. 33:6-9)

After making the heavens and the earth and everything on it, the Lord made a man and a woman in His image—also able to hear and speak. He instructed them in His ways and blessed them.

But there was another voice in the Garden. It was the first voice with a question: "Did God actually say, 'You shall not eat of any tree in the garden'?" (Gen. 3:1), asked the Serpent. For the first time, another speaker challenged the authority and the very words of God. Adam and Eve responded to that voice. With that volley, war was declared and is still being waged today.

But, praise God, the story didn't end there. Into this war, God decided to send His Son, the Word, into this fallen world to take on our flesh and be our substitute for the punishment of our sins. John 1:14 says, "And the Word became flesh and dwelt among us, and we have seen his glory, glory as of the only Son from the Father, full of grace and truth." Reflecting on this glorious truth, Paul Tripp writes:

Think of this. The God who created speech and spoke the world into existence, the God who used human words to reveal himself to his people throughout the ages, comes to his world as the Word, to people who have forsaken him. He is not only a speaker of truth, he is Truth, and only in him is there any hope for us. Only in the Word do we find hope to win the war of words and speak again according to our Maker's example and design. The Word became flesh because there was no other way to fix what was broken in us.[2]

Here is our provision for the heart overhaul. Because the Word became flesh to fix what was broken in us "from his fullness we have all received, grace upon grace. For the law was given through Moses; grace and truth came through Jesus Christ" (John 1:16-17). With this grace and truth, we now have all that we need to speak in a godly manner. We also have an amazing assignment for our words: "we are ambassadors for Christ, God making his appeal through us" (2 Cor. 5:20). We are to go and communicate the message of the gospel to those who have never heard it or understood it.

The problem, however, is that the ambassadors keep getting potshots from the enemy within. We open our mouths to speak for Him, and instead we find our words issuing forth from the sinful overflow of our hearts. James 3:6-10 is starkly candid:

> And the tongue is a fire, a world of unrighteousness. The tongue is set among our members, staining the whole body, setting on fire the entire course of life, and set on fire by hell. For every kind of beast and bird, of reptile and sea creature, can be tamed and has been tamed by mankind, but no human being can tame the tongue. It is a restless evil, full of deadly poison. With it we bless our Lord and Father, and with it we curse people who are made in the likeness of God. From the same mouth come blessing and cursing. My brothers, these things ought not to be so.

From the same mouth come blessing and cursing—how very true! How are we ever to reconcile the problem of a restless tongue, full of deadly poison, with the role of being an ambassador who is commanded to speak with grace and truth?

We must examine our words to see what is stored up in our hearts. Once we see what's there, James says we are to be patient and establish our hearts (James 5:8). That Greek word translated as "establish" is *sterizo*, which means literally to turn resolutely in a certain direction.[3] That's a big command, but we have everything we need for victory, for we have grace upon grace from the Word Himself.

Let's see how this looks in the account that opened this chapter.

WORDS REVEAL

Bo's simple question was: "What's your schedule like this afternoon?" If I had been establishing my heart on brotherly love and patience, I would have answered a different way. Yes, I was tired, hungry, and hormonal.

Yes, I had a lot of work on my plate. But those circumstances, and even Bo's question itself, didn't *make* me respond sinfully. His question revealed what was *already* stored up in my heart and waiting to escape. As best as I can understand it now, here's what my words revealed in that situation:

1. *I was self-centered.* I didn't respect the position and authority of my boss. I'd forgotten that my role is to serve my boss, not the other way around. If I had been establishing my heart on that proper perspective, I would not have responded through a self-centered perspective.

2. *I sinfully judged his motives for asking the question.* Bo was asking for information, but *I* determined *why* he was asking and then responded according to my assumption of his motives. (Ladies, this is one common female sin pattern—and it provokes many men around us. If we would just learn to answer the question put before us—and *only* that question—we would have a lot fewer conflicts on our hands.) If I had been establishing my heart on thinking the best about other people, I would have assumed he was asking merely for information.

3. *I sinfully judged my boss for not noticing or caring how many assignments I was juggling.* This judgment was contrary to the ongoing record of spoken and written evidence that he *was* concerned. I *assumed* that since he was asking this question, he wanted to give me more work.

4. *I was ready to complain about my workload.* Instead of being grateful for a job or even for an opportunity to help my boss with one of his tasks, I was going about my work with resentment.

5. *I was counting myself more significant than others.* Bo's question revealed my functional belief system that my life and agenda shouldn't be interrupted. In other words, I believed that my plans and interests were more important than the needs of my colleagues, which is the opposite of the orientation Philippians 2:3-4 tells us to have: "Do nothing from rivalry or conceit, but in humility count others more significant than yourselves. Let each of you look not only to his own interests, but also to the interests of others."

6. *I gossiped (and shifted blame) when I dragged in my evaluation of someone else's perceived lack of help.* This person wasn't there to offer a defense against my evaluation, and the individual's efforts weren't even relevant to the original question Bo asked me.

Wow. That's a sobering list. There was a lot going on in my heart. (And probably there's more than I know right now, too.) Proverbs 12:18 (NIV) says: "Reckless words pierce like a sword, but the tongue of the wise brings healing." This is an accurate portrait of my encounter with my boss. He asked a question for information, and I parried with sword thrusts of the tongue.

Words Can Heal

Are you discouraged about your speech? I would be if I didn't remember one important fact: Because of the cross, I have a new resident in my heart—the Holy Spirit—who is renewing me inwardly every day. Despite my sinful tendencies, the Holy Spirit provides the grace to respond in a godly way. He gives me the power to be one whose wise tongue brings healing. The Holy Spirit can make me into a Proverbs 31 woman who "opens her mouth with wisdom."

Practically speaking, we can start with The Pause.

James 1:19-20 says: "Know this, my beloved brothers: let every person be quick to hear, *slow to speak,* slow to anger; for the anger of man does not produce the righteousness that God requires" (emphasis mine). If I am slow to speak, if I pause and consider my words, I have time to ask God for help to speak wisely—even when I'm physically weak, as happened in that conversation with my boss. Bo modeled that for me. When I went to him a few hours later to confess my sin and to ask his forgiveness, he was gracious to extend it. As we spoke, I remarked that I felt even worse about my sinful reaction because I knew that he too was sick that day. In reply, he said that he was grateful he remembered to stop and ask the Holy Spirit for the grace to respond properly to me. The Holy Spirit told him to hold his tongue, which he did. As I listened to this wise counsel, I wished I had done the same thing.

The Pause, however, is only a tool to access the wisdom we should be depositing in our hearts. If we haven't been making those deposits, we will only have a breather before we start spewing sin. But how do we make those deposits? First Corinthians 1:30 (NIV) says: "It is because of him that you are in Christ Jesus, *who has become for us wisdom from God*—that is, our righteousness, holiness and redemption" (emphasis mine). Jesus is our wisdom from God, and the apostle Paul defines that as "our righteousness, holiness and redemption." Therefore, the deposits we need to make in order to overhaul our hearts are thoughts of the gospel, the cross, and our Savior!

As we think of our King, we will speak redemptively, as worthy ambassadors, with words that heal instead of wounding.

These deposits can be made in five simple ways, according to Pastor C. J. Mahaney:

1. Memorize the gospel. "All God's promises and commands are precious, but those verses that tell us of the Son of God who gave His life in our place are the most precious of all."

2. Pray the gospel. "There's nothing complicated about this. To pray the gospel, simply begin by thanking God for the blessing of eternal life, purchased through the death of His Son. Acknowledge that Christ's work on the cross is what makes our very prayer possible."

3. Sing the gospel. "A Christian's heart should be brimming every day with the song of Calvary. . . . There are countless worship CDs available, but it's important to choose ones that draw our attention to the amazing truth of what God has done on our behalf."

4. Review how the gospel has changed you. "Even if your story doesn't involve drugs or immorality, it is still a miracle of God's grace. You didn't write it by yourself. God intervened. God changed your heart. God saved you. Take time to think about that."

5. Study the gospel. "Never be content with your current grasp of the gospel. The gospel is life-permeating, world-altering, universe-changing truth. It has more facets than any diamond."[4]

Now let's see how the gospel can change our words from reckless to redemptive in the five sinful areas I identified in my conversation with my boss: disrespect, anger, gossip, complaining, and sinful judgment.

Disrespect—>Respect

I believe women have a specific mandate for our speech that is especially needed in our culture today. This mandate is respect. Ephesians 5:31-33 says, "'Therefore a man shall leave his father and mother and hold fast to his wife, and the two shall become one flesh.' This mystery is profound, and I am saying that it refers to Christ and the church. However, let each one of you love his wife as himself, and *let the wife see that she respects her husband*" (emphasis added).

Respect is a slippery concept. It's an intangible quality, but the effect of respect, or lack of it, is quite real. It's a heart quality that is hard to measure except when we examine our speech. I think this is why we have these warnings from Proverbs:

It is better to live in a desert land
than with a quarrelsome and fretful woman. (Prov. 21:19)
A continual dripping on a rainy day
and a quarrelsome wife are alike;
to restrain her is to restrain the wind
or to grasp oil in one's right hand. (Prov. 27:15-16)

And just in case the point isn't sinking in, Proverbs 21:9 gives us this portrait and then repeats it *word for word* a few verses later in 25:24.

It is better to live in a corner of the housetop
than in a house shared with a quarrelsome wife.

These proverbs are emphatic that it's better to live exposed to the elements in either the desert or on a rooftop than exposed to the corrosive words of a quarrelsome, nagging wife. That is quite the picture of how our words affect men.

Our sinful selves, however, don't like to give respect. We like to wag our heads and swivel our necks, and with a roll of the eyes announce, "I just don't *hand out* the respect. I will give it when it is *earned*." Well, don't get quarrelsome now! The Bible doesn't tell the *men* to see to it that their wives respect them. No, God's Word tells *wives* to police themselves in this regard. Why? To show the mystery of how Christ and the church relate— the joyful response of a wife to her husband is supposed to emulate the joyful response of the Lamb's bride. This is the gospel deposit we need to make in our hearts!

Men seem to come with a factory-installed respect sensor. They are acutely aware of women's disrespect and are affected—for the better or the worse—by our words. I remember when one of my friends encountered this sensor. About two weeks prior to her wedding, her fiancé gently confronted her about her quarrelsome attitude, which he rightly perceived was a lack of respect. He gave her some examples of how she "dripped" away at him when she didn't like the decisions he was making. Her constant displeasure was wearing him down, and he felt himself pulling away from her. As a result, her words were wounding them both. She was horrified to hear how he felt because of her speech and immediately asked his forgiveness. "My words make him feel like either a king or a heel," she lamented. "I've been tearing down this wonderful man when I could have been building him up and making him feel like the king of the world!"

Ladies, there are a number of ways we can cultivate the feminine quality of respect prior to marriage. Romans 13:7-8 commands us this way: "Pay to all what is owed to them: taxes to whom taxes are owed, revenue to whom revenue is owed, *respect to whom respect is owed*, honor to whom honor is owed. Owe no one anything, except to love each other, for the one who loves another has fulfilled the law" (emphasis added). This admonition is set in the context of governing authorities. We may not have husbands now, but we all have governing authorities—parents, pastors, bosses, and more. Are we giving the proper respect to these people because of their position in our lives? How are we speaking *of* and *to* these governing authorities?

As we saw in an earlier chapter, Proverbs 7 shows us the fruit of the wayward, foolish adulteress and the impact of her words. Verses 25 and 26 say: "Let not your heart turn aside to her ways; do not stray into her paths, for many a victim has she laid low, and all her slain are a mighty throng." The New King James Version translates this phrase as "for she has cast down many wounded." Author Nancy Leigh DeMoss explains what casting down or laying low the men in our lives looks like:

> The foolish woman is an instrument of "cast[ing] down" *many* men. She may do so by means of sexual seduction, as does the woman in Proverbs 7, or she may do so more subtly, by means of discouragement, spiritual pride, or intimidation. I have found that I can walk into a meeting with a group of men and in a matter of moments change the climate of that room by my spirit. . . .
>
> One politically correct way that women "cast down" men is by verbally bashing them—making "men jokes" or cutting comments about men. Of course, it is equally inappropriate for men to bash women, but the woman is the glory of man (1 Cor. 11:7). When we speak words that cut, diminish, and wound—even in jest—we are tearing down those we were intended to lift up. . . .
>
> As I read this passage, I find myself wondering how many wounded or strong men I have cast down—perhaps not morally, but spiritually. How many men have I discouraged or intimidated? Our calling with the men God has placed in our lives is to be a cheerleader, to lift up their hands and to pray for them. Yes, they have weaknesses, as do we; but we need to encourage them and pray and trust God to make them mighty men of God. That is our high and holy calling.[5]

We will be countercultural women if we refuse to bash men. That takes constant vigilance, though, for man-bashing is the stuff of our culture's humor, entertainment, and media. I have found this to be a particularly per-

nicious weed in my life—worse than summer dandelions with their stubborn roots. If I only try to change the content of my conversations, I will be
doing no more than pulling off the dandelion head. I have to examine and
change my thought patterns so that I can completely pull up that weed
before it blooms again.

One related thought here: We can cast down men by casting down their
opinions—even their good opinions of us. When a man (or anyone for that
matter) offers us a compliment, let's do our best not to dismiss it. A simple
"thank you" is the proper answer. I used to deflect people's compliments out
of false humility. I say "false" because true humility values the opinions of
others. To deflect someone's compliment is, in essence, to dismiss his or her
assessment. To receive it is an opportunity to thank God for the grace that
others are seeing in us.

Anger—>Meekness

Scripture describes God as being slow to anger; so we should be, too. "The
LORD is gracious and merciful, slow to anger and abounding in steadfast
love" (Ps. 145:8). Meekness is the quality that restrains anger and is the
redemptive quality we should cultivate. Seventeenth-century theologian
Matthew Henry wrote in his classic work, *The Quest for Meekness and
Quietness of Spirit*, "as patience in case of sorrow, so meekness in case of
anger, keeps *possession* of the soul."[6]

Meekness is not being a doormat. It is the strength to govern our unruly
passions so that we can fulfill the James 1:19 mandate to be slow to speak
and slow to anger. Proverbs 16:32 compares meekness to a valiant warrior
and says that meekness is better: "Whoever is slow to anger is better than
the mighty, and he who rules his spirit than he who takes a city." Proverbs
15 also shows the wisdom of meekness: "A soft answer turns away wrath,
but a harsh word stirs up anger" (15:1).

David gives us a great example of meekness in Psalm 39. As Matthew
Henry writes:

> When our hearts are hot within us it is good for us to keep silent and hold
> our peace; so David did (Psalm 39:3) and when he did speak it was in
> prayer to God and not in reply to the wicked that were before him. . . .
> Those who find themselves wronged and aggrieved think they may have
> permission to speak, but it is better to be silent than to speak amiss and
> make work for repentance. At such a time, he that holds his tongue holds
> his peace; and if we soberly reflect we shall find we have been often the

worse for our speaking, but seldom the worse for our silence . . . [f]or there is nothing said or done in passion but it may be better said and better done afterwards. When we are calm, we shall be likely to say it and do it to a better purpose. *A needful truth, spoken in a heat, may do more hurt than good, and offend rather than satisfy* (emphasis added).[7]

Friends, meekness is required for that priceless inner beauty. The "gentle and quiet spirit" of a woman with inner beauty (1 Peter 3:4) is sometimes also translated as a "meek and quiet spirit." As author Barbara Hughes notes, this quality "isn't weakness or spinelessness or timidity or even niceness. This word in classical Greek was used to describe tame animals, soothing medicine, a mild word, and a mild breeze. It is a word with a caress in it."[8] I like that idea. When we speak, we can either pierce like a sword or soothe with a verbal caress. That's the redemptive quality of meekness.

Gossip—>Discretion

I love "scoop." If you've got good news, I want to know about it. I can't help it. My professional training is as a journalist. It's not that I'm a busybody, of course. Well, okay, maybe a *little* bit of a busybody. All right, all right. I'll be honest. It's a significant temptation for me! I'm writing this section with a bit of trepidation because I know one of my wonderful friends is going to quote this to me in the future as sure as the sun rises and sets! And that's not because *they* are predictable but because *I* am.

Let's be candid here: We all have "itching ears" because we like to be in the know. Information is power. That's why we don't want to be the last to hear of something, good or bad. I call good news "scoop" and differentiate it from damaging gossip or backbiting slander. But at its root, I think it's not all that different. It's still news about someone else.

When I was new to my church, I'd sometimes hear people ask with genuine concern, "Do you think what I just said cast anyone in a bad light?" That was an odd question to me then. *"Cast anyone in a bad light?" Well, is it true? If so, who cares? It's the truth.* I had not yet learned one powerful aspect of gossip: "The words of a gossip are like choice morsels; they go down to a man's inmost parts" (Prov. 18:8 NIV). In other words, gossip settles into our guts and stays there, poisoning our whole system. I also wasn't accounting for the fact that truth is rarely complete in only one person's account. Proverbs 18:17 says: "The one who states his case first seems right, until the other comes and examines him."

Ladies, Scripture says this is an area of particular weakness for us. When Paul was instructing Timothy, the apostle advised the young pastor not to allow young widows to join the widow's roll—the local church charity for these women—because it would, among many things, tempt the younger women to indulge in gossip: "As for younger widows, do not put them on such a list. For when their sensual desires overcome their dedication to Christ, they want to marry. Thus they bring judgment on themselves, because they have broken their first pledge. Besides, they get into the habit of being idle and going about from house to house. And not only do they become idlers, but also gossips and busybodies, saying things they ought not to. So I counsel younger widows to marry, to have children, to manage their homes *and to give the enemy no opportunity for slander*" (1 Tim. 5:11-14 NIV, emphasis added).

Give the *enemy* no opportunity for slander? When I first read that verse, I thought the apostle meant that single women were a reproach to the church and thus were the *objects* of slander. But I think a more accurate understanding is that we can be a *tool* for our spiritual adversary's goal of slandering God and His creatures. We can fall into repeating lies from the very pit of hell itself! This is very serious. Gossip is deadly to fellowship. It has split numerous churches throughout history. It has ruined friendships and damaged marriages. It is a demonic weapon, and the enemy looks for every opportunity to wield it.

The apostle Paul has an additional concern here. He notes *two* ways in which we can say things that we ought not to—as gossips and as busybodies. I think of these two words as the difference between slander and scoop. A gossip passes on reports that damage other people's reputations, are sinfully motivated, and are possibly untrue. A busybody repeats matters that aren't negative or gossip—and may even be good news—but that aren't really necessary for *her* to repeat. It's taken a long time to sink in, but I think I've finally learned that this applies even to good news like engagements. Why steal thunder from other people? Let them tell their own good news. (Please don't misunderstand me. It's not that I think we can *never* share good news. But are we human news stations, broadcasting to everyone within hearing range? That's a busybody.)

The redemptive quality for sinful and even idle talk is discretion. It's a quality we touched on in the previous chapter. Discretion is a fruit of cultivating wisdom. In Proverbs 2, the writer is instructing his son in the benefits of calling out for insight and crying aloud for wisdom. He says the fruit of seeking wisdom is that "discretion will protect you, and understanding will guard you" (Prov. 2:11 NIV). Discretion protects us from saying things we will later regret. I like to think of discretion as God's "blurt control."

Here are some helpful guidelines for cultivating discretion:

• Would I be embarrassed if the person I am talking about were to overhear what I am saying?

• Am I, or the person I am talking to, part of either the problem or the solution? If not, I am probably gossiping.

• Do I need to use someone's name in this account, or would a generic version get my point across just as well?

• Am I thinking through the impact of my words? I once read that THINK is a great memory aid for evaluating our words. Is it True? Helpful? Important? Necessary? Kind? If not, it's probably about to become a tool in the enemy's hands.

The beauty of discretion is that it is loving: "Whoever covers an offense seeks love, but he who repeats a matter separates close friends" (Prov. 17:9). This is what Jesus did for us on the cross—in love He covered our offenses with His blood and brought those who were separated from Him into eternal life. When we use The Pause and consider whether our words are discreet, we are seeking to love others as Jesus loves us.

Complaining—>Thanksgiving

I mentioned Mark Dever's insightful message on Ruth in chapter 3. During that sermon, he drove home a great point about Naomi's complaints against God. He said that every breath we have is from God; thus we should steward well every word that comes out of our mouths. Have you ever thought of stewarding your breath in this way? I had not until then.

Philippians 2:14 says, "Do all things without grumbling or questioning." All things? Yes. The next verse goes on to tell us why: "that you may be blameless and innocent, children of God without blemish in the midst of a crooked and twisted generation, among whom you shine as lights in the world." The New International Version translates this passage as "do everything without complaining or arguing." Complaining, grumbling, arguing, questioning—these are the hallmarks of a crooked and twisted generation. When we avoid those behaviors, we shine as bright lights.

Why is the Bible concerned about complaining? Because complaining drowns out our witness that God is good and His ways are best. This is significant when we think of our singleness. As we grumble, question, argue, and complain about our status, we are contradicting our gospel witness. We are saying, in effect, that salvation is good but *not as good* as getting married. We might think we're justified in complaining about this (or other issues), but as one of my pastors, Chris Silard, said in a recent sermon: "When we justify our complaining, we are crossing out the word *all* from this command."

Why is this so serious? For one reason, Chris says, in the church it's serious because of the way it disrupts the harmony of the people and hinders the work of grace and the advancement of the gospel. He adds, "But it's more serious than that. When we grumble and question and complain, we have become God's judge. We have told Him at least two things: 1) You are not enough for me. I cannot be content with things the way they are. This difficulty is too great for me to respond to in a way that pleases You. You are deficient, and ultimately You do not satisfy me. I want a different God. 2) You are not wise. If I were You, God, I would do things differently. You should have consulted me before You allowed this difficulty in my life or before You chose to keep that good thing from me that I want and don't have."[9]

So what is the redemptive quality we can exchange for complaining? It is thanksgiving: "Pray without ceasing, give thanks in all circumstances; for this is the will of God in Christ Jesus for you" (1 Thess. 5:17-18).

My niece Natalie and my nephew Patrick came with me to church on the Sunday that Chris gave this message. Afterward we went out to lunch. On the way, we talked about how to apply what we'd heard at church to our time together at lunch. We all agreed we wouldn't complain about how long it takes us to get our food at the restaurant. Why? Because no matter how long it might take to get our food, we could reasonably expect we would end up with something to eat—which is more than many children around the world receive. We can offer thanksgiving for the provision of food and stifle the complaining about the rest of it because we have been richly blessed. In light of all that we have, our complaining is doubly scandalous.

"Through Jesus, therefore, *let us continually offer to God a sacrifice of praise*—the fruit of lips that confess his name" (Heb. 13:15 NIV, emphasis added).

Sinful Judgments—>Charitable Judgments

I've found it to be true that at the root of most sinful speech is a sinful judgment. Sinful judgment is when we assume we know all the facts of any given situation and haven't overlooked anything, that we know why someone has done or said (or *not* done or *not* said) something, and that there is no possible reason why this situation could have happened in any other way. Thus, when we speak, we skip over asking questions for more information and head straight to judgment. Examples of sinful judgment in our speech usually start with these phrases:

- "I know why you did (or said) this . . ."
- "You/I always . . ."
- "You/I never . . ."
- "I'm tired of always . . ."

Ken Sande, president of Peacemaker Ministries, teaches with great clarity about this topic. He writes:

> This is not to say that it is inherently wrong to evaluate or even judge others within certain limits. Scripture teaches that we should observe and evaluate others' behavior so that we can respond and minister to them in appropriate ways, which may even involve loving confrontation (see Matthew 7:1-5; 18:15; Galatians 6:1).
>
> We cross the line, however, when we begin to sinfully judge others, which is characterized by a feeling of superiority, indignation, condemnation, bitterness, or resentment. Sinful judging often involves speculating on others' motives. Most of all, it reveals the absence of a genuine love and concern toward them. When these attitudes are present, our judging has crossed the line and we are playing God.[10]

Proverbs calls us foolish for doing this. "A fool takes no pleasure in understanding, but only in expressing his opinion" (Prov. 18:2). "He who answers before listening—that is his folly and his shame" (Prov. 18:13 NIV).

The redemptive quality that is an antidote to sinful judgment is a "charitable judgment" or a loving judgment. When we are tempted to think the worst about a situation, we have to remind ourselves we simply don't know the whole picture and resolve to *believe the best* until our questions reveal something different. When a friend doesn't call us, for example, we can sinfully judge her for not caring about us. Or we can make a charitable judgment—assuming that her silence is for a reason wholly unrelated—until we have the facts. More often than not, we will later find out that she's been traveling, sick, swamped at work, or caring for someone else.

The gospel deposit we can make here is humility—recognizing that each of us in these situations is a sinner for whom Jesus died. We shouldn't be self-righteous about the sins of others—real or imagined. Instead, we should follow the principles of Philippians 4:8: "Finally, brothers, whatever is *true*, whatever is *honorable*, whatever is *just*, whatever is *pure*, whatever is *lovely*, whatever is *commendable*, if there is any *excellence*, if there is anything *worthy of praise*, think about these things" (emphasis added). The truest, most honorable, most just, purest, loveliest, most commendable, and excellent thing we can consider is the cross, the place where mercy and justice meet.

PREPARED TO ANSWER

Finally, I'd like to address one area of wise speech that I think is unique to single adults, one that requires every bit of the wisdom and kindness we find in the Proverbs 31 woman.

Do you remember the awkward scene in chapter 1 at my high school reunion? I was asked all those "unhelpful questions" about being single. Here is a situation requiring wise, grace-filled speech, especially when worldly wisdom is offered to us as a "solution" for our current singleness. First Peter 3:15-16 (NIV) says, "But in your hearts set apart Christ as Lord. *Always be prepared to give an answer* to everyone who asks you to give the reason for the hope that you have. But do this with *gentleness* and *respect*, keeping a clear conscience, so that those who speak maliciously against your good behavior in Christ may be ashamed of their slander" (emphasis added).

When I hear one of those questions coming my way, my instinct is to bat it away as hard as I can and avoid the topic. But that's not the counsel that Peter gives us. He says that first we need to set apart Christ as Lord. Christ is Lord over our singleness and over the current conversation. If we lose sight of that, we are already walking away from the path of wisdom. Second, we need to be prepared. We shouldn't be surprised when someone makes a crack at a wedding or when a colleague wants to know if we have a "hot date" for Valentine's Day. We should be prepared with a thought-out, rehearsed, and gracious reply that is delivered with gentleness (a caress, not a sword thrust) and respect. In fact, a question like this is an opportunity to thank God rather than complain. Questions can be open doors for sharing our faith if we are prepared to walk through them.

This mind-set, however, runs contrary to my natural instincts. I like to hide behind humor instead. When someone asks, "How's your love life?" I am tempted to say, "My love life? Enough about me! Let's discuss *your* love life." When someone asks, "Why are you still single?" I want to reply, "Why are you still obnoxious?" And so on. But those aren't answers that set apart Christ as Lord; neither are they gentle or respectful.

We should anticipate both the longer, more intimate discussions with good friends and family, as well as the casual conversations that require a prepared, pithy response. One comment many singles hear frequently is that we need to be out and about, running from one event to another so that we can "broaden our horizons." People who advise single women that way may mean well, but they don't have a place for God in their thinking. They can't imagine a God who orchestrates the events and timing of our lives to the tiniest details. This is a wonderful opportunity to testify to the One who sees the beginning from the end, who always was and will be, who is everywhere present. You can't get broader horizons than this, and this same God has His eye on us and hears our prayers.

Ladies, our Proverbs 31 woman models God's standard for our words, and by the grace of God, we can grow into it. In all of our conversations, may we pause, remember the gospel and our roles as His ambassadors, and ever strive to emulate the wisdom of Proverbs 16:24:

> *Gracious words are like a honeycomb,*
> *sweetness to the soul and health to the body.*

For Further Study

❖ I highly recommend *War of Words: Getting to the Heart of Your Communication Struggles* by Paul David Tripp (P&R Publishing). The quotes I chose for this chapter give a brief overview of the fine teaching in this book, but they don't do it justice. Though there are tremendous numbers of practical application points in this book, the heart of it is the gospel.

❖ *The Quest for Meekness and Quietness of Spirit* by Matthew Henry is carried by Soli Deo Gloria Publications, which reprints classic Christian literature. Though you will encounter little-known words in this book, like "froward" (which means stubbornly contrary and disobedient; obstinate), overall it's not a difficult read and well worth any extra effort you may put into it. Here's a classic quote: "A meek and quiet Christian must needs live very comfortably, for he enjoys himself, he enjoys his friends, he enjoys his God, and he puts it out of the reach of his enemies to disturb him in these enjoyments."

❖ I quoted from some of Ken Sande's articles on the Peacemaker Ministries Web site. That Web site is a tremendous resource itself. The address (I hope it will not change in the near future) is www.hispeace.org. Ken is also the author of *The Peacemaker: A Biblical Guide to Resolving Personal Conflict* (Baker Books). You will never look at conflict the same way after reading this book—it's an opportunity to glorify God! This Web site also carries Alfred Poirer's excellent article, "The Cross and Criticism."

12

REACHING OUT TO THE NEEDY

She opens her hand to the poor and reaches out her hands to the needy.

PROVERBS 31:20

These days we've hardly gotten Christmas cleaned up and put away before stores are festooned in red and pink. The buildup for Valentine's Day—or "National Singles Awareness Day" as a friend coined it—is a solid three to four weeks of diamond ads, rose peddlers, heart-shaped candy, and photos everywhere of smiling couples gazing at each other in rapt, adoring attention. When you're single and unattached, it's hard to go anywhere and not be reminded that you aren't part of this national love fest.

One year I left my local shopping mall with a heavy, gray blob of self-pity bobbing behind me. As I got into my car, I looked across the street to the looming assisted-living center. The facility is attractive and blends in with the surrounding neighborhood, but suddenly it caught my attention. I wondered how many people there might not receive anything on Valentine's Day either. With that thought, I heard a small pop in my soul and felt a sudden release. The gray blob of self-pity had dissipated.

A few weeks later, I was standing with a group of friends in one of the reception rooms of this assisted-living center. We were a small army importing a party. We had brought in fine china, linens, candles, tea, and dessert to host a Valentine's tea for some of the residents. The men in my caregroup (the term my church uses for our small groups) typically would do something nice for the ladies around this time, a mass Valentine's Day activity.

But this year we decided to turn our focus outward. One of the women in my caregroup—Joanie—visited this home regularly to see her grandmother. So we decided to make Joanie's grandmother the guest of honor for Valentine's Day and invite her friends to join us.

As our guests arrived, we seated them at small tables with different members of our group. The conversation at each table soon grew animated as my friends asked open-ended questions to become acquainted with our guests: "What's your earliest Valentine's Day memory?" "What was your most memorable Valentine's Day?" "What's one piece of advice you would give young adults now about this holiday?" And so on. In some cases, those questions led to conversations about the gospel and our church. At the end, we prayed for our guests and thanked them for coming.

The evening passed remarkably fast, leaving fond memories and dirty dishes. As we cleaned up, we agreed that this was one of our best Valentine's Days. By turning our attention away from ourselves, we became vessels to demonstrate the love of God in a practical way to others. There was nothing particularly heroic about this event. We didn't solve the problems of the world. We simply gave away a small amount of time and material resources to surprise and delight others.

A CALL TO CHANGE FOCUS

Let's be honest. One great temptation of singleness is an unrelenting self-focus. We need to be reminded to look outside of our circumstances and ourselves. I chose this Valentine's Day story for that specific reason, even though it's not a remarkable story of outreach or investment. In fact, it's rather ordinary. But it strikes at the heart of a common temptation, don't you think? If Valentine's Day is hard because we think everyone else is out celebrating their romances (which isn't as common among married couples as we'd like to speculate), then we can turn our gaze inward and start pondering that gray blob of self-pity. We translate singleness into loneliness.

Ladies, when those temptations come, those are grace moments. That's when we need to literally, *out loud*, ask for God's grace to respond differently. In those moments, I have a mental picture of our Father peering intensely at us with a big encouraging smile—the way parents do as a child is just starting to walk: "Come on, come on—you can do it! Ask Me for the power to respond differently. Take the next step. Hold out your hand and ask Me for help." Our Father is ready and willing to give us all we need to step out.

His outpouring of grace is not dependent on our requests, but it's a wonderful exercise to ask Him.

To encounter loneliness through the eyes of faith is to see opportunities to minister love. Grace translates singleness into outreach. There are plenty of people on, say, Valentine's Day or New Year's Eve, or at parties or weddings—single *and* married—who need someone to carry God's love to them. With this perspective, let's resolve when we next feel lonely or awkward, to use those emotions to remind us that others nearby may be feeling the same way.

The opportunities to minister love abound, and that's the point of our Proverbs 31 verse for this chapter: "She opens her hand to the poor and reaches out her hands to the needy" (v. 20). There are three spiritual benefits to serving the poor and needy around us: 1) It glorifies God and blesses others; 2) It builds our local churches; 3) It's a great antidote to self-pity. That's our topic for this chapter, and we'll be looking at various ways we can fulfill this in our lives.

WHO ARE THE POOR AND NEEDY?

When we hear "poor and needy," we often think of the overwhelming poverty of various developing nations. Their desperation is so critical it can be numbing to consider. From a distance, it's hard to know how to make a difference. We are tempted to think that one individual really can't change anything, and thus we end up not doing anything at all.

I think we need to start where the Proverbs 31 woman did. The verbs here—*opens, reaches out*—demonstrate active concern. There is initiative in these concepts. I get the picture from this verse that the poor and needy aren't too far away, but just enough out of reach that they could be ignored or overlooked unless this woman was stretching to meet their needs. She reached out to those she could touch—those whose paths crossed hers.

But this is only a start. Because our mass media allows us to "cross paths" with nearly everyone in the world, we will have a broader awareness of the poor and needy than women of biblical times. I hope that instead of producing "crisis fatigue," this will remind us of how limited we are—and inspire us to pray fervently to the One who is not limited. We need to ask our Father to intervene where we cannot go and seek His direction for the strategic use of our resources (time, talent, treasures). We may not be able to personally end genocidal wars, but we can intercede each day on behalf

of the terrified victims. We may not be able to end famines, but we can partner financially with church ministries and Christian relief agencies that not
only meet the physical needs in these areas but also address the eternal ones.
And who knows? As we seek the Father's will, He may direct us to become
more personally invested in such causes.

Such was the case for my friend Joanie by the way. She spent two years
teaching and serving in the African country of Burkina Faso. When she
returned, she continued this pattern of service in her local church—serving both the elderly and children alike in her daily life. I know of other single women who are serving and investing in their church's ministry for AIDS
orphans. The examples abound.

As the old saying goes, a journey of a thousand miles begins with a single step. Where is the next step we can take to purposefully emulate this
Proverbs 31 virtue? Who are the poor and needy within our reach? Who are
those in our churches, our communities—even our families—who would
benefit from our outreach to them? The Hebrew word for "poor" in this verse
is *'ānî*, which broadly means those who are objectively "depressed in mind
or circumstances, afflicted, humble, lowly, needy, poor."[1] The word for
"needy" in this verse is *'ebyôn*, which emphasizes the sense of want (especially in feeling) or the state of being destitute, as a beggar.[2]

This applies to many people right around us. We don't have to look very
far to find them. In fact, the Lord has a way of putting them right in front
of us.

AN ARRANGED RELATIONSHIP

I was standing near the receptionist's desk when Sheree first called my
church. She'd found an invitation to our upcoming Christmas Eve service,
and she wanted a ride. I couldn't help overhearing the conversation.
Seriously. The receptionist was shouting very loudly: "Yes! That's right,
Christmas Eve, *not* Christmas Day. . . . No, *no* bus. We don't have a bus.
Someone can give you a ride. Where do you live? . . . *Live.* Where is your
house? . . . Your *house.* Where is it?"

Sheree lives in the neighborhood where my caregroup was then meeting. So I thought that someone in that area would be glad to give her a ride.
The Lord apparently had other ideas. No one else could help her. Evidently,
there was a reason I was there when she called, and it wasn't just to arrange
a ride for her. The Lord wanted me to arrange a relationship.

That was more than five years ago. We've been friends ever since. Sheree is a single woman only two years older than I am. Whenever we go out, I wheel her up to my car and help her get in. Then I stow her wheelchair in the trunk. When we drive, conversation only happens at stoplights so that I can turn to her when I speak. She needs to see my lips to make sense of the muffled words. Even though her eyesight is too weak to read anything other than the occasional large print publication, she can always spot the coffee shops as we drive past. Coffee is one of her sole consolations.

Sheree's life changed when she was thirteen. Her headaches had grown severe, and tests revealed the dreaded reason—a benign tumor growing in her brain stem, too entangled among vital nerves and arteries to risk surgery. By the time Sheree was seventeen, radiation had slowed the tumor's growth, providing Sheree with a brief window of "normal" life. She graduated from high school and lived and worked on her own for a few years. But slowly the tumor took her independence hostage, eroding her sight, hearing, and physical coordination.

But it didn't take away her desire for the pleasures of normal life. Now, at age forty-two, she lives in a group home for those with various head injuries and traumas. One of her roommates, Kathy, was injured in a drunk-driving accident when she was a teenager, and she's been in a wheelchair ever since.

One time the three of us sat in their house looking at high school yearbooks and talking about our memories. It was a sobering reminder of how similar our upbringing and backgrounds were. In high school, none of the three of us expected then that our futures would be what they are now. But to her credit, Sheree looked forward to her twentieth high school reunion—unlike me, her self-conscious friend. She wasn't concerned about being in a wheelchair. She wanted to see her old friends. My caregroup pitched in and bought her a new dress to wear, and one of the ladies did her makeup while I did her hair. Sheree looked very pretty that day, but I think it was her eager smile that made her appealing.

I am aware that I had a choice that December day in the church office. I believe God was putting Sheree in my path—there was no mistaking that. But I've never seen her as an "outreach project." It just blesses her when I reach out my hand to her in friendship. In fact, Sheree has pursued the friendship in some ways more than I have. Is she one of the poor? She doesn't have income of her own, but she's not destitute—thanks to her fam-

ily and various government agencies. Is she one of the needy? She is definitely physically afflicted, but to her credit I've never heard her complain
about this. She doesn't have a wide circle of friends, however, and so I count
it a privilege to be among them.

Open Wide Your Hand

Our generosity to the poor and needy honors God and reflects His generosity to us. Proverbs 14:31 says, "Whoever oppresses a poor man insults
his Maker, but he who is generous to the needy honors him." It is God's
nature to be generous and compassionate, and He is the ultimate deliverer.
That's why Psalm 72:12-13 refers to God in this way: "For he delivers the
needy when he calls, the poor and him who has no helper. He has pity on
the weak and the needy, and saves the lives of the needy."

God has said a lot in the Bible about our treatment of the poor. In
Deuteronomy 15, the Lord gives the Israelites a series of commands
designed to keep them from being stingy toward their brothers and sisters
in need. Verse 11 says: "For there will never cease to be poor in the land.
Therefore I command you, 'You shall open wide your hand to your brother,
to the needy and to the poor, in your land.'"

Open wide your hand. This is a command. It's not just a guideline for a
certain group of people living in a certain period. The Old Testament commands are actually expanded and amplified in the New Testament. Luke
12:33 presents an invitation to outrageous generosity: "Sell your possessions, and give to the needy. Provide yourselves with moneybags that do not
grow old, with a treasure in the heavens that does not fail, where no thief
approaches and no moth destroys." In Acts 4:34-35 we find a rare model of
obedience to this command. Referring to the first days of the church in
Jerusalem, it says, "There was not a needy person among them, for as many
as were owners of lands or houses sold them and brought the proceeds of
what was sold and laid it at the apostles' feet, and it was distributed to each
as any had need."

Contrast this praise to the condemnation of Sodom, found in Ezekiel
16:49: "Behold, this was the guilt of your sister Sodom: she and her daughters had pride, excess of food, and prosperous ease, but did not aid the poor
and needy." Referring to this city as a feminine entity is a biblical literary
device, but doesn't it strike a little closer to home to read it this way? Pride,

excess of food, prosperous ease—I think these adjectives accurately and fairly describe current American culture.

I was shamefully reminded of this Scripture a few years ago when I got talked into an expensive visit to the hair salon. But I had agreed to all the steps involved, never asking how much they cost. I don't fault my stylist; this is her job, her focus. She was offering a creative solution to me. It's not her responsibility to consider if this is money wisely spent or not—that's *my* burden. I was still smarting when I got home and retrieved the mail. In the wise, loving providence of God, I had received an urgent plea from a relief agency I support. This group was appealing for designated gifts to alleviate a famine crisis in an African country. I was stunned when I read that for the exact amount I had just spent on my hair, I could have purchased *a metric ton of food* for the victims of this famine.

I received that loving adjustment from my heavenly Father. On my next visit to the salon, I explained to my stylist what had happened. I then said that when I viewed my expenses through the grid of my faith, I couldn't justify dumping that much money on my head when that amount could spare someone's life. She understood and proceeded to offer less expensive alternatives.

I certainly have more room to grow in honoring my Lord and Savior through my generosity to the poor and needy. But ultimately I want to make sure, by God's grace, that what was said of the residents of Sodom is not said of me.

Not a Needy Person Among Them

I have mentioned Christian relief agencies a few times in this chapter, but I don't want to give anyone an improper perspective. I do think that it is imperative for us to give generously to relieve the physical suffering and religious persecution of those in other places. But I am always brought up short by that simple statement from Acts 4:34: "there was not a needy person among them." *Among* them!

Here again is that idea of helping those who are within our reach, namely right within our own churches. In my church, we have the privilege of serving a single man in his sixties who has been a quadriplegic since a diving accident in his twenties. Like Sheree, Richard is not destitute, but he has no income other than various government programs—and these certainly don't cover all of his needs. For years a faithful troupe of families, couples, and singles alike has been helping Richard with a variety of needs from personal care to transportation. My friend Susan is among them. For several years, she has used her nursing experience to help Richard with routine medical care. For a long period, she gave up every Friday night to help him. Sometimes she would go over several times a week when others on the team couldn't make it. She always said it was her joy to serve Richard. Her life backed that up—she was my roommate during that time, and I witnessed her service up close. (By the way, Susan met the man who would become her husband while they were both helping Richard. Just another proof that you don't have to be seen out and about "broadening your horizons" to meet the man God has for you.)

In the same way, those within churches are to care for their family members. In 1 Timothy 5:16, Paul instructs Timothy: "If any believing woman has relatives who are widows, let her care for them. Let the church not be burdened, so that it may care for those who are really widows."

Here is clear instruction to women to care for our own relatives, especially those who are among us in the church. Dear sisters in the Lord, you may be young and your parents active and healthy. This duty might seem very far away to you. But I hope that reading this section will help prepare you for whatever God has in the future. I am the executor for my parents' estates, and we've had numerous conversations about their preferences for the future. No doubt we still have much to discuss. Given the family obligations of my sisters, I assume that as a single woman, the privilege will be mine to care for my parents in the future. (Though they may have another preference!) And I do mean *privilege*. Not only would it be a blessing to care for two precious people who have lavished so much care on me, but it would also honor and glorify God.

I am watching another friend of mine serve in this way. She is caring for her widowed father now. Do you remember my friend Vivian Saavedra, with the top ten list in the first chapter? Last year Vivian lost her mother to pancreatic cancer. Her mother's illness was brief but intense—and her funeral was a God-glorifying event.

I visited Mrs. Saavedra twice in the last week of her life. The image of one visit is burned indelibly in my memory. Vivian had moved back into her childhood home to help her father care for her mother. As her mother's cancer progressed, Vivian and her father performed all the routine nursing care. One evening when I visited, Vivian gave her mother her pain medicine and insulin shots and then sat by the bed rubbing cream into her mother's swollen legs. Her mother lay in a cotton nightgown, illuminated only by the soft lamp on the nightstand. Mrs. Saavedra didn't have the energy to talk, but she was luminously peaceful. I sat quietly by, somewhat stunned by the dying process. I had never spent this much time before with someone in the last hours of life.

The only sound in the room was a worship CD playing a beautiful melody sung by a vocalist with a sweet, bell-like tone:

And when the storms swirl and rage
There are mercies anew
In affliction and pain
You will carry me through
And at the end of my days
When Your throne fills my view
I will sing of Your mercies anew.[3]

When I looked over at Vivian, both of us were crying. The sweet truth of what the cross promised for Mrs. Saavedra elicited our bittersweet tears and our heartfelt worship.

Since her mother's death, Vivian continues to live with her father. Though he is in reasonably good health, she helps him with the household chores. After more than fifty years of marriage, Mr. Saavedra has to create a new rhythm of life, and Vivian is there to help her dad with this transition. She's declined other offers to change her living arrangements because she considers caring for her father her priority right now. This means she commutes longer to work and to church, but she considers neither a sacrifice. In this way, Vivian is fulfilling the 1 Timothy 5:16 requirement.

PERSONAL APPLICATION

This chapter just skims the myriad of ways we can be others-oriented and bless the poor and needy. I hope it has triggered some ideas of your own for additional ways to serve. Are there people in your church who could benefit from your friendship, your help, and your generosity? What about the mercy ministries in your church—prison ministries, after-school programs, international outreach ministries, etc.? Whom do you see in your community on a regular basis who might need to receive the love of Jesus through you?

I hope you will prayerfully consider these ideas. As you do, I would also want to pass along the wisdom I've gleaned from others in my own ventures. Though we single women may have more time and flexibility to serve, we still need to proceed "in community." Our actions aren't conducted in a vacuum. For example, if we bring a homeless hitchhiker home on the spur of the moment, the others in our household may not understand. We need to be mindful of all those affected by our service. I know of a single women's household years ago that reached out to a prostitute and let her live with them for a period. Everyone in the house was in agreement on this matter before it happened; so there was harmony in their service.

There are also benefits for us being "in community" as we serve. One is the counsel of others about our approach. I learned this when I was a mentor or "big sister" at a crisis pregnancy center for several years—one of the outreach ministries of my local church. I gleaned so much from those days. The first thing I learned is that I default to "fixing" other people instead of helping them to find solutions on their own. This tendency is motivated by pride—"Here, let *me* fix you!" The executive director suggested that I change my approach. She said my help ultimately would be ineffective because I wasn't enabling these women to find solutions on their own, and conflict could result when they would come to resent my heavy-handed advice. She was right on both counts. I'm glad I had her oversight and input.

The second benefit of serving "in community" is that we can't do it all by ourselves. I need the help of others in my church. Not only am I called to my church to serve *them*, but I believe I am also called to serve *with* them. I found that to be particularly true when helping at the pregnancy center. I may have been the primary volunteer, but my whole caregroup (a mix of singles and families at that time) was involved. They helped me with baby showers and attended with gifts. They helped with rides. They contributed finances. They offered parenting advice when I had none. They even helped with legal problems in one case (it was great to have a lawyer in the group). Because this community ministry was a priority for my local church, my church in effect served with me.

A third benefit to serving "in community" is that because there can be risk involved in outreach, we can ask for advice and assistance. In my experience, poverty in this country is more complicated than a simple lack of available resources. We are a prosperous nation, by the grace of God. So in our country, there are usually several contributing factors to poverty—ranging from substance abuse to immigration obstacles. Sometimes these problems are too much for one person to tackle, and they can also become quickly compounded by our sin natures. For example, when we volunteer, we usually would like to be appreciated. That can quickly tip over to demanding gratitude. Those we help may sense they are a "project" and not a friend, and they might respond with resentment or anger. When those problems arise, we need the wisdom of others to help us sort out our reactions and the limitations we perceive. We also need their wisdom regarding physical risk. Some situations just aren't appropriate for single women.

Finally, I would caution against one-on-one service to men. Minimally, it might create romantic expectations where none were intended. Men were designed to want women's help and support, and this is an attractive quality, as we've already considered. But generally I've found it's not fruitful. (There's a reason why men generally find it easier to receive ongoing correction from other men but call it nagging when it comes from women!) One woman I befriended through the pregnancy center was still involved with her baby's father. Both became my friends, and on several occasions I presumed to counsel and correct this man. Over time I saw little change, and I began to doubt my usefulness. I remember after one difficult evening asking the Lord why this man wasn't changing. Par for the course, the Holy Spirit didn't answer my proud question about another person. Instead, He corrected *me*. I felt strongly impressed that I had overstepped my bounds in attempting to disciple the man. I should have gotten out of the way and encouraged him to build this kind of relationship with another man. Fortunately, because I was volunteering "in community," I was able to ask my caregroup leader to help me—and he was more than willing to do it.

THE WATCHING WORLD

I hope these practical applications didn't dampen your zeal to be one who "opens her hand to the poor and reaches out her hands to the needy." This is a convicting verse in the Proverbs 31 collection because we can't overlook its importance in our witness to a watching world. James 2:14-20 is point blank about the implications of faith without good works:

> *What good is it, my brothers, if someone says he has faith but does not have works? Can that faith save him? If a brother or sister is poorly clothed and lacking in daily food, and one of you says to them, "Go in peace, be warmed and filled," without giving them the things needed for the body, what good is that? So also faith by itself, if it does not have works, is dead. But someone will say, "You have faith and I have works." Show me your faith apart from your works, and I will show you my faith by my works. You believe that God*

is one; you do well. Even the demons believe—and shudder! Do you want to be shown, you foolish person, that faith apart from works is useless?

When the early church was faithful to the scriptural mandate to give generously to those in need, unbelievers were drawn to them. Concluding a section about the church's giving, Acts 5:14 says, "And more than ever believers were added to the Lord, multitudes of both men and women." May this be true in our own churches! As author and professor Donald Whitney writes, "The goal of each of us should be to serve in the church in such a way that it is stronger because we are there."4

More importantly, when we care for the poor and needy, we are serving Christ Himself. This is the lesson Jesus taught his disciples on the Mount of Olives (Matt. 25:34-40):

> *Then the King will say to those on his right, "Come, you who are blessed by my Father, inherit the kingdom prepared for you from the foundation of the world. For I was hungry and you gave me food, I was thirsty and you gave me drink, I was a stranger and you welcomed me, I was naked and you clothed me, I was sick and you visited me, I was in prison and you came to me." Then the righteous will answer him, saying, "Lord, when did we see you hungry and feed you, or thirsty and give you drink? And when did we see you a stranger and welcome you, or naked and clothe you? And when did we see you sick or in prison and visit you?" And the King will answer them, "Truly, I say to you, as you did it to one of the least of these my brothers, you did it to me."*

What a sweet commendation from the One who gives us the grace and ability to do these righteous acts in His name! May the promise of such words from our Savior make us known as disciples like Dorcas, a woman commended as being "full of good works and acts of charity" (Acts 9:36).

FOR FURTHER STUDY

❖ If you realize you lack a heart for the local church and a vision for serving there, I'd like to recommend *Spiritual Disciplines Within the Church: Participating Fully in the Body of Christ* by Donald S. Whitney (Moody Press).

13

LAUGHING AT THE TIME TO COME

Strength and dignity are her clothing, and she laughs at the time to come.

PROVERBS 31:25

Lisa sipped quietly from her china teacup, staring thoughtfully at the remaining scone on her plate. The late afternoon autumn sunlight bathed her in a champagne hue as she mulled over her memories. Outside the window, I could see the colonial-era buildings of Annapolis, Maryland. Inside, baroque classical music floated above the quiet female conversations and clinking of teapots.

Breaking her reverie, Lisa returned to the present and fixed her gaze on me. "I've just lately realized why I've been discontented with being single all these years," she said. "I've been thinking God has been withholding marriage from me; so I've been withholding my affection from Him. But if I'd known Him better, I would have known this isn't His character; this isn't His heart for me."

Sensing this was a moment to capture, I set down my teacup and grabbed a pen to take notes on the paper doily.

"I wish I hadn't wasted my forties being discontented about my single-ness," she continued. "I mean, it wasn't easy in my thirties either, but I *really* took it hard in my forties. Now that I've turned fifty, I'm suddenly a lot more aware of eternity. What do I have to show for those years? When you're young, with so much time ahead of you, you have expectations for your life. But as you get older, you find out it's true—time *flies*! And you become aware of how 'light and momentary' our afflictions are. I don't think I ever thought about eternity when I was younger. But now I see how close eternity is and how short this life is—and I wonder what I've been building that will last."

I nodded sympathetically, marveling with her at God's grace in showing her these things.

"I think people tried to tell me over the years that I was more discontented than I realized, but it was always someone who had gotten married at twenty who told me that! I didn't think they could possibly understand me. I had so many expectations wrapped up in a husband. In a way, I'm glad I didn't get married earlier because I would have dumped all of it on this poor guy, and who could handle that?"

Undistracted by my scribbling, Lisa grinned wryly and continued, "Of course, I still want to get married. I'd rather be at home right now with my husband, watching a football game. But I don't have a husband; so here I sit having tea with you. And you know what? That's an answer to prayer because I just asked God for something fun to do—I've been working so much lately. I guess I've just learned to be a lot more thankful for my life. I talk to God a lot now about my life, and I take even the smallest requests to Him. And this is a good thing because in the past my bitterness kept our conversations short."

As Lisa spoke, her earnestness was confirmed by her countenance. She is a beautiful woman, but as she spoke, she glowed. I was amazed that inner beauty could be this tangible. But there was a tinge of regret in her expression, too.

"I wish I hadn't judged God for so long. He's been nothing but merciful and compassionate to me."

I've known Lisa for ten years. One of my earliest memories was watching her stand amidst the many families at church, crying about being single. I remember looking at her then, wondering why she wasn't married—as though any of us can evaluate that from outward appearances. But I would not have characterized her as a bitter woman. She is generally gracious and grateful, though I knew she was periodically disappointed about not being married.

However, now Lisa can clearly see how her earlier distrust curtailed her *full* involvement in her church. So she decided to stop holding back, waiting for the change she craved. Instead, she asked where she might serve. She started as a greeter in the new members class and joined a Bible study that challenged her to spend lots of time in the Word. Her faithfulness as a greeter led to various other assignments at church. Most recently she was asked to facilitate the next round of this Bible study she enjoys. Lisa is amazed to see how God is using her in a group of mostly married women. And that difference between them doesn't seem to be such a big deal to her anymore.

Though Lisa would still like to get married, she is more aware of eternity and what she is investing for that time than what she is or is not receiving here. As we talked that afternoon, I heard her make five important points:

- There's only one relationship that's most important eternally.
- Our fruitfulness is more important than our blessings.
- God is sufficient and will provide for our needs and righteous desires.
- God is creative, and He delights in showing us His creative provision.
- We shouldn't judge God but walk trustingly with Him through our years.

Smiling at the Future

Our final Proverbs 31 verse for this book is verse 25: "Strength and dignity are her clothing, and she laughs at the time to come." It might not seem appealing to be clothed in such somber qualities: Where's the fun? Where's the dazzle in that? You'll find it right there in those concepts. The Hebrew word for "strength" is ʿōz, which means strength in various applications, such as force, security, majesty, praise, or even a loud boldness.[1] That sounds like a SWAT team and a royal coronation all in one—hardly a dull moment there. The Hebrew word for "dignity" is *hadar*, which means magnificence, as ornamentation or splendor, with a connotation of excellence, glory, honor, and majesty.[2] This woman is looking *fine!* She has chosen glorious garments, and they speak of her royal association with the King. That relationship is her source of joy, and she can rejoice in her future.

I recently read about a group of women who are literal examples of merry women clad in loud, bold garments. They are the Red Hat Society, whose slogan is "greeting middle age with verve, humor, and élan." This "disorganization," as the Red Hatters call it, has few rules except that its members are women over fifty who meet wearing clashing red hats and purple clothes for the sole purpose of enjoying each other. The group gets its name from the opening lines of a poem by Jenny Joseph:

When I am an old woman I shall wear purple
With a red hat which doesn't go and doesn't suit me.

Women under fifty are welcome to attend, but they must wear more muted hues. As the group's Web site stipulates: "We also suggest rather strongly that women under 50 stick to the pink hat and lavender attire until THE BIRTHDAY. This adds an element of fun to aging, which we think is invaluable to women in our society who have learned to dread aging and avoid it at all costs. We believe that aging should be something anticipated with excitement, not something to dread."[3]

I like their spirit and their embrace of the whole spectrum of life, but I couldn't sing their theme song: "All my life, I've done for you. Now it's my turn to do for me." That's where the party hits a sour note. A woman who has nurtured many others throughout her life should be encouraged to stay the course, not to suddenly become self-centered or frivolous. Though my friend Lisa could now wear the garments of the Red Hat Society, she had decided instead to put on the garments of the Proverbs 31 woman—a much wiser choice.

As we conclude this book, we will be looking at the Proverbs 31 woman's example of how to finish well in the eyes of the Lord in a youth-oriented world. We will see why, no matter how old we are, the best is truly yet to come. Whether your next birthday will be your eighteenth or your eightieth, if you belong to God, you can smile at your future. Why? Because the One who loves you more than any of His creatures *ever* would is already there in your future, and He is beckoning you to follow Him with a trusting heart.

YOUTH SHOWS BUT HALF

I've always liked the sentiment of a popular wedding song, "Grow Old with Me." The opening lines are, "Grow old along with me; the best is yet to be." Though I was generally aware that the opening lyrics were from a poem, I had not read the full poem until recently. Now I understand why the song's lyrics stop short of Robert Browning's complete thought in the first stanza:

Grow old along with me!
The best is yet to be,
The last of life, for which the first was made:
Our times are in his hand
Who saith, "A whole I planned,
Youth shows but half; trust God: see all, nor be afraid!"[4]

Without the acknowledgement of God's loving providence for our lives, we just have the sweet, vaguely hopeful sentiment of the first two lines. But in the third line, the poet throws open the doors and ushers truth into the midst of the frilly emotion—God has planned a *whole* life, of which youth is only a *part*. Our times are in His hands, and He is fully worthy of our trust. There's nothing random about our futures.

Jim Elliot once said, "Wherever you are, be all there." *Be all there.* That can seem like bumper-sticker wisdom—intriguing but ultimately without much depth. However, when you consider Jim's brief twenty-eight years and his demise as a martyred missionary to the Auca Indians of Ecuador,[5] this sentence resonates with godly truth. Wherever you find yourself in God's sovereign plan for your life, be *all* there. We never know how much time we have, but we can be fully engaged in each day we have—living life with an eye toward the eternal.

No doubt we all know women who live like grayed-out software functions—visible but not completely accessible. We are probably like that at different times, too. Despondency drains us of vibrant colors and energy, leaving a dotted-line impression behind. During those times, we are a far cry from the loud boldness of the woman clothed in strength and dignity who can laugh at the days to come.

Why don't we smile at our futures? I think it's because we view that time with the vague dread of a blind date—we're unsure of whom we've committed this time to, where we're going, and whether we're going to like this time together. But I think we'd have a big smile on our faces if we viewed our futures with the happy idea of a honeymoon—anticipating uninterrupted time with the One we love in a beautiful setting. Surely this is what we will experience in eternity, and we will have foretastes of this joy throughout all of our years.

Have you ever noticed how many times the Bible records the faithless reactions of God's people to their uncertain futures and how many times God tells them to recount His faithfulness in the past to them? As John Piper says, this is because "past grace is God's down payment on the fullness of future grace." He continues:

> Actually that image of a one-time down payment doesn't quite work. Past grace is continually accumulating every day. The infinite reservoir of future grace is flowing back through the present into the ever-growing pool of past grace. The inexhaustible reservoir is invisible except through the promises. But the ever-enlarging pool of past grace is visible; and God

means for the certainty and beauty and depth to strengthen our faith in future grace.[6]

As we face our futures, let's examine two common situations that tempt us to be afraid: being alone and death.

Going On Alone

I think that when mankind was banished from the Garden of Eden, it bred in us a legitimate fear of being alone, of being separated from God's presence. But thanks to Jesus, we are fully reconciled to God and will never be alone again. We have full assurances of God's constant care for us. I like the way Jerry Bridges presents this truth:

> One such promise we will do well to store up in our hearts is Hebrews 13:5: "Never will I leave you; never will I forsake you." The Puritan preacher Thomas Lye remarked that in this passage the Greek has five negatives and may thus be rendered, "I will not, not leave thee; neither will I not, not forsake thee." Five times God emphasized to us that He will not forsake us. He wants us to firmly grasp the truth that whatever circumstances may indicate, we must believe, on the basis of His promise, that He has not forsaken us nor left us to the mercy of those circumstances.[7]

God will never leave us; neither will He forsake us. We have to hold onto this portion of God's Word as firmly as we do the promises of forgiveness of sin, our salvation, and eternal life. Either all of the Bible is true, or none of it is. So for professing Christians, this means we are assured we will never be alone. Christ was forsaken so that we would be forever accepted.

Not only do we have God's eternal companionship, but we also have the companionship of the rest of the body—specifically the members of our local churches. We have been added or joined to others, which ensures that we will not be alone. Have you ever noticed how often the book of Acts describes the process of conversion as being *added*? Acts 2:47 gives the account of the first days of the church as "the Lord added to their number day by day those who were being saved." Acts 5:14 says, "And more than ever believers were added to the Lord, multitudes of both men and women." Acts 11:24 records: "And a great many people were added to the Lord." We have been added to the "church, which is his body, the fullness of him who fills all in all" (Eph. 1:22-23).

We may be unmarried, but as Christians we are not solitary. Admittedly, it can sometimes feel like that, but may I gently suggest that this feeling of isolation can be overcome by reaching out to other parts of the body of Christ instead of waiting for them to reach out to us? After all, these are the people with whom we will spend eternity; so why not get to know, invest in, and love some of them now?

Now consider the "ever-growing pool of past grace" in your life. Even in your greatest trials, hasn't God provided companionship? In my experience, every time a friend marries or I've moved or someone leaves, He shortly ushers a new friendship into my life. No, it's not always the same; nor is it always at the same depth as before, but I've never been left completely on my own. I'm teaching myself that whenever I feel alone in a crowd, I should look around for someone else who may be feeling the same way—so that I may be used by God to extend grace and kindness instead of being consumed by my own feelings.

In saying this, I'm not trying to sugarcoat the realities of growing older or of being part of a church full of imperfect people. There will be challenging circumstances in our futures, but we will not walk through them utterly alone. We are part of the Lord's body now, and both the Head and the other members will be with us for all time.

DEATH'S DOORWAY

Death should sober us because it is the payment for sin (Rom. 6:23). Yet, as John Piper writes, "it is astonishing how disinterested people are in the reality of dying." He continues:

> Few things are more certain and universal. The possibilities for joy and misery after you die are trillions of times greater than in the few years on this earth before you die. Yet people give almost all their energies to making this life secure, and almost none to the next. The Bible compares this life to a vapor that appears on a cold winter morning and then vanishes (James 4:14). That's about two seconds. But it describes the time after death as "ages of ages" (Revelation 14:11, literal translation)—not just one or two ages that last a thousand years, but ages of ages—thousands and thousands of ages. It matters infinitely what happens to you after you die.[8]

The good news is that as a Christian, death is only a doorway into the resurrection life of Christ. We no longer have to be slaves to the fear of death. Hebrews 2:14-15 says that through death Christ destroyed "the one who has the power of death, that is, the devil, and deliver[ed] all those who through fear of death were subject to lifelong slavery."

While we shouldn't fear death, we *should* fear dying with regrets. We should fear living small, self-centered lives that will earn few eternal rewards. As Randy Alcorn writes:

> Evangelicals reject the doctrine of a second chance for unbelievers. We recognize there's no opportunity to come to Christ after death. But it's equally true that after death there's no second chance for believers. There's no more opportunity for us to walk by faith and serve our Lord in this fallen world.
>
> We can't do life here over again. . . . When the trumpet heralds Christ's return, our eternal future begins and our present opportunity ends. If we have failed by then to use our money, possessions, time, and energy for eternity, then we have failed—period.
>
> "But we'll be in heaven and that's all that matters." On the contrary, Paul spoke of the loss of reward as a great and terrible loss. The fact that we're still saved is a clarification, not a consolation—"If it is burned up, he will suffer loss; he himself will be saved, but only as one escaping through the flames" (1 Corinthians 3:15). Receiving reward from Christ is an unspeakable gain with eternal implications. Forfeiting reward is a terrible loss with equally eternal implications.[9] . . .

Isn't it amazing that the God who spared us His righteous wrath by sacrificing His Son would also then reward us for the deeds we do that He planned and empowered us to do through His grace? The promise of reward in heaven is the future grace that is flowing back into the present through the opportunities we have here to do good to one another. John Piper says this is why he thinks about what comes after death. I have highlighted one section of his book *Future Grace* that spoke to me specifically about how considering life after death affects my singleness now:

> We don't dream our most exciting dreams about accomplishments and relationships that perish. We don't fret over what this life fails to give us (marriage, wealth, health, fame). Instead, we savor the wonder that the Owner and Ruler of this universe loves us, and has destined us for the enjoyment of his glory, and is working infallibly to bring us to his eternal kingdom. So we live to meet the needs of others, because God is living to meet our needs (Isaiah 64:4; 41:10; 2 Chronicles 16:9; Psalm 23:6).[10]

We don't fret over what this life fails to give us because God loves us. This is why the Proverbs 31 woman laughs at the time to come. Being so loved, she understands that the best is yet to come.

HEAVEN: AN EXPLOSION OF JOY

"God is joy spilling over," Joni Eareckson Tada writes.[11] In heaven we will be in His overflowing joy for ages of ages. As a Christian, this is your future. Aren't you smiling already? I am much encouraged by Randy Alcorn's writings on heaven, including this bright passage: "What does God say to his faithful servants when their work on earth is done? 'Come and share your master's happiness' (Matthew 25:23). The contagious joy of our Lord will permeate every square foot of heaven and every square inch of us."

Randy also introduced an idea to me that I'd never considered: We will be ourselves there, only better.

> People in heaven are called by name—Abraham and Isaac and Jacob (Matthew 8:11) and Lazarus (Luke 16:25). A name denotes a distinct identity, an individual personality. The fact that it's the same name used on earth demonstrates we'll be the same people. I'll be Randy Alcorn throughout eternity, just without the bad parts. You'll be who you are throughout eternity, just without the bad parts.[12] . . .
>
> Some think we won't be male or female in heaven, based on what Jesus says in Matthew 22:30. ("At the resurrection people will neither marry nor be given in marriage; they will be like the angels in heaven.") But that passage doesn't teach we'll be genderless. Gender is a God-created aspect of humanity. Jesus simply states there'll be no marriage in heaven but the marriage of Christ and his bride. . . . Before Mary recognized Jesus in his new body, she addressed him as "Sir," showing she saw him as being male (John 20:15).[13]

Consider the implications of this. We will not be given in marriage in heaven, but we will continue to be male and female in heaven. All that we do now to glorify God in our femininity will also be rewarded in heaven. *So, then, isn't it tragic to waste years of our lives being more concerned about marriage—a temporary state—than investing ourselves into what will outlast even that?*

FINISH WELL

We know our destination, but we have to stay the course now. The apostle Paul wrote in 1 Corinthians. 9:24, "Do you not know that in a race all the runners compete, but only one receives the prize? So run that you may obtain it."

Let's run to receive eternal rewards, dear sisters. May we follow the course laid out for us in Proverbs 31 and not look to the sidelines. May we esteem the gift of singleness that's been given to us now so that we will be called wise stewards of that gift and invited to share in our Master's happiness. Let's cultivate noble characters and not let bitterness, jealousy, or disappointment steal from us the rewards for trusting God. May we guard our hearts and affections for the Lord and not be concerned with whether or not a fellow creature pursues us for the temporary state of marriage.

May we freely love and serve others, especially those members of Christ's body who are in our local churches. Let's show hospitality to others and use our homes as mission fields and places to refresh others. May we earn, spend, and invest wisely—storing our treasures in heaven. By God's grace, let's not worry whether or not we will bear children, but let us love, encourage, and disciple the children we encounter now. May we never put our trust in physical beauty that decays, but always cultivate the inner beauty that will likely be part of our femininity for all time. Let's resolve to use our words to build up and edify others so that when we give an account of every careless word, it will be short rather than long. And may we never be known as "needy" women who require lots of emotional support because of our disappointment over being single, but may we be known as women who reach out to the needy and generously give to the poor.

In a youth-oriented world, may we never lose sight of heaven. By following in the footsteps of the Proverbs 31 woman, I pray that we also will receive her blessing of the closing verses:

> *A woman who fears the Lord is to be praised.*
> *Give her of the fruit of her hands,*
> *and let her works praise her in the gates.*

AFTERWORD:
WHAT IS THIS GOOD NEWS?

The bright morning sun momentarily blinded me as I approached the intersection. Squinting, I looked left at the crest of the hill just a few yards away. This was always a tough intersection to negotiate because cars would speed suddenly into view. No cars were coming; so I quickly turned right and continued on my way to work.

The flashing red and blue lights in my rearview mirror caught my eye. Unconcerned, I looked for a place to pull over, expecting that the policeman would quickly pass me on his way to arrest some criminal. To my great surprise, he followed me as I eased right and came to a stop behind me. *What in the world?* I thought.

This officer would not have won any congeniality awards. In the cold January morning, my electric window motor wasn't working well; so I shouted a greeting through the crack while prying my window open manually. I smiled sheepishly, but he was stone-faced. *Not even the tiniest hint of amusement. This isn't good.*

"License and registration, please," he said.

I handed him both and waited for him to tell me why he had pulled me over. I didn't think it was a good idea to display my ignorance by asking. He ducked into his car with my documents, and I waited. And waited. *Is it a good thing or not that this is taking so long?* I wondered.

Finally he came back to the car. I tugged down the window. He extended a ticket book toward me. "Sign here at the bottom," he said, pointing. The sun was blinding me again. I squinted and shifted, trying to read what he was holding. I don't believe in signing something I haven't read, but his impatience was palpable.

"I'm sorry," I finally said. "I can't really see this. So I'm sorry I have to ask, but, um, why am I getting this ticket?"

"It's a warning," he replied gruffly. "You didn't stop at that intersection. But if you get stopped again, you'll get a ticket and two points because of this warning."

"Thank you very much," I said, signing the ticket. Pausing a moment, I—unwisely—added, "You're right. I rolled through that stop. That intersection is so close to the top of the hill that I just pause and scoot through whenever I see it's clear."

For the first time, the policeman looked me directly in the eye. "Your logic is backward. That's precisely the reason you need to stop. We've had a lot of accidents at that intersection," he said. Then he walked away.

I tugged my window up, started the car, and drove away—still stunned that I'd almost been ticketed. I turned on the radio, and an old hymn flooded the car:

> Whatever my lot,
> Thou has taught me to say,
> It is well, it is well, with my soul.

I burst into tears. I had been guilty of making a rolling stop, but I had received mercy instead of punishment. Even if I had received that ticket, however, it was still well with my soul, for I've received mercy for far graver matters.

You see, on that day I received a warning; it didn't cost the officer anything personally to extend mercy to me. That's where the analogy breaks down.

The good news of the gospel cost God the Father a great deal—His Son. But what's true about this analogy is that there is a real law. I was guilty of rolling through a stop sign whether or not I thought I had a better plan to preserve my life. The same is true with God's laws.

God created the world and still rules it, despite our continued rebellion against Him. God's laws are real, and they reflect His perfect character. God's ways are perfect, and He desires what is best for us. The problem is that ever since the first man and woman, we think we have a better idea about how to live our lives. And yet the truth remains, whether or not we acknowledge it, that there is a loving God, and we break His laws every day of our lives.

No matter our background, most of us are generally aware of the existence of the Ten Commandments, even if we can't name them all. These are the basis of God's moral law, intended for us to know something of Him, as well as ourselves—namely that we can't keep these commands in our own strength.

Sin might not be a current concept in our vocabulary these days, but it has never gone out of God's vocabulary. First John 1:8 says, "If we say we have no sin, we deceive ourselves, and the truth is not in us." The apostle John goes on to write, "Everyone who makes a practice of sinning also practices lawlessness; sin is lawlessness" (1 John 3:4). That might be easier to understand—sin is lawlessness. We can pick up any newspaper in any town in the whole world, and this lawlessness is graphically chronicled for us. We can read about millions of dollars being embezzled by corporate executives; children being beaten to death by their parents; teen girls being abducted, raped, and murdered; angry sports fans brawling with each other; impatient commuters exploding in road rage and ramming other cars; dictators executing anyone who opposes them; insane world leaders refusing to feed their people and creating political famines; college fraternity members hazing one another to harm and even death, and so on. Sin and lawlessness abound in shocking proportions.

But you might say to yourself, "Well, that's stuff about other people. I'm not a bad person; I've never murdered anyone." And this is what Jesus said to those who thought the same thing: "You have heard that it was said to those of old, 'You shall not murder; and whoever murders will be liable to judgment.' But I say to you that everyone who is angry with his brother will be liable to judgment; whoever insults his brother will be liable to the council; and whoever says, 'You fool!' will be liable to the hell of fire" (Matt. 5:21-22).

And you might say, "The Ten Commandments say not to commit adultery, and I never have." But Jesus taught, "You have heard that it was said, 'You shall not commit adultery.' But I say to you that everyone who looks at a woman with lustful intent has already committed adultery with her in his heart" (Matt. 5:27-28).

That is the impossibly high standard of a perfect and holy God. But that's perfection, you might object. Yes, that's true. Jesus said, "You therefore must be perfect, as your heavenly Father is perfect" (Matt. 5:48). No one can meet that standard! Romans 3:23 says, "for all have sinned and fall short of the glory of God." That's all of us, every last one of us. *No one* is "good enough." We have all sinned and will continue to sin, and the penalty of our sin is serious: "For the wages of sin is death, but the free gift of God is eternal life in Christ Jesus our Lord" (Rom. 6:23). Because of our sin, we live in a fallen world abounding in sin, and our end is death.

That's a grim picture, a severe reality. However, there is good news. God is *both* wonderfully merciful and perfectly just. He does not sweep our sin under the carpet. He cannot. He is a just God, and He cannot overlook our sin. So how can sinners like you and me relate to a holy God? Through His work on the cross. That is why the cross is so important to humanity.

On the cross He did what no other human being could ever do—He paid the penalty for our sins Himself.

Jesus came to live a perfect life and meet all the requirements of the Law so that He could receive the punishment for our sins without deserving any punishment Himself. "Do not think that I have come to abolish the Law or the Prophets; I have not come to abolish them but to fulfill them. For truly, I say to you, until heaven and earth pass away, not an iota, not a dot, will pass from the Law until all is accomplished" (Matt. 5:17-18).

Jesus' claims about Himself were clear—we can't ignore their plain meaning. Here is some of His testimony about Himself:

• "I am the way, and the truth, and the life. No one comes to the Father except through me." (John 14:6)

• "I am the resurrection and the life. Whoever believes in me, though he die, yet shall he live, and everyone who lives and believes in me shall never die. Do you believe this?" (John 11:25-26)

• "I am the light of the world. Whoever follows me will not walk in darkness, but will have the light of life." (John 8:12)

• "For this reason the Father loves me, because I lay down my life that I may take it up again. No one takes it from me, but I lay it down of my own accord. I have authority to lay it down, and I have authority to take it up again. This charge I have received from my Father." (John 10:17-18)

• "For God so loved the world, that he gave his only Son, that whoever believes in him should not perish but have eternal life." (John 3:16)

• "For even the Son of Man came not to be served but to serve, and to give his life as a ransom for many." (Mark 10:45)

• "Greater love has no one than this, that someone lays down his life for his friends." (John 15:13)

The proof of the Father's acceptance of Jesus' finished work on our behalf is in the Resurrection. Despite the sophistication of a unit of Roman guards at His tomb and the opposition of the political leaders at that time, no one could produce His body. Even though Jerusalem would have been extremely crowded during the Passover due to the thousands of pilgrims there to celebrate this religious feast, no one saw any tampering of His tomb.

Instead, this band of frightened disciples who abandoned Jesus during His arrest and execution suddenly were filled with faith, enduring persecution and execution, to proclaim the good news of salvation:

> *For while we were still weak, at the right time Christ died for the ungodly. For one will scarcely die for a righteous person—though perhaps for a good person one would dare even to die—but God shows his love for us in that while we were still sinners, Christ died for us. Since, therefore, we have now been justified by his blood, much more shall we be saved by him from the wrath of God. For if while we were enemies we were reconciled to God by the death of his Son, much more, now that we are reconciled, shall we be saved by his life. More than that, we also rejoice in God through our Lord Jesus Christ, through whom we have now received reconciliation.* (Rom. 5:6-11)

The gospel is the good news that the One who would be our judge is instead our Redeemer. If we receive and believe this tremendously good news, when we die, we will face a Judge who extends His pierced hand from the robes of justice and beckons us to join Him in everlasting life because of the blood He shed for us. But if we do not receive this good news—if we don't believe it, don't think it is important, or if we try to justify ourselves on the basis of a "pretty good life"—then we will find no mercy at the judgment seat, for we will be spurning the most valuable gift of all.

Dear friend, if you have turned from your sins and believed that Jesus died on that cross for them, you are now no doubt rejoicing and praising Him as you read these words. *If you have not yet turned from your sins, I appeal to you to seek mercy while it is being offered to you.* Your most pressing, eternal problem has been solved at the cross—if you will acknowledge your sin, turn from it, and receive forgiveness from the One who paid your penalty to fulfill perfect justice and extend perfect mercy.

This is the gospel—that Jesus fulfilled the demands of God's holy law and took the punishment for those who could not meet those demands. Your response today could usher you into paradise.

Please don't walk away from the most important gift you could ever receive.

NOTES

CHAPTER 1: "YOU'RE STILL SINGLE?"

1. Joshua Harris, *Boy Meets Girl* (Sisters, Ore.: Multnomah, 2000), p. 213.

CHAPTER 2: ESTEEMING THE GIFT

1. *New Bible Commentary*, ed. G. J. Wenham, J. A. Motyer, D. A. Carson, R. T. France (Downers Grove, Ill.: InterVarsity Press, 1998), pp. 1170-71.
2. *The IVP Bible Background Commentary: New Testament*, ed. Craig S. Keener (Downers Grove, Ill.: InterVarsity Press, 1993), pp. 464-66.
3. W. E. Vine, *The Expanded Vine's Expository Dictionary of New Testament Words*, ed. John R. Kohlenberger III (Minneapolis, Minn.: Bethany House Publishers, 1984), pp. 476-77.
4. Ibid., p. 477.
5. Gordon D. Fee, *God's Empowering Presence: The Holy Spirit in the Letters of Paul* (Peabody, Mass.: Hendrickson Publishers, 1994), p. 86.
6. Ibid., p. 159.
7. Wayne Grudem, *Bible Doctrine: Essential Teachings of the Christian Faith* (Grand Rapids, Mich.: Zondervan, 1999), p. 399.
8. Elisabeth Elliot, *Quest for Love* (Grand Rapids, Mich.: Fleming H. Revell, 1996), p. 215.

CHAPTER 3: GOD'S QUIET PROVIDENCE

1. Mark Dever is senior pastor of Capitol Hill Baptist Church, Washington, D.C., and founder of Nine Marks Ministries.
2. Quoted in *The Student Bible New International Version* (Grand Rapids, Mich.: Zondervan, 1992), p. 250.
3. Jerry Bridges, *Trusting God* (Colorado Springs, Colo.: NavPress, 1988), p. 18.
4. Herbert Lockyer, *All the Women of the Bible* (Grand Rapids, Mich.: Zondervan, 1967), p. 145.
5. Bridges, *Trusting God*, pp. 49-50.
6. *New Bible Commentary*, ed. G. J. Wenham, J. A. Motyer, D. A. Carson, R. T. France (Downers Grove, Ill.: InterVarsity Press, 1998), p. 292.
7. Ibid.
8. Ibid., p. 293.

CHAPTER 4: A WOMAN OF NOBLE CHARACTER

1. I acknowledge my debt here to Elizabeth George's book, *Beautiful in God's Eyes: The Treasures of the Proverbs 31 Woman* (Eugene, Ore.: Harvest House Publishers, 1998), pp. 11-12.
2. Douglas Wilson, *Her Hand in Marriage* (Moscow, Ida.: Canon Press, 1997), pp. 84-85.
3. *Strong's Greek and Hebrew Dictionary*, in English Standard Version software, Hebrew word 802.
4. Ibid., Hebrew word 2428.
5. Ibid., Hebrew word 6443.

6. English Standard Version, Matthew 25:15 note.
7. I acknowledge my debt for this illustration to a sermon on contentment given by Pete Greasley at Covenant Life Church a few years ago.
8. Thomas Watson, *The Art of Divine Contentment* (Glasgow, U.K.: Free Presbyterian Publications, 1885). Permission granted to publish the book on the Internet, from which this quote was taken. www.ccel.org/w/watson/contentment/contentment.html
9. Robert D. Jones, "Learning Contentment in All Your Circumstances," *The Journal of Biblical Counseling*, Vol. 21.1 (Fall 2002), p. 55.
10. *The New Bible Commentary*, ed. G. J. Wenham, J. A. Motyer, D. A. Carson, R. T. France (Downers Grove, Ill.: InterVarsity Press, 1998), p. 574.
11. John Piper, *Desiring God: Meditations of a Christian Hedonist* (Sisters, Ore.: Multnomah, 1996), p. 250.
12. Ibid.
13. Ginny Owens, "Free," as recorded on *Blueprint* (Rocketown Records, 2002).
14. *Strong's Greek and Hebrew Dictionary*, Greek word 5463.
15. Jerry Bridges, *Trusting God* (Colorado Springs, Colo.: NavPress, 1988), p. 102.
16. *Strong's Greek and Hebrew Dictionary*, Greek word 4982.
17. Ibid., Greek word 5281.
18. Elizabeth George, *Loving God with All Your Mind* (Eugene, Ore.: Harvest House Publishers, 1994), p. 21.

CHAPTER 5: DO HIM GOOD ALL THE DAYS OF YOUR LIFE

1. *Strong's Greek and Hebrew Dictionary*, in English Standard Version software, word 3820.
2. Carol Potera, "Get Real About Getting Married," *SHAPE* magazine, September 2003, p. 36.
3. *Strong's Greek and Hebrew Dictionary*, word 8444.
4. Michelle McKinney Hammond, *Secrets of an Irresistible Woman* (Eugene, Ore.: Harvest House Publishers, 1998), pp. 113-14.
5. Executive summary, *Hooking Up, Hanging Out, and Hoping for Mr. Right— College Women on Dating and Mating Today* (Washington, D.C.: Independent Women's Forum, 2001), www.iwf.org/news/010727.shtml.
6. Laura Sessions Stepp, "Modern Flirting," *The Washington Post*, October 16, 2003, p. C8.
7. "Sex Without Strings, Relationships Without Rings," The National Marriage Project, 2000 (Rutgers, The State University of New Jersey), marriage.rutgers.edu/Publications/pubsex-wostrings.htm.
8. Ellen Fein and Sherrie Schneider, *The Rules: Time-Tested Secrets for Capturing the Heart of Mr. Right* (New York: Warner Books, 1995), pp. 7, 9.
9. Hammond, *Irresistible Woman*, pp. 125-26.
10. ABCNEWS.com, online chat with Ellen Fein and Sherrie Schneider, as archived on abcnews.go.com/sections/community/DailyNews/chat_rules0511.html.
11. Paul David Tripp, *Instruments in the Redeemer's Hands* (Phillipsburg, N.J.: P&R Publishers, 2002), p. 85-88.
12. Robert Murray McCheyne, *Journal of the Grace Evangelical Society*, Spring 1992, Vol. 5:1 (Irving, Tex.: Grace Evangelical Society), www.faithalone.org/journal/1992i/McChey.html.

CHAPTER 6: RESPECTED AT THE CITY GATE

1. Ray Vander Laan, (c) 1995-2003, That the World May Know Ministries, as originally recorded in the *Faith Lessons* video series and then posted online at community.gospelcom.net/Brix?pageID=1577.
2. Douglas Wilson, *Her Hand in Marriage* (Moscow, Ida.: Canon Press, 1997), p. 88.
3. Matthew Henry, *Concise Commentary*, on Genesis 24:54-67, English Standard Version software.

222   D I KISS MARRIAGE GOODBYE?

4. Andrew Farmer, *The Rich Single Life* (Gaithersburg, Md.: Sovereign Grace Ministries, 1998), pp. 116-17.

5. Steve Watters, "Taking a Relationship from Good to Great," *Boundless* webzine (Colorado Springs, Colo.: Focus on the Family), October 9, 2003, www.boundless.org.

6. Michelle McKinney Hammond, *Secrets of an Irresistible Woman* (Eugene, Ore.: Harvest House Publishers, 1998), p. 70.

7. Quoted in the "Grace Gems" e-mail newsletter of June 11, 2003. Adapted from J. C. Ryle's commentary, *The Gospel of John*.

8. Carolyn Mahaney, *Biblical Womanhood in the Home,* ed. Nancy Leigh DeMoss (Wheaton, Ill.: Crossway Books, 2002), pp. 23, 25.

9. Carolyn Mahaney, *Feminine Appeal* (Wheaton, Ill.: Crossway Books, 2003), p. 125.

10. Wayne Grudem, *Bible Doctrine* (Grand Rapids, Mich.: Zondervan, 1999), p. 116.

11. Ibid., p. 121.

12. Elisabeth Elliot, *Let Me Be a Woman* (Wheaton, Ill.: Tyndale House Publishers, 1976), p. 121.

13. Ibid., p. 99.

CHAPTER 7: FOOD FROM AFAR

1. Elisabeth Elliot, *Let Me Be a Woman* (Wheaton, Ill.: Tyndale House Publishers, 1976), p. 33.

2. Alexander Strauch, *The Hospitality Commands* (Littleton, Colo.: Lewis and Roth Publishers, 1993), pp. 21, 22.

3. *Strong's Greek and Hebrew Dictionary*, in English Standard Version software, Greek word 5382.

4. Strauch, *Hospitality Commands*, p. 35.

5. Herbert Lockyer, *All the Women of the Bible* (Grand Rapids, Mich.: Zondervan, 1967), p. 87.

6. Marilyn Yalom, *A History of the Wife* (New York: Perennial Publishing, 2001), p. 102.

7. Ibid., pp. 102-3.

CHAPTER 8: OUT OF HER EARNINGS

1. Betsy Israel, *Bachelor Girl: The Secret History of Single Women in the Twentieth Century* (New York: William Morrow, 2002), p. 15.

2. Ibid., p. 16.

3. Ibid., p. 19.

4. Ibid., p. 100.

5. John Piper, *Don't Waste Your Life* (Wheaton, Ill.: Crossway Books, 2003), p. 139.

6. Ibid., pp. 143-44.

7. Joshua Harris, *Not Even a Hint: Guarding Your Heart Against Lust* (Sisters, Ore.: Multnomah, 2003), p. 42.

8. The Women's Institute for Financial Education, San Diego, Calif. Posted on the Facts & Fun web page. www.wife.org/facts_didyouknow.htm.

9. Randy Alcorn, *Money, Possessions & Eternity* (Wheaton, Ill.: Tyndale House Publishers, 1989), pp. 16-17.

10. Randy Alcorn, *The Law of Rewards* (Wheaton, Ill.: Tyndale House Publishers, 2003), p. ix.

11. Based on Covenant Life Church's *Our Journey Together: New Members Course,* Lesson Nine. Copyright 2003 Covenant Life Church, Gaithersburg, Md.

12. Ada Lum, *Single & Human* (Downers Grove, Ill.: InterVarsity Press), p. 27.

13. Matthew Henry, *The Quest for Meekness and Quietness of Spirit* (Morgan, Penn.: Soli Deo Gloria Publications, 1996), p. 22.

14. Ibid., p. 35.

15. Herbert Lockyer, *All the Women of the Bible* (Grand Rapids, Mich.: Zondervan, 1967), p. 78.

CHAPTER 9: THE BLESSING OF CHILDREN

1. George Barna, *A Revealing Look at Three Unique Single Adult Populations* (March 11, 2002), www.barna.org.
2. Andrew Farmer, *The Rich Single Life* (Gaithersburg, Md.: Sovereign Grace Ministries, 1998), p. 153.
3. *Women Helping Women: A Biblical Guide to Major Issues Women Face*, Elyse Fitzpatrick and Carol Cornish, eds. (Eugene, Ore.: Harvest House Publishers, 1997), pp. 335-36.
4. C. J. Mahaney, *Gospel-Centered Parenting*, audio message (Gaithersburg, Md.: Sovereign Grace Ministries, 2001).
5. Wade F. Horn and Tom Sylvester, *Father Facts, 4th ed.* (Gaithersburg, Md.: self-published, 2002), www.fatherhood.org/fatherfacts.htm.

CHAPTER 10: DECEPTIVE CHARM

1. Carolyn Mahaney, *Feminine Appeal* (Wheaton, Ill.: Crossway Books, 2003), p. 80.
2. Nancy Leigh DeMoss, transcript of *Revive Our Hearts* broadcast of June 10, 2003, www.reviveourhearts.com.
3. *Strong's Greek and Hebrew Dictionary*, in English Standard Version software, Hebrew word 1892.
4. *The Classic Hundred Poems: All-Time Favorites*, William Harmon, ed. (New York: Columbia University Press, 1998), p. 126.
5. Joshua Harris, *Not Even a Hint: Guarding Your Heart Against Lust* (Sisters, Ore.: Multnomah, 2003), pp. 85-86.
6. Herbert Lockyer, *All the Women of the Bible* (Grand Rapids, Mich.: Zondervan, 1967), p. 270.
7. Nancy Leigh DeMoss, ed., *Biblical Womanhood in the Home* (Wheaton, Ill.: Crossway Books, 2002), pp. 92-94.
8. *Classic Hundred Poems: All-Time Favorites*, p. 126.
9. Carolyn Mahaney, "True Beauty," *Biblical Womanhood in the Home* (Wheaton, Ill.: Crossway Books, 2002), pp. 37-38.
10. Joni Eareckson Tada and Steven Estes, *When God Weeps* (Grand Rapids, Mich.: Zondervan, 1997), pp. 202-03.
11. Randy Alcorn, *Edge of Eternity* (Colorado Springs, Colo.: Waterbrook Press, 1999), pp. 46-47.

CHAPTER 11: WISE SPEECH

1. Paul David Tripp, *War of Words* (Phillipsburg, N.J.: P&R Publishing, 2000), p. 55.
2. Ibid., p. 36-37.
3. *Strong's Greek and Hebrew Dictionary*, in English Standard Version software, Greek word 4741.
4. C. J. Mahaney, *The Cross-Centered Life* (Sisters, Ore.: Multnomah, 2002), p. 56-67.
5. Nancy Leigh DeMoss, ed., *Biblical Womanhood in the Home* (Wheaton, Ill.: Crossway Books, 2002), pp. 96-97.
6. Matthew Henry, *The Quest for Meekness and Quietness of Spirit* (Morgan, Penn.: Soli Deo Gloria Publications, 1996), p. 27.
7. Ibid., pp. 32-34.
8. DeMoss, ed., *Biblical Womanhood in the Home*, pp. 126-27.
9. Chris Silard, "Living As Lights in the World," a sermon given at Covenant Life Church, December 21, 2003.

10. Ken Sande, "Getting to the Heart of Conflict," as posted on the Peacemaker Ministries Web site, www.hispeace.org.

CHAPTER 12: REACHING OUT TO THE NEEDY

1. *Strong's Greek and Hebrew Dictionary*, in English Standard Version software, Hebrew word 6041.
2. Ibid., Hebrew word 34.
3. "Mercies Anew," music and lyrics by Mark Altrogge and Bob Kauflin. (c) 2002 PDI Praise (BMI). Sovereign Grace Music, a division of Sovereign Grace Ministries. From *Upward: The Bob Kauflin Hymns Project*. Featuring vocalist Shannon Harris. Used by permission.
4. Donald S. Whitney, *Spiritual Disciplines Within the Church: Participating Fully in the Body of Christ* (Chicago, Ill.: Moody Press, 1996), p. 112.

CHAPTER 13: LAUGHING AT THE TIME TO COME

1. *Strong's Greek and Hebrew Dictionary*, in English Standard Version software, Hebrew word 5810.
2. Ibid., Hebrew word 1921.
3. Poem and guidelines as posted on The Red Hat Society Web site, www.redhatsociety.com.
4. Robert Browning, "Rabbi Ben Ezra," *Poems of Robert Browning*. Great Literature Online. 1997-2004, www.underthesun.cc/Classics/Browning/PoemsOfRobertBrowning/PoemsOf RobertBrowning15.html
5. Jim Elliot was author Elisabeth Elliot's first husband. He was a missionary to the Auca tribe in Ecuador, and was slain in January 1956.
6. John Piper, *Future Grace* (Sisters, Ore.: Multnomah, 1995), pp. 101-2.
7. Jerry Bridges, *Trusting God* (Colorado Springs, Colo.: NavPress, 1988), p. 197-98.
8. Piper, *Future Grace*, pp. 356-57.
9. Randy Alcorn, *The Law of Rewards* (Wheaton, Ill.: Tyndale House Publishers, 2003), p. 70-71.
10. Piper, *Future Grace*, p. 369.
11. Joni Eareckson Tada and Steven Estes, *When God Weeps* (Grand Rapids, Mich.: Zondervan, 1997), p. 35.
12. Randy Alcorn, *In Light of Eternity* (Colorado Springs, Colo.: Waterbrook Press, 1999), p. 45.
13. Ibid., pp. 50-51.